ROYAL CRUISING CLUB
JOURNAL 2000

Edited by CHRISTOPHER CORBET

Editorial Acknowledgements

My particular thanks are due to the many contributors who have put in time, thought and effort to produce material which is worthy of the Journal. A more muted paean of praise goes out to those who had interesting and amusing tales to tell but were either too busy or too unmindful to check or to correct their typescripts and track charts in accordance with simple conventions of spelling and punctuation and in accordance with the recommendations of the Blue Book.

There are many who help in the putting together of each edition of Roving Commissions and they all deserve our gratitude: I am grateful also to those who write for and compile the various 'Club Matters' sections at the end. Jonathan Virden deserves special thanks for his compilation of the contributions relating to the Round Britain Rolling Meet.

There are again some fine illustrations this time from the hand of John Webster at pages 133 and 269. Also I thank David Taylor of the National Maritime Museum for his seeking out the pictures at pages 181 and 183 and for the permission given to publish them.

There has been careful proof reading by Catherine Pitts, Catriona, Richard and Leila Corbet and Matthew Thom. James Pritchard-Barrett, who is also extremely generous with his time and resources in the distribution of the Journal, gave yet further time in proof reading.

Finally, thank you to the conscientious staff at Bookcraft and Footnote Graphics, who work hard to ensure that Roving Commissions is produced to a consistently high standard.

ISBN 0 901916 21 8

Typeset by Footnote Graphics, Warminster 01985 215322
Printed and bound by Bookcraft, Midsomer Norton 01761 419167

Contents

TILL THE SEA ITSELF FLOWETH IN YOUR VEINS

You never enjoy the world aright, till the Sea itself floweth in your veins, till you are clothed with the heavens, and crowned with the stars..... Till you can sing and rejoice and delight in God, as misers do in gold, and Kings in sceptres, you never enjoy the world.

From Centuries of Meditations by Thomas Traherne

These words of Thomas Traherne invite us to recognise the Sea as not merely a place where we can enjoy ourselves but as an element of our own selves which lives in us while we delight in it. And the logs in this Journal show how the Sea courses through the veins of the membership of this club. Even when the circumstances are adverse and simple enjoyment seems to be entirely absent, where icebergs are being fended off for the third night in a row or carefully planned voyages come to nothing, nevertheless the rejoicing and delight in being part of the Sea and in the Sea being part of the author is ever present.

Some of the logs in this book record a grappling with adversity or discomfort, fear or failure or debility, but there is a strange elation throughout, sensitive and not always heroic, which drags the reader into the writer's predicament to exult somehow in all the good and bad things that nature has to offer. There are voyages to the deep south of South America, a couple to, or at least towards, Greenland's icy mountains, one to the Russian Arctic, one to the Antarctic and an octogenarian single handed transatlantic venture; each of these voyages may give us cause to wonder why the participants enjoy the world in the way that they do. But there is no doubt that they enjoy it and that those reading their accounts will enjoy that world through their eyes.

Other logs, and I would cite as examples Keith Gems' *The North Western Edge* and Heather Howard's *Underneath the Arches*, contain no such tales of adversity but are still in complete sympathy with the world about them. Again there is no doubt about their enjoyment; even though Heather does not tell us that she sang the *Jubilate* or some other paean of joy as she sailed up Loch Etive, I would expect that she did. And I have no doubt that their enjoyment will be infectious towards the readers of their accounts.

Sadly this editorial has to contain an apology for the delay in publication of the book. I have to take full responsibility. Farmers, according to a survey, average a 70 hour week and I have recently become a full time farmer and I put in more hours than that. Other editors have been more successful in the management of their time and in delegation; I have not. The practice of including at least a part of almost every voyage submitted cannot be sustained, given the large number of submissions and the heavy editing that many of them require. In 1947 seven logs were submitted and were printed, I suspect, with very little editorial input. This year there were at least forty-eight submitted and forty-eight included. It would be sad to disappoint those who have spent time and effort on their submissions to the Journal and it would be sad to exclude good tales even when they require a lot of editing to bring them up to the standard required by Roving Commissions. I have heard of gaps of twenty years and more before a once disappointed author would write again for the Journal. This year neither writers nor readers should be disappointed, but I fear that next year a new approach is required.

WITH APOLOGIES TO TILMAN – AGAIN!

by The Rev Bob Shepton

A very persuasive fellow our Hon. Editor, and so I must write something for the Journal. By the same token I had better make a long summer short. The aim of the expedition then was to sail round to the west coast of Greenland again, and climb mountains from the boat in the Tilman tradition, but this time with special reference to a huge rock wall above the Arctic Circle near Upernavik.

In true Tilman style the sailing crew were not finalised till almost the last moment. But finally this comprised two Brits who had done some offshore sailing, two Australians who flew over specially but had done no sailing or virtually none, and myself. Fortunately by contrast my hard climbing team who were to fly out to Greenland to join us later were in place months before, due to the good offices of Graham my climbing co-ordinator. So we set off from Loch Linnhe rather late in the summer, on 26 June. No two Atlantic passages are ever the same, and the abiding memory of this crossing was of too little wind, in distinct contrast to last time when we had two gales, a storm and a knock-down. We took our offing through the Sound of Mingulay, and had to motor in high pressure for two days till the wind came in, at last. There followed three days of reasonable sailing before a huge high pressure system began to establish itself right across the Atlantic from Greenland to Scotland. Becalmed again, we inched along with the engine running on low revs to preserve fuel, sailing in anything above 4 knots of wind. It was fast becoming Ancient Mariner stuff but at least we did have fresh water, for the moment.

A small navigational error on behalf of the skipper brought us into some mild ice off the south coast of Greenland, and near Kap Desolation the helmsman got a nasty shock when a big iceberg loomed suddenly dead ahead out of the mist. The Reverend chose to become hard of hearing all of a sudden! And in the Davis Strait we launched the dinghy so that Jim with his height and strength could lift bits of brash ice into the

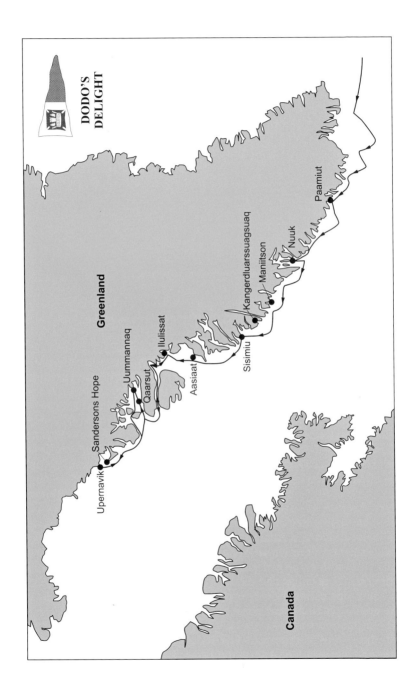

DODO'S
DELIGHT

Greenland

Sandersons Hope
Upernavik
Uummannaq
Qaarsut
Ilulissat
Aasiaat
Sisimiu
Kangerdluarssuagsuaq
Maniitson
Nuuk
Paamiut

Canada

dinghy and so into the boat. These we melted down to replenish our fast dwindling fresh water supply. Rather an intriguing solution to water shortage afloat, we thought, and the odd piece in a celebratory wee dram went down well too. We enjoyed meeting a Danish retired ship's carpenter building his own wooden gaff-rigged sailing cutter in Paamiut – a rare occurrence in Greenland. And of course we enjoyed renewing friendships at the Boat Club in Nuuk where we stayed for a few days' rest and refreshment, seeing Queen Juliana on a visit to Greenland and re-stocking the boat.

As we continued up the Davis Strait, we put into Kangerdluarssuagsuaq fjord on the way. This cuts fifteen miles into the 'near island' just to the north of Kangerlussuaq, or Søndre Strømford, and the pilotage was somewhat exciting as it was one of those places where the Danish chart suddenly ceases to give soundings. So we proceeded cautiously on the echosounder aiming carefully for our plotted waypoints, particularly on the way out northwards later. It is always difficult to know whether it is going round twice or whether it really is one metre below the keel! We did our usual trick of two years ago in the alluvial silt at the head of the fjord, but this time through not believing the new echosounder when it said one metre until we slid gently to a halt. We were still 'miles' away from the head of the loch; it was going to be a long row to shore. But we turned the boat round and motored out to 4 metres and put the anchor down.

That evening we made a brief walking reconnaissance to align the various ridges and peaks with the 1:250,000 Saga map. Excellent as these are for most uses, not least coastal sailing, they are far too small a scale for mountain work but there is nothing else. Over a period of three days we climbed two peaks. These were mountaineering peaks not requiring technical climbing, though the Australians being really one pitch rock-climbers – there are no mountains in Western Australia – did have a tendency to go straight up the rock buttress on the side of the valley rather than choosing the longer, but easier, 'mountaineering' route. And the first peak did involve a round trip of 20 kilometres and 1510 metres (nearly 5000 feet) of ascent from sea level. The Old Man perforce, not having climbed a mountain except by ski lift since the last expedition, was *almost* suffering from what Tilman used to call 'Mountaineer's Foot' by the end – the inability to put one foot in front of the other! But at the top of each peak we looked carefully for a cairn or sardine tin with names within. We found none and, with great relief after all that effort, built our own cairn and claimed the first ascent of the peaks. And the Australians were ecstatic at climbing their first proper mountains!

From Ilulissat onwards the sailing crew gradually left, but not before enduring one of the skipper's less successful short-cuts which inadvertently led to weaving and pushing through close packed ice for twenty-five miles in the Torssukatak. I then began to pick up the hard climbers.

Dodo anchored at Kangerdluarssuargsuaq.

This became a case of 'desperate means demand desperate measures' – Tilman was always fond of quoting proverbs and aphorisms. The climbers having no means, I invented the measure of picking them up off the beach just below the airstrip at Qaarsut, to save them the expense of the helicopter hop to Uummannaq. This was fine except when there was a sea running, in which case launching a rubber dinghy, with people and climbing gear, was not an easy matter. But after finally picking up the two groups of climbers who arrived in shifts over a two week period, and meeting *Northanger* when we put into an anchorage in inclement conditions, we began to make our way north to Upernavik. This should have been a straightforward two day passage, but the next morning I came on deck to find Graham struggling with the helm in increasing wind. We reefed the main, turned off the engine, and tacked out to avoid an awkward outlying reef off Svartenhuk, but when our Austrian member came up for her watch she was quite frankly terrified. This was under-standable: there is not a lot of sea in Austria, and she had never been on a boat before. On the other hand when she had been on watch for a while and realised the boat was not going to tip over and could on the whole handle the conditions, she regained her confidence. By contrast I was never quite convinced that my friend, her hard climbing, British, male partner did ever gain real confidence at sea, which in some ways rather surprised me. But then as he said, mountains and not sea were his thing, and that's fair enough.

We pressed on getting some protection from the seas after we had passed the headland to the north, but when the wind gusted to 51 and 56 knots, I decided enough was enough, handed all sail, lashed the helm and lay-a-hull and drifted. Now climbers by nature have a yearning for land, and there was land in sight, and all my seaman-like protestations, 'in a storm it's better to stay out at sea' did not seem to be that well re-ceived. But since I had been doing all the helming and was exhausted, I fell into my bunk and was instantly asleep. And the poor Italians – not a lot of sea in Italian mountain villages either – had been confined to theirs throughout. Waking half an hour later, I bowed to the inevitable and put the engine on and motored at a slant to the wind and waves for the coastline. It was a long haul. I did say as we approached, I hope not out of sour grapes, 'I have to say I do not think this will work' (anchoring in a gale). But eventually we made it into a U-shaped harbour formed by an incredible natural gravel breakwater which we had discovered on a pre-vious passage. It was however open to the east and the gale was from south east, but by tucking into a small inlet close to the refuge hut on shore, presumably to do with the winter dogsledding route, we had protection from the wind and waves raging a little further out. I have seldom been so glad to be wrong! But by then we had down 40 metres of chain in 4 metres of depth, with an angel down the chain, and another anchor with chain and warp as a back-up. I arranged an anchor watch, fell into my bunk, and was again instantly asleep. On waking four hours later, what had happened to the anchor watch? But by then it was flat calm anyway.

And when we reached Upernavik the team made the first ascent of the North Wall of Sandersons Hope at 72° 43′N, though it was not quite as simple as that! This was a direct ascent of the prime line up this huge sweeping compact granite wall involving 1045 metres (3,400 feet) of highly technical, specialised climbing, and of course it had never been done before. And whilst this may be the biggest wall there, it is also in an area laced with big walls and sweeping climbs in dramatic fjords, all so far unknown and undeveloped. So hopefully the significance of the ascent will be to open up this area for climbers in the future, and yachtsmen too as we attempted some pilotage of further likely anchorages in this scenic cruising area whilst we were there, all of course now dutifully submitted to the appropriate editor of the Pilotage Foundation! It took the team six days of climbing over a period of fourteen days, employing siege tactics and coming down to the comfort of the boat each evening. And it was just as well they did too because the course of the climbing was continually interrupted by bad weather in this year's strangely poor Greenlandic summer. On occasion they had frustratingly to wait for two or three days before the weather cleared and the rock dried. Indeed they had finally to force the last section in icy conditions climbing on into the by now dark night; and then of course the next day dawned clear and sunny.

To me this was a tremendous, ground-breaking achievement on behalf of the 'lads', my international team of star climbers. I can write in such terms because I found it necessary to stay and look after the boat (well, somebody had to)! But as a sailing and climbing explorer, self-styled, in my old age it was for me eminently satisfying that it was an ascent from a boat in the Tilman tradition, up this famous navigational headland named by John Davis in 1587 as his offing from Greenland to Baffin in search of the Northwest Passage. But really I suppose it was taking Tilman to extremes, since it was only possible to get the team onto the wall in the first place directly from the boat as the cliff dropped straight into the sea. This involved all sorts of adventures, and was really 'no way to treat a lady', or even my boat! To establish a system at all we had first to nose the bow right up to the cliff, even though in places nearby the echosounder read only one metre with the wall shelving a little underneath, so that our tallest member Alberto could step from the pulpit to gain a ledge system on the wall above. We then tried a system of pallets suspended on lines from climbing bolts driven into the wall which was especially good for landing the immense amount of equipment needed for such a specialised climb, and initially also for the lads to jump onto from the boat as I gingerly motored past in the swell. But soon the spring tides and the big swell of some days destroyed that system. So we reverted to backing the dinghy against the wall, to let the lads grasp the trailing lines and jump onto the wall at the top of a swell before jumaring up their fixed lines to the previous day's high point. All rather unusual boating, and climbing, but it worked.

The passage south afterwards was not without incident, involving as it did a night crossing of the forty mile wide open mouth of Uummannaq fjord – we had six hours of darkness now – in ice, with inexperienced crew, forced on us by a steeply plummeting barometer. The Vaigat too between Disko Island and the mainland was somewhat lively and with plenty of ice around, but we did find a 'new' anchorage which should make passages there more user friendly in the future for those who might want to stop. And now the boat is resting at Aasiaat for the winter, ready for more adventures next year.

But one day I am going to try sailing for pleasure ....

EIGHTY-EIGHT YEARS LATER

by Stephen and Sue Lennane

This is the cruise for which the Juno Cup was awarded.

We had spent some seasons in the Baltic and it was time to move on. Sue wanted to see the Lofotens. How to get there from Stockholm? Idly looking at an atlas last winter I realised that there is a fairly narrow isthmus between the Gulf of Bothnia and the Barents Sea and thus the Lofotens. Why not take the boat overland? There has always been a tradition of portage be it across the Alps by Hannibal, across Panama before the canal and, of course, by Tristan Jones who carried his boat from the Dead Sea to Lake Titicaca. Like all the good ideas I have had, someone has always thought of it first. I think it was Oliver Roome who told me that C.C. Lynam, the famous headmaster of the Dragon School at Oxford, had done it by train in 1912 and had written it up in Roving Commissions that year. Indeed he had. His cruise of 1912, which made him well known both in the RCC and nationally, was from Trondheim to the North Cape and then back to Narvik where Blue Dragon II was put on a train for Stockholm. He said in his log that he wished he had chosen Luleå rather than Stockholm so that he could have sailed down the Gulf of Bothnia. So our cruise this year was decided – we would do his route eighty-eight years later but in reverse. However it seemed better not to go to Narvik but to try for Kirkenes on the Norwegian Russian border as that opened up two unexplored stretches of water and anyway there would not be time to get beyond Tromso.

Lynham had the help of one Captain Björnstad and the British Vice-Consul who arranged matters for him but I had the advantage of the internet and, after a number of false trails, managed to track down a haulage firm in Skellefteå almost at the top of the Gulf of Bothnia. After several months and many faxes and e-mails, all was arranged and we set off, as luck would have it, from near Lidingo island in Stockholm where *Blue Dragon II* had eventually arrived, at the beginning of July.

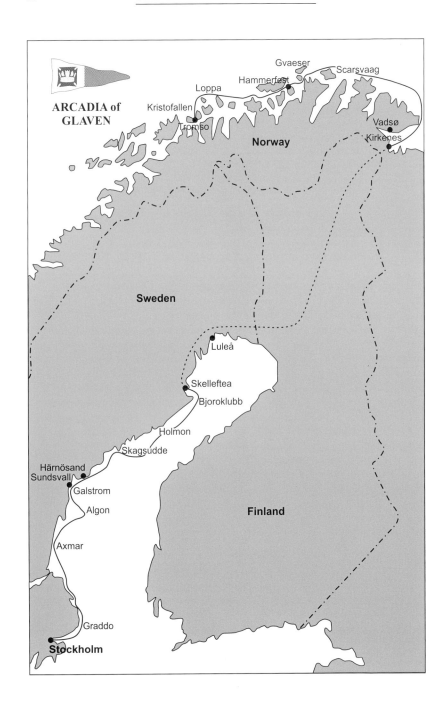

ARCADIA of
GLAVEN

Gvaeser
Scarsvaag
Hammerfest
Loppa
Kristofallen
Tromso
Norway
Vadsø
Kirkenes

Sweden

Luleå
Skelleftea
Bjoroklubb

Holmon
Skagsudde
Härnösand
Sundsvall
Galstrom
Algon

Finland

Axmar

Graddo
Stockholm

We reached Graddö, in the Stockholm archipelago, having experienced the first of the light northeast winds that were later to plague us. There was a nice notice in the marina saying that the showers are 5 kroner and that the harbourmaster will help you change! We then passed through the Vaddö canal and under an electricity line not marked on the chart. The height was shown as 17 metres. Our air draught is about 15. No problem said Sue, as on these occasions I never look, but I did notice she took her hand off the stay she had been holding on to. We anchored at Kulbadviken just across the water from Öregrund where we called for stores next morning. From this point all yachts seemed to disappear, as this is the limit for most Swedish yachtsmen. Indeed we saw nothing all day and, with no wind, had to motor to Axmar where we moored beside a little restaurant where they said they had never seen an English boat before. Next day we beat northwards and anchored at Agön, a small island with a fascinating eighteenth century church.

We were now 180 miles from Stockholm but, with another 240 to go and a lorry to catch, we were glad of a westerly wind to Galström. This tiny harbour was once used as a port for iron ore with fascinating old kilns for producing the iron. The forecast next day was for light southeast winds which turned out to be rather more east and more than light. Up to 24 knots, needing a reef but with the pleasure of eventually hiding in the islands. We moored at a peaceful pontoon amongst lovely vegetation with wild strawberries and dark blue Canterbury bells. A motor cruiser called Mickey Mouse came alongside the pontoon with a Dalek voice in English telling him where he was and where to go. We could have done with that later!

Next day the weather started to deteriorate and there was fog and rain with a lumpy sea and no wind. Most unpleasant. We used the radar to find the gap between two islands which form the harbour of Ulvöholm. Visibility was down to 100 metres or less at times and never more then half a mile the whole day. There were a few brief moments of evening sunshine and then the rain started, the like and duration of which we had not experienced before. It was regatta week at Ulvöholm and crowded so we left in spite of the poor forecast and in fact had a brisk sail to Trysunda in sun before the mist came down again with the rain. During this brief period we saw the High Coast for the first time. This is a lovely cruising area of hills, deep water and many anchorages. An undiscovered part of Swedish waters and the most attractive we have seen. It would be a good place for a week's cruise for anyone going north of Stockholm.

We were weather bound in Trysunda for three days. There was a Russian high and a Norwegian high, which sandwiched a series of depressions coming from the Baltic States into a pathway up the Gulf of Bothnia. For the next week fog and rain reduced visibility till in the end we chose harbours with entrances that had no off-lying dangers and which would be radar friendly. We could have stood off the coast altogether as there was little shipping to avoid but being lightly crewed the depressions were off putting and anyway we wanted to explore the coast. At one stage we closed on the lighthouse at Skagsudde and heard the white water on the rocks before we could see it and make the necessary turn to starboard. Not a moment to be revisited.

Over the next few days we pushed on further north, seeking windows in the weather and getting paranoid that any blurring of the horizon would turn into a fog bank, which as often as not it did. Stockholm radio began to issue navigational warnings because of the trees that were being washed down into the Gulf and we found out later that the hospitals had been put on alert because of the flooding.

Dense fog at the island of Holmön gave us a day to visit one of the best museums we have seen. It had sections on boats and their construction in the last century, on seal hunting, on fishing and on the textiles that the women made. It was very much worth the visit. The white camouflaged seal hunting boats gave us the feel that we were getting near the Arctic. One final night at the famous old pilot station at Bjoroklubb and we arrived at Skellefteå, our port of embarkation as it were.

As we moved north various people who had asked where we were going seemed amazed at the idea of going to Norway via the Gulf of Bothnia. A German we met rushed off with gales of laughter at our foolishness to tell his wife. When we met Karl-Hendriik, who had organised the transport, he spoke of merriment in his office at the mad Englishman who was coming. We accepted the role of eccentric English but were secretly worried that the whole thing might not succeed, everything being dependent on a crane. I was therefore delighted on arrival to see one, as cranes in this part of the world are not two a penny. However on closer inspection it had a maximum lift of half our displacement and depression set in until we could contact Karl-Hendriik next day. It would have been so disappointing to have had to return to Stockholm. He reassured us that there was a suitable machine half a mile up the river and a day later we were ready to load *Arcadia* onto the waiting lorry. Before this we just had time to return to Stockholm by overnight train so that Sue could fly back to see her patients and I could bring the car north for the overland part. I returned to unstep the mast and found myself having to be craned up to the spreaders. The crane was paid for by the hour so speed was the order of the day. Eventually *Arcadia* was on board the lorry with the mast tied alongside. I left the burgee up as I thought at that stage I would still be near the yacht and in effective control within the meaning of the Act. It was also decidedly more classy than the usual rag hanging off the end of a load. I thought of e-mailing the Hon. Sec. about flag etiquette in these circumstances but decided that life was too short.

The schedule was that loading was to take place on Wednesday with the boat arriving in Kirkenes on Friday afternoon. I had not reckoned with Karl-Gunnar, the driver, and his desire for speed. He left at 1500 on the Wednesday while I had to wait for John Phipps, who was coming to help crew the next leg of the cruise. He arrived at the airport at 2100 and we set off to follow the boat. By 0400 next morning I had driven non-stop through the night (not that it ever got dark) and eventually found *Arcadia* in a lay-by somewhere above the Arctic Circle. By this time I was desperately tired and parked across the lorry to prevent a quick getaway. I climbed on board to sleep. Two hours later, woken by the lorry engine, we were up again and off to Kirkenes where we arrived somewhat tired. An enormous crane was waiting on the quay and within minutes of arrival *Arcadia* was floating in the Barents Sea. The mast was lowered into place and having been just about secured at four points I was again craned up. At this moment there was a long blast from a ship's horn and I saw from my elevated position that we were in the middle of the famous Hurtigruten coastal ship's dock and she wanted it. Down the mast again and with help from the crowd that had collected we moved *Arcadia* round the end of the dock with the Hurtigruten's bow ending up about ten feet from our stern. All was nearly finished with the re-rigging when I went below to find the wind speed instruments lying on the table. In view of his speed Karl-Gunnar had wisely asked that they should be removed. So up the mast again, this time to the top, bosun's chair attached to an enormous shipping crane hook. John helpfully suggested that if I had the hook pointing away from me I was less likely to be garrotted. Very kind. I had climbed in my youth but I have less of a head for heights now. All of a sudden at the top of the mast a thought flashed through my head, 'What am I doing here, at my age, hanging from the top of a crane in the Arctic? Would not Bognor be better?' Eventually both instruments were reattached and later, to my surprise, they both worked. A friendly Norwegian showed us the way to the small boat harbour, which was just as well, as at that stage I would never have noticed the leading marks placed about 600 feet up on a hill.

The Norwegians we met in Kirkenes were very friendly as one might have expected in such an isolated place. No one had ever moved a yacht overland before to Kirkenes from Sweden although our imminent arrival had been talked about in the town. We were ahead of schedule and had two days to wait for the arrival of Oliver the other crewmember. So we sailed round the Varanger fjord and spent a night at a tiny fishing village where John caught an enormous cod, which filled our protein requirements for several days. We also visited by car Grensle Jacob, the village – well two houses and a church – on a tiny estuary, which marks the Russian border. We could not cross because visas were too expensive but contented ourselves by throwing stones across the river into Russia but no one was in. Oliver Barnes, an ornithologist and botanist, arrived and we set off on the next leg of the cruise.

The FPI for North Norway is a little depressing about the North Cape to the Russian border. 'No yacht is known to have sailed into these

Blue Dragon II at the North Cape, August 1912.

waters. No inner lead or protection from the Arctic Sea. Hazards in the shape of bad weather, few harbours of refuge and no attractions or facilities'. Fortunately there was no bad weather, only the very light northeast wind that the locals had prophesied. With the yankee and the engine and the tide we progressed slowly along this barren and slightly awesome coast. The cliffs are about 1000 feet high with patches of snow, no trees and little vegetation. With Oliver's help we spotted arctic skuas, puffins, red necked phalaropes and many other species. It was interesting that Oliver and I had different perceptions of the same thing. He saw a fulmar happily sitting on a piece of wood. I saw a large baulk of ship-damaging timber with a bird on it. The shoreline is littered with timber from the Russian rivers but the height of the wood above the high water mark serves as a reminder of the potential ferocity of the northeast wind in these waters. The old gun emplacements reminded us of the war and the appalling conditions the Murmansk convoys must have endured.

The FPI was inaccurate about harbours of refuge as there are several between the Russian border and the North Cape and we visited five as well as collecting information about four others. One night we anchored in a small fjord used as a bolt hole by trawlers in poor weather. On other occasions we used the small fishing harbours where there was always a berth or a vacant buoy. We were warned to keep well offshore at Sletnes, a low peninsular with the most northerly lighthouse in the world and offshore shoals. Passing on a good day we had no trouble but later a Hurtigruten captain told me he keeps one and a half miles off and four miles off in bad weather.

Arcadia at the North Cape, August 2000.

Our last stop before the North Cape was at Scarsvåg, the most northerly fishing village in the world. After dinner we decided to walk up the hill to see the North Cape at midnight. While preparing to go John slipped on the companionway steps and there was a large hiss as the fire extinguisher went off covering everything with white powder. I've always wondered what a fire extinguisher could do and now I know. The scene was like one of those Christmas cards with artificial snow over everything – quite Arctic in fact. Eventually, helpless with laughter at the devastation, we left on our walk on the flimsy pretext that we had better let all the dust settle. We were rewarded with a magic sunset just before midnight over the North Cape. An unforgettable moment. Getting back to the ship there was a forgettable moment lasting about two hours while we attempted to clear up. Fire extinguisher powder should not be allowed overboard, however inert the manufacturers say it is. It floats embarrassingly all over the harbour unless treated with washing up liquid.

Next day we caught up with Lynam, as it were, at Hornviken, the cove on the east side of the North Cape. Oliver and I went ashore in the dinghy, making fast to the disused landing stage for tourists described by Lynam. We climbed the thousand feet or so to the plateau from which we could see the tourist site. No longer the refreshment room secured by wire stays of Lynam's day but a vast complex with dozens of cars, coaches and camper vans. We went no further. Instead Oliver kindly gave me a short tutorial on how the vegetation had adapted to so barren a site. The weather was sunny and there was no wind, only a slight swell. Exactly the conditions Lynam had had eighty-eight years and four days before. The

crew were therefore dispatched into the Barents Sea in the dinghy to take
a photograph of the yacht as Lynam had done.

On to Gjesvær where Lynam bought half a halibut and we bought a
seven pound salmon. Obviously a good place to shop for fish. We saw
our first sea eagle here. Later at Bustadhamn where Lynam fished John
caught nothing. Presumably *Blue Dragon II* had scooped all the fish. To
the amazement of the locals the crew of *Blue Dragon II* swam each day.
They did have an exceptional summer though. Not to be outdone this
skipper swam for a short time (microseconds) while the crew just stood
by and laughed. What wimps. There is a photograph to record the occasion and it shows the extreme agony as the cold water reached the outlying parts.

The winds remained very light and we had to motorsail a lot in order
to get to Tromso on time. Hammerfest, now no longer the most northerly town in the world (Honningsvåg has taken the honours) was shut on
Sunday morning and quite empty except for tourists from the cruise ships
wandering round looking for something to buy. On to Loppa where we
spent a happy day in the sun. Oliver who knows about cruise ships says
that it is called 'Day at Leisure'. I went walking, John went fishing and
Oliver was in his element and recorded forty species of birds on the one
day. A glass of whisky with one of the four all-the-year-round inhabitants
was rewarded next morning with a large amount of cod. No chance of a
protein deficiency disease in Norway. And Oliver promised to find a
special anti-scurvy grass that grew there. Such health! On towards
Tromso via the glacier at Jokulfjord. It rained for about forty-eight hours
making for cold sailing, and after getting hopelessly lost in poor visibility,
we eventually found the harbour at Kristfallen for our last night. Then to
Tromso where Sue was to rejoin and Oliver was to go back to England.
After one further week's cruising round the outer islands Sue and I left
on the Hurtigruten ferry to collect the car from Kirkenes. It was wonderful to have someone else doing the navigation and a good chance to see
the Arctic scenery inland on the return journey.

Looking back we were well pleased with this eccentric cruise. It opened
up two relatively unexplored European cruising areas and there cannot
be many of those left. It also showed that there could be a fairly quick
route from the Baltic to the Lofotens. It was fun comparing Lynam's
journey with ours. Modern electronics and a more reliable engine spared
us the many navigational scrapes he got himself into but his weather was
far kinder than ours. Yet, however different the conditions, eighty-eight
years later we shared with him the same object of exploration and of
course all the fun involved in doing the unusual.

¿DONDE VA LA LANCHA?

by Andrew O'Grady and Ulla Norlander

Where is the boat going? To Anihue, for a winter cruise. It could have been to any one of the picturesque little communities with wooden churches and shingled homes that abound in the archipelago of Chiloé. The *lancha vela*, a traditional Chiloé sailing boat that conducted trade in the islands under sail, is no more. *Balaena* with her varnished spars, traditional lines and gaff rig is closer to the boat in the song than the multitude of colourful motor launches whose crews wave cheerfully or toot on their horns as we sail by.

We had arrived in the islands of Chiloé from New Zealand via the roaring forties. Good food and wine, friendly people, folk music and dancing complement the natural beauty of the islands. Castro, the main town, is one of the safest anchorages that one could wish for. Here in the south of Chile we have found perfect cruising.

Leaving Castro on one of the still, cloudless days that seem so common in winter we headed south. Despite the beautiful weather, an approaching front encouraged us to hurry in order to be snugly at anchor before it arrived. Estero Castro and Canal de Yal led us south through rural scenery that can hardly have altered in the 440 years since the Spanish arrived. Oxen were pulling the ploughs, pigs fattened themselves noisily and apple trees were preparing for spring. Only after leaving the canal did the Andes remind us that this was Chile and not Devon in a bygone age. Monte Melimoyu, the most southerly of four snow-capped volcanoes, was clearly visible at a distance of 100 miles. Anihue lay below the horizon betwixt the toes of the mountain.

After a long day in which the breeze only aided us on one or two occasions we found our way in the dark into Estero Huildad. We had been there before, so the absence of the usual entrance light did not upset us and allowed us to practice our skills with radar.

The following day the wind was still fickle for our crossing of the gulf to Puerto Juan Yates in the shadow of one of those snowy volcanoes.

This anchorage is within a pretty group of islands in Bahia Tic Toc. The day had been quiet as we sailed over to the wildside from cultivated Chiloé. However by evening it was clear that we needed a secure anchorage. The barograph was falling and the sky lowering. We knew from experience that we had to choose a spot with protection from both the northwesterlies preceding the front and from the southwesterlies following it. We had fun setting the anchor on a rocky bottom. Each time we tested with full power astern *Balaena* took off on a new trip. Finally, as dusk came, we finished our preparations with two anchors ahead and two stern lines ashore. We felt a little unsure of how secure this place was going to be.

All the work was not in vain. When the gale arrived it brought violent *ráfagas* from the north. These tumbled down the slopes of Monte Yanteles and were a reminder of how different conditions are close to the mountains. Topography can be as important as the coastline when choosing your anchorage. This was the kind of night that nightmares can be made from. Rain thundered down and *Balaena* was swung to and fro on her lines. Occasionally a strong *ráfaga* would lay us over while the wind screamed through the rigging and tore at any loose rope end or fitting. It was dramatic to experience. One has to have absolute trust in the mooring. Thankfully we have had only two nights like that in a year.

The following day was bright and gusty from the southwest. It was fascinating to explore our anchorage. It is an idyllic spot with abundant bird life and many resident dolphins and seals. Timid, comical steamer ducks paddle off in a cloud of spray at the approach of a dinghy. This is typical of almost all spots away from larger towns where nature is still in charge.

The next strong blow saw us running at 6 knots under staysail alone for Bahia Anihue. This spot typifies the peculiarities of anchoring near the mountains. It is almost open to the north and would not appear very secure. However the towering peak that rises from the southern shore of the cove buffers the wind. Even in severe northerlies all that was felt were a few gusts reflected off the cliff.

Ulla was suffering from debilitating back pain and had to stay in bed most of the next few weeks. This gave me an opportunity to show what a good husband I can be when put to the test. We were in a flawless anchorage and the winter weather just at the base of the Andes was a succession of cloudless days. I was able to catch up with repairs and to explore the rivers and bays.

One rising tide we conned our way up a narrow creek into a completely landlocked saltwater lake. Here nature ruled and the only sign of mankind was a long abandoned midden from pre-European times. Otters and seals patrolled the lake competing with pelicans and cormorants for the abundant fish-life. *Balaena* is probably the only yacht ever to have visited this mountain hideaway.

At last Ulla was able to spend a little time on her feet and we made the short trip to Rio Buta Palena. This river is the second largest in Chile and is navigable for many miles once inside the bar. We found five metres at high water at the entrance making it essential to have settled weather. Our friends from Bahia Anihue also have a home on the Palena and helped pilot us in. Once again we enjoyed many hours of their hospitality. In the wide river there was excellent shelter and holding. Our only concern was with the possibility of floods. How did those enormous piles of driftwood including substantial trees arrive along the riverbank? It was a novelty to anchor in fresh water, which we could use straight from the river. In Chile water is generally not a problem aboard *Balaena*. We collect rain directly from the deck into our tanks.

Of course the weather had to change as soon as we decided to head back to Chiloé. Now the wind came from the northwest and blew across the Golfo Corcovado creating a nasty little sea. *Balaena* waited in Bahia Tic Toc for a swing to the southwest. We tried to leave but were unable to stomach the awful conditions and ran back to our anchorage. Returning we covered the same ground in thirty minutes that had taken three hours of beating. After a night's rest we realised that we had to face the gulf once again. It was unpleasant to set off with sleet, snow and gale force winds from right ahead. Yet after five hours of hard going there was a magical change. The sun shone and the wind swung to the southwest (which is what the weather chart had been showing for two days). Once again we discovered that the mountains create their own weather. We could look back to Tic Toc and see the black clouds and squalls obscuring the mountains as *Balaena* flew north with a bone in her teeth.

A POLICEMAN'S TIP FOR THE PENTLAND FIRTH

by Christopher Thornhill

Sai See was tucked into a corner of Kirkwall harbour. It was a skilful bit of parking by Mary, jammed into a right angle of the quay wall and hemmed in by fishing boats: Tommy Duncan was impressed.

A squad car braked sharply on the quay and a policeman in uniform strode towards us. 'Oh ho! What have we done?' He had come to admire the best looking vessel in the harbour and I suppose he had to make it look official in case his sergeant was watching.

Our new friend was of course a yacht owner and told us that he raced regularly across the Pentland Firth to Wick. This was our destination for tomorrow and the Pentland Skerries were on my mind; which side to pass them with a strong east-going tide? I was expecting to go clear to the east of the Skerries, be swept out into the North Sea and have to beat back to Wick. 'No problem,' the officer said, 'keep close round the shore of South Ronaldsay as far as the Lother Rock and leave the Skerries to port. From Lother Rock head firmly for Stroma and the tide will bring you half a mile off Duncansby Head'. It sounded easy. He explained that a useful eddy runs westwards from the Old Head from three and a half hours before HW Dover, while the Pentland Firth tide is setting southeastwards at full strength. The edge of the eddy is clearly marked by rough breaking water. 'Keep to the north of the breakers, close to the shore, until near the Lother Rock, the nearer the better.'

We left Kirkwall at 1230 on 10 August (HW Dover 2100 BST). The log records: 'Fast run to Mull Head Deerness: then a fast reach to the Copinsay Sound and in far too strong wind to the south of Ronaldsay. Hove-to at 1640 in Wind Wick (sic) to await the policeman's eddy – hope it's not too windy for this caper'. We had arrived too early.

The wind blew at 35 knots while we were hove-to, fore-reaching to and fro across the bay, but when we let draw at 1715 it dropped suddenly and, to our surprise, we unrolled the jib and took out the deep reef in the

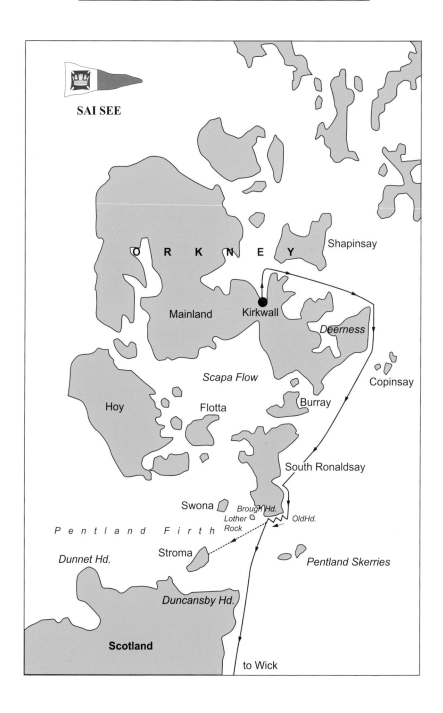

SAI SEE

ORKNEY

Shapinsay

Mainland

Kirkwall

Deerness

Scapa Flow

Copinsay

Hoy

Flotta

Burray

South Ronaldsay

Swona

Brough Hd.

Lother Rock

Old Hd.

Pentland Firth

Stroma

Pentland Skerries

Dunnet Hd.

Duncansby Hd.

Scotland

to Wick

mainsail. At 1740 (−0320 Dover) we found the promised eddy at Old Head. The sea was calm but the white water was clearly visible where the tidal streams met.

Visibility was poor; we could just see the Muckle Skerry but nothing of mainland Scotland. We tacked westwards close to the shore until we were about 2 cables southwest of the coastguard lookout on Brough Head, which we judged sufficiently close to the Lother Rock; then we headed for an invisible Stroma. The copper did not tell us which bit of the two mile long island to head for, so, as it was neapish, we made for the middle. The course was about 240°T (at springs it should probably be the north end, Swilkie Point, about 250°T). The time was 1805 (−0255 Dover) and it was 5.3 miles to Duncansby Head.

The overfalls were no trouble (at neaps) as we plunged into the main tide, but the fog thickened. At first it seemed touch and go with the misty Muckle Skerry, but we cleared it easily. A huge ore carrier came out of the fog and went close astern, heading at a crazy angle to cross the tide. Another passed close ahead. It was not much fun! But at 1850 the GPS told us that Duncansby Head was indeed abeam, half a mile to the west. We never saw it.

It was a most efficient crossing that took forty-five minutes. The fog cleared and we sailed on to Wick in the lee of the land where Mary found a good berth alongside the quay for supper.

Note:

This passage is not described among the Pentland Firth routes in the Clyde Cruising Club's pilot, nor in a very useful article *Passage Plans for the Pentland Firth* published in *Cruising*; Spring 1999. The reasons for its efficiency and comparative safety can be found in the *Admiralty North of Scotland Pilot (NP52)*, in the sections '*Tidal Streams − Old Head to Swona*' and '*Tidal Streams − east part of The Pentland Firth: between Duncansby Head and Muckle Skerry*'; and on chart 2162. The Liddel Eddy begins to run westwards from Old Head towards Brough Head and the Lother Rock about −0330 Dover. There is a race off Old Head, but the tide is with you and it does not last long. There are some rocks, the Skerries of Skaigram, up to 1 cable off Old Head and it is wise to pass the point around the 30 metre contour, or further out according to the race (but keep in the eddy). There are rocks close inshore between Old Head and Brough Head, extending out a cable midway between the heads; it is wise to tack on the 20 metre contour. When Brough Head bears northeast it is time to head for Stroma. You should be swept clear of the race off the Lother Rock, although there will be some breaking water where the streams meet. The southeast going tide, which runs up to 8 knots at springs, will push you neatly in the direction of Duncansby Head, but should keep you 1½ miles clear west of the Muckle Skerry. Timing is vital, not only to make proper use of the Liddel Eddy, but to avoid the notorious Duncansby Race, which is described as 'extremely violent and dangerous, when the southeast going stream is opposed by E or southeast gales'. It is not to be trifled with at any time and it is often the sting in the tail of the Pentland Firth on the passage east, even in the finest weather. The beauty is that by −0230 Dover the main race will have swung round to the northwest of Duncansby Head, leaving our route clear, although there is always some degree of disturbed sea near the headland. So be off Old Head between −0330 and −0300 Dover. There is a lit beacon on the Lother Rock (Q) and lighthouses on the Muckle Skerry; Swona; Stroma (Swilkie Point) and Duncansby Head.

PILOTS OF THE WILD WEST

by Tom Cunliffe

Western Ireland is the sort of place that can tip you off your cloud of complacency with a hard bump. In the fantasy world of cruise preparation, you imagine days drifting past bird cliffs of impossible splendour followed by nights in gaily-painted, turf-scented pubs. I suppose it could be like that. If you believe the accounts of others, it apparently sometimes is. There is only one problem. Old Man Weather.

The 'retro' pilot cutter *Westernman* and her crew put out from the English Channel in May to leave the major landmarks of Mizen Head, Malin Head and the Dublin Guinness brewery to starboard. We made an improbable beginning at Cape Clear Island where for once neither wind nor wave disturbed the tranquillity, but soon we were served with the sort of conditions that led to poor Jonah being converted into a fun-sized whale snack. The rain it rainèd every day, the gales howled mercilessly and the seas ran so high that we suffered the unprecedented unpleasantness of a cockpit-full while rounding Kerry Head. That sort of thing doesn't happen on pilot cutters.

Against this general background of comfort-threatening violence, we rocketed through the breaking seas of dread Blasket Sound, squared off and ran away to round the far Maharees into Tralee Bay. Here, the small port of Fenit now boasts a first class marina in the form of a sort of high-class concrete box built on the end of the pier. It was hard to imagine the sea walls would guard us from the mayhem outside, yet the water was carpet flat as the incumbent vessels heeled to the storm.

I had learned about Fenit while researching a book on sailing and pulling pilot craft. It turned out that this port for the provincial city of Tralee had been one of the last places in Europe regularly to use such vessels. My correspondent had been Bob Goodwin, a retired local pilot, who grew up on the Maharees learning his family trade by boarding ships from canvas curraghs with his father. The islands are several miles from the marina, but Bob happened to be out there as *Westernman* tore by under deep-reefed main. He instantly recognised her for a pilot boat. Later, he came aboard and invited us across to his sometime family house on St Seanach's Island, Illauntannig. Now deserted except for occasional 'summer lets', it was here that he and generations of pilots before him had been raised.

'Bring your boat across in the morning. I'll come off and guide you in.'

The approaches were tortuous and the only possible shelter looked hopeless. The island is tiny and, as W. M. Nixon observed about Tory a little further north, the place enjoys a fine lee from Bermuda.

It was blowing a gale as we put to sea for the four-mile passage. We considered aborting, but the question of pride when confronted with this sea-hardened professional ran stronger than any considerations of bourgeois judgement. Half a mile from a pile of rocks breaking like Armageddon, Bob appeared in a small motor boat out of the mother of all squalls. There seemed no hope of anchoring, but we followed him closely and were brought to a secret pool among shoals and sandbars where the seas subsided with a suddenness only matched by improbability. The storm blew itself out, the sun flirted with the day and, as the tide fell, the clear shallow water over white sand took on a West Indian colouring. Bob moored his boat and transferred to a curragh, rowing us to the kelpy beach with the bladeless oars of the west.

The Maharees have been uninhabited since World War II except for occasional visitors and the birds who nest willy-nilly, their eggs and chicks all around. At the southern end, Bob showed us a monastic settlement

Westernman in Cape Clear.

with intact beehive huts and the bones of monks gleaming white as the ocean eroded their burying ground. On the windward margin, the fields were under threat from waves breaking over them. Bob indicated a battered wall whose job was to stabilise the soil rather than keep out poachers. Beyond it were only the rocks, the madness of the breakers and the scattered sky.

We drank strong dark tea in the house which remains undisturbed since the family moved ashore in the late 1930s. There is no power and no telephone. The hearth is painted brick in the traditional fashion, below roof timbers dark with the smoke of ten thousand fires. Bob told us of his childhood when the Goodwins and a second pilot dynasty lived on the island, competing for the same ships. Sometimes, one family would put to sea long before dawn to be out of sight before the others realised they were gone. It was not enough to watch from the shore for a ship, then hope to out-row the others. Such head-to-head rivalry led to boats being launched in heavier weather than was remotely safe, yet loss of life was surprisingly small, perhaps a tribute to the unlikely sea-keeping capability of the frail, ultra-light-displacement curragh.

Bob Goodwin recalled his father describing a failed gun-running attempt during World War I when a German ship carrying a consignment of arms for the IRA had somehow missed her pilot off Fenit. The ship was apprehended, but the pilots were arrested anyway and taken to Dublin in chains. Only last-minute evidence saved them from the firing squad.

'How can you follow that,' we wondered as we beat out of Tralee Bay into the left-over slop the following day. Yet Ireland, as always, provided the answers. It was a long way to the North Channel, a passage involving broken bones, poetry, light-footed girls tripping their sprightly measures to wavering concertinas in pipe-black bars, the world's most creative scrapyard at Malin Head where unwanted cars are literally kicked over the cliff, then finally, calm summer sunshine in the Irish Sea.

There are no prizes left for being first round Ireland, but if it's romance and adventure you want, take my advice. Don't bother hacking all the way to the South Seas. Steer northwest from the Scillies instead. You'll soon be there.

A SHORT VOYAGE TO ALBANIA

by David Edwards

It is a sad consequence of the long isolation of Albania under the Communists that practically nobody has heard of Butrint. Yet for over two thousand years it was a port on the mainland commanding the Straits of Corfu. It was on the trade route from Venice to Constantinople. In the time of Alexander the Great it already had a flourishing harbour and a theatre. The Romans used it as a supply base and Julius Caesar established a veterans' colony there. In the Byzantine era its harbour continued to flourish. The Normans completed a basilica there in the thirteenth century and from the fourteenth to eighteenth centuries it was part of the Venetian Empire. As John Julius Norwich has said, 'it is a microcosm of three thousand years of Mediterranean history.' Then in 1993 Lord (Jacob) Rothschild, who has a fine villa on Corfu overlooking Butrint, joined with Lord Sainsbury of Preston Candover, and established the Butrint Foundation to help the Albanian Government to save and preserve the city and to secure international support. This was a turning point. Richard Hodges, professor of archaeology at the University of East Anglia, was appointed director of the Butrint Foundation, and many UEA students go there each summer to dig. It is a huge task, but the rewards will be immense. 'When we have finally uncovered everything that is in Butrint', said Richard Hodges, 'it will make Pompeii seem like Kettering.'

One who had heard of Butrint was Nicholas Barber, who is a trustee of the British Museum. He was one of our crew in *Mehalah* in September 2000. He persuaded us that we must go to Butrint – and we did. We sailed to Corfu, and there Nicholas spoke to the Director at Butrint and arranged for us to have a guided tour the following Sunday. We scoured the chandlers of Corfu, and managed to find an Albanian courtesy flag (Hapsburg eagles on a fierce red ground) and a Greek chart which showed as a right angle the tiny quay at Sarande which was the only port through which Butrint could be approached.

The Venetian tower, Butrint.

We had been advised to go to Sarande but to give warning of our arrival by VHF. We duly called up the harbour but voice communication was not established because of language difficulties. We arrived just before our scheduled time of 0900 (1000 Corfu time) to find that the concrete quay was a wreck. It reminded me of the utter dereliction of the customs quay at Kronstadt when we visited St Petersburg in 1997.

On the quay was a large and cheerful reception committee, port officials, customs, shipping agent, and Gjoni, the assistant director at Butrint, who smoothed our arrival in the country and commandeered from its owner a taxi – the usual Mercedes – to take us the fifteen miles to the site at Butrint. Gjoni, who had been to an American university and spoke excellent English, was living with his young family in Sarende. Although poverty was everywhere, despair was not. The odd hotel had been built, and we saw small motor boats which brought tourists over from the harbour at Corfu. One felt sad for a people who for so long had a rough time from a fanatical government.

The first building you see in the city at Butrint is one of the most modern, the Venetian tower which guards against attack from the river. The whole area is full of gems of Venetian masonry. Near the tower is a small, probably Roman, bath house. From there we walked through an avenue of gum trees to the Roman theatre, built in the third century BC, and originally seating 2500 people. We walked along the Sacred Way, in front of the theatre which dates from the fourth century BC, to the large bath house, dating from the second century AD, which has a superb mosaic floor. Here you are surrounded by the tantalisingly unexcavated

The Basilica, Butrint.

remains of the heart of the ancient city. The diggers will uncover here the Prytaneum, which was the magistrates' building, the Sanctuary of Asclepius on which were carved inscriptions detailing such matters as the release of slaves, the Stoa and the open area which was the market and place of assembly.

We left the ancient centre and walked to the Baptistery, built in the sixth century AD and an important early christian building with a well-preserved mosaic pavement. We passed the remains of the aqueduct which fed water to the city from 4 km away, and then we came upon the Basilica, reminiscent of the great Yorkshire abbey ruins, and itself constructed and rebuilt over a period of more than a thousand years.

We finished with a tour of the city walls including the Scaean Gate which was built in the fourth century BC but remained in use throughout the city's life. Above the city is an Acropolis castle, largely unexplored and unexcavated, from which there is a superb view of the surrounding country and Ali Pasha's castle at the mouth of the river.

Without a trace of archaeological indigestion we were then driven back to the boat by Gjoni, and were greeted at the port by various officials who had arrived with bills. We had apparently been treated as if we were a small cargo ship, for example paying US $16 for light dues. It all added up to US $130, which we did not mind, because it was a small contribution to a country in desperate need and a modest charge for a unique experience.

SUNLESS IN ALASKA

by Ann Fraser

This is the cruise for which the ICC Ships Decanter was awarded.

Gollywobbler II arrived on the west coast of the USA, after a 3000 mile trip from Florida, drawn by a fiery steed (Okay, a red truck!) and handsomely escorted by her chauffeur, Gus. We were 100 miles north of Seattle with 900 miles of Inside Passage to get to Juneau.

We left Anacortes on 11 May and the CCA cruise was due to start in Juneau on 16 June, so we knew we had to make good speed. I was aware that the going would be tough during the cruise to Glacier Bay, because the CCA members, although all very experienced sailors, were all in power cruisers capable of about eight to twelve knots, the Inside Passage being notorious for lack of wind. The planned daily run varied from about forty to seventy miles, so to keep up we would have to leave earlier and get in later. And so it proved, despite groans from the crew.

We entered British Columbia at Bedwell Harbor, one of the Gulf Islands. 'Welcome to a cold country,' the friendly customs officer greeted me. 'Had I any potatoes, apples or avocadoes on board? How much alcohol?' Fortunately, I had been warned of the restrictions and shopped accordingly, but I was amused to see in the first Canadian supermarket large bags of Idaho potatoes.

Before us we had 900 miles of fiords, mountains and wild life – orca and humpback whales, Dall's porpoises, bald eagles, Steller's sea lions, harbour seals and river otters. There were also the hazards of whirlpools, rapids, eddies and tide-rips, and currents up to fourteen knots. Much advice was given by experienced Inside Passage sailors, including not to assume that slack water was coincident with high or low water at a nearby port. Also warnings about floating logs and, even more dangerous, deadheads – waterlogged tree-trunks floating vertically and almost submerged. Someone who knew I wanted to sail to Alaska suggested I should read Jonathan Raban's *Passage to Juneau*. I did, and was so

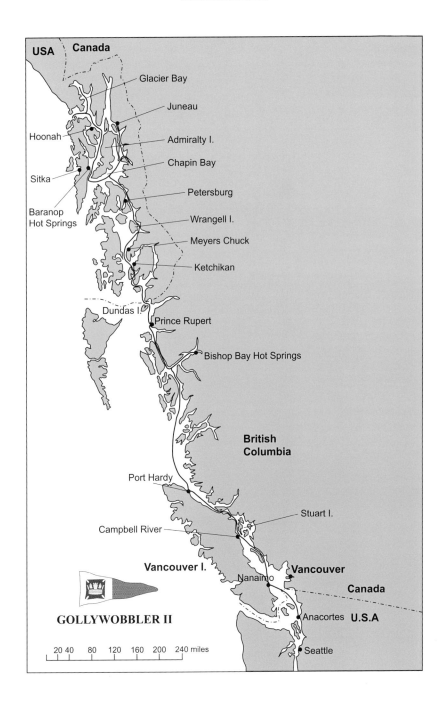

USA Canada

Glacier Bay

Juneau

Hoonah

Admiralty I.

Chapin Bay

Sitka

Petersburg

Baranop
Hot Springs

Wrangell I.

Meyers Chuck

Ketchikan

Dundas I.

Prince Rupert

Bishop Bay Hot Springs

British
Columbia

Port Hardy

Stuart I.

Campbell River

Vancouver I.

Vancouver

Nanaimo

Canada

Anacortes U.S.A

Seattle

GOLLYWOBBLER II

20 40   80   120   160   200   240 miles

alarmed by his tales of dangers, I was tempted to call the whole trip off!

The scenery was magnificent. 3000 foot mountains stretched down to the water's edge, thickly covered with the dark green of pine trees, spruce, hemlock and Douglas firs. At first it appeared merely a uniform green, then one began to see the variation in shades and texture, added to by alders and salmonberry bushes. Waterfalls tumbled through gaps in the trees and, in the near distance, snow-capped mountains peaked and caught the early morning and evening sun, becoming tinged with pink and gold. We glimpsed the occasional small house amongst the trees, but we might sail for five or ten miles before seeing another small community in this wilderness. Roads were rare or non-existent. Transport between islands and houses was by boat or the ubiquitous float planes, which often landed alarmingly close. Supplies and materials for Alaska were towed up on gigantic barges.

Our first experience of coping with rapids came early on at Dodd Narrows, six miles south of the city of Nanaimo on Vancouver Island, where we hoped to pick up more charts. Based on Peter's low water slack calculations, we would be able to carry the flood on to Nanaimo and were there waiting, half an hour early. Two small tugs were also waiting, but it was not until they moved that we realised they were towing a log boom (a huge raft of logs chained together) from which several logs broke loose as they started to take it through the narrow gap. The smaller tug scurried about like a dog herding the errant logs, while we took the opportunity to slip past. To port, after the Narrows, lay the smoking pulp mill of Harmac, where the logs would be sawn up and pulped, contributing to British Columbia's economy.

As I sat on the verandah above the marina at Nanaimo, I had my first glimpse of wild life when a large, bewhiskered, furry brown animal with a long flat tail ran across in front of me. It was a river otter foraging for food. They are wonderful swimmers underwater, but are also at home on land.

Up to then, the weather had been good and not much rain. The wind, light but southerly, allowed us to motor-sail to make progress. Now the wind had become 10–15 knots and northerly – on the nose – as it was to be for most of the way to Juneau. So more motor-sailing, with main hard in to help push *Gollywobbler* through short seas, was our only means of keeping up five knots. We altered course towards the mainland side of the Inside Passage, stopping off at Stuart Island, just before the Yuculta Rapid. There are three sets of rapids close together, Yuculta, Dent and Greene Point Rapids, requiring careful timing for slack water.

Although late May, it was cold as we moved north. After a night at anchor, Peter Shaw found ice in the mainsail and there is a note in the log that I was wearing ski-mitts and goggles, as well as thermals, fleece and oilskins. Alaska and British Columbia are not always ice and glaciers, snow and rain. The sun can shine, as it did when Peter came up with the bright idea of heading for Bishop Bay Hot Springs, where we enjoyed the pleasure of a hot bath followed by a gift of crab from another boat for supper.

Our next goal was Prince Rupert, where we cleared out of British Columbia and headed across the open water of Dixon Entrance, which marks the international border between Alaska and Canada. Dixon Entrance is open to swells from the Pacific and is famous for throwing up a nasty sea in bad weather. Not taking this risk, we anchored overnight in Brundige Inlet on Dundas Island, before heading on to Ketchikan, Alaska, where we cleared in at U.S. customs.

It was now 30 May. We aimed to be in Juneau, another 220 miles, by 13 June, when new crew were to join. We hurried on up the Tongass Narrows, and anchored in the pretty fishing community of Meyers Chuck. We were invited to have a drink with the crew of *Sundowner*, a longliner fishing boat (deep-fishing on the bottom for halibut). We learned about the woes of the industry which are not unlike our own – overfishing over many years, so that salmon fishing is now limited to specific days for licensed boats when the salmon are running to spawn.

Then on through Zimovia Strait towards the fishing port of Wrangell, set against the magnificence of the Stikine Mountains. Approaching Wrangell, the water became murky yellow with patches of foam as if a washing machine had emptied. This was caused by glacier effluence from the Stikine River, which rises 200 miles away in British Columbia.

Wrangell had a rather depressed air. We looked in vain for a lively bar and eventually settled for a hotel where an alcoholic beverage seemed a possibility. But when ordering dinner, we were offered nothing stronger than iced tea. I never did work out the licensing laws.

We pressed on to the busy and friendly fishing port of Petersburg, through the rapids and strong tides of the tortuous Wrangell Narrows with its sixty-six 'ignore-at-one's-peril' marker buoys. Because of the big tidal range, the three fish canneries are built over the water on stilts. Over a beer at Kito's Kave, a lively bar and fast food dive, the bell rang. This was the signal for drinks all round on the house, or rather on the winners of a golf tournament in nearby Wrangell. On the way we had already sighted humpback whales and Dall's porpoises, but in Petersburg a sea lion surfaced right under our stern catching his salmon breakfast before our eyes.

We were now on the home run up Stephen's Passage towards Juneau. A spell of bad weather had set in – no wind, but rain, mist and cloud down to the water, making a sharp lookout for tugs towing immense barges a quarter mile behind them even more necessary. We explored Tracy Arm briefly, but did not get as far as the glaciers due to lack of time. We made a final stop-over in Taku Harbor, where the mist lifted temporarily, as did our spirits, before passing, mast intact, under the Juneau-Douglas Bridge (minimum clearance 50ft at springs) and arriving at Aurora Basin in Juneau on 9 June.

The organisers of the Pacific North West CCA Cruise, Bill and Lu Whitney in *Wojo* and Lou and Phyl Scott in *Traveler*, were already in Aurora. Other CCA boats were arriving at Auke Bay a few miles north near the airport. Of the nineteen crews, half were members of the Pacific Northwest Station, but others had come from the east coast and had chartered. I was delighted to meet Edmund and Ottsie Kendrick (RCC) from Massachusetts. There was also one other sailboat, the elegant 72 foot *Shanake II*, from southern California.

Juneau lies on a strip of land on the east side of the Gastineau Channel, with mountains towering above the city on both shores. Tourism is of major importance to Juneau and there are often several cruise ships in together. The main streets are full of gift and art shops and attractive bars and restaurants, but there are also many challenging trails to explore in the mountains. Peter and I took the Perseverance Trail up to the waterfalls and made a visit to Mendenhall Glacier while waiting for Chris Powell to arrive (which she did with the Mayor of Juneau, whom she had met on the plane from Seattle). Caroline Pulver (RCC) was due to arrive from New York at 0100 on 17 June to complete the crew for the cruise to Glacier Bay, when Peter left for some mountaineering on Mt McKinley. Meanwhile we all provisioned for two weeks at the excellent super-markets, because the cruise itinerary featured few stopovers where food or fuel would be available. Caroline arrived behind schedule by which time the CCA boats were a day ahead of us at Tracy Arm Cove.

It was grey, drizzling, cold. The wind was dead on the nose from the southeast. After two hours motoring to windward, the crew looked miserable. I decided a couple of hours' break might help and suggested going into Taku Harbour, and we could still reach Tracy Arm Cove before dark. Inside the harbour the murk cleared, the sun came out and we took a walk on the beach and met up with another yacht, *¿Que Pasa?*, Stan and Bronwen Lindskog, whom I was to meet up with later. In more cheerful mood, we departed under main and genoa with – yes, 18 knots of wind – and anchored in Tracy Arm Cove near two CCA boats, still in broad daylight at 2100. At this time of year, it is light until 2300.

The following day we explored Tracy Arm. Mountains over 3000 feet high rose sheer from the water, the granite often bare and of a beautiful purplish colour, waterfalls tumbling from the heights, bergy bits floating past with bald eagles perched on them.

The next day was again wet and cold with bad visibility. In drifting fog and a bumpy sea, we ploughed down the east coast of Admiralty Island to Chapin Bay. But we were much cheered by a welcome party in inflat-able dinghies of Bill Whitney and Dave and Sharon Heaps (*Sounder III*) and others greeting us with music and enthusiastic waves.

Thereafter, things improved. On the summer solstice we arrived in Baranof Hot Springs, moored alongside *Sounder III*, and within minutes

Gollywobbler close to Margerie Glacier.   (C.W. Guildner)

were drinking *Carronade*'s very welcoming Margaritas. After a bath in the hot springs, three natural pools which empty into the thundering water-falls immediately below, we were then invited to a cocktail party on *Avanti*, so life was definitely looking up.

We arrived at Hoonah on Chichagof Island, a large Tlingit (pronounced Klink-et) Indian settlement, and then spent the night at Elfin Cove.

Next day, 25 June, several of us were booked for entry to Bartlett Cove and Glacier Bay National Park. To be late on entry risked losing one's 'slot' and the whole five-day permit, so despite protests from the crew we left at 0520. The orientation contained advice on anchorages, injunctions not to get within 200 yards of whales, dolphins, sea-lions. There were warnings about bears, one in particular, a grizzly near Reid Glacier, having a reputation for being 'pesky'.

We anchored for the first night in peaceful Spokane Cove, where someone had said we would probably see bears on the beach in the evening. Nary a bear, but we did see a grey wolf and heard on the VHF that someone had seen a moose swimming. Later I heard that in the next cove *Silver Eagle II* had seen about twenty bears foraging on the beach and fishing. Que pena! The following day we headed for Reid and Lamplugh Glaciers, which had been recommended by Dave Heaps. We anchored in Reid Inlet and were joined by *Silver Eagle II*, with whom we had also chummed up. We went ashore and walked towards the impressive snout of the glacier. Caroline and Chris continued up to the glacier, while I went back to haul the dinghy up further. They returned looking rather nervously over their shoulders, having realised that the footprint they had just photographed was of the afore-mentioned grizzly. We learned later that a party of kayakers had landed there the next day and their tent and kayaks had been roughhoused by the same grizzly, causing them to leave rapidly.

We left Reid Inlet, threading our way under power through a field of bergy bits descending from adjacent Lamplugh Glacier, and heading towards Tarr Inlet and our goal of spectacular Margerie and Grand Pacific Glaciers. Seeing a clear patch developing to starboard, I headed for it and heard voices on the VHF saying '*Gollywobbler* seems to be doing all right'. By now, several of the CCA boats were around and we encountered another field of bergy bits coming down from Grand Pacific, which although vast, was rather unattractive and menacing, being flat with a dark brown horizontal band disfiguring its top.

A plaintive voice came over the VHF from Fred Hayes in *Annabelle* saying he would like to take a picture of us in front of Margerie 'but you have a fender over'. Much laughter all round and I retorted swiftly: 'The crew say it is for fending off icebergs!' as it was hurriedly removed.

We all hovered around Margerie Glacier taking photographs, mesmer- ised by the vertical splits in the ice which widened perceptibly each time a thunderous crack reverberated round the bay. It seemed as if at any moment a huge piece would ultimately calve and crash into the water, causing a massive wave that would swamp the boats passing too close in front.

We made our way back to Juneau, this time into Auke Bay where most of the boats had gathered. There was a final dinner at a hotel in Juneau at which we all thanked Bill Whitney for a very successful cruise and learned that he is to be the next Commodore of the CCA.

During the speech-making, I suddenly heard *Gollywobbler*'s name mentioned and realised someone who had heard the exchange on VHF at Margerie Glacier had set-up a big leg-pull about our fender-dangling episode. Bill Whitney was reading aloud from a paper, which in mock legal language recounted the tale of *Gollywobbler*'s transgression. Although Bill denied all knowledge of the author, I have my suspicions. But it ended the cruise on a high note.

THE NORTH WESTERN EDGE

by Keith Gems

Cashla, 16 miles west of Galway, looks open and bleak. Little houses, like cows, scatter the boggy hummocks. New visitors' moorings bob, courtesy of EU, empty and as yet undiscovered. Management was in dispute, John Donnely, the harbourmaster was uninterested so Pat Brethinack, a local fisherman, was in charge for a moderate fee. Pat had our dinghy ready. *Passim* was a white speck in the expanse of water and sky. Three trips and we were stowed, dry, fed and awash in charts and tide tables. 'All ships, all ships, all ships, crackle, pause, silence, crackle. This is – er – Valencia – Valencia radio, pause, Good evening, Meteorological situation at 1600hrs ... Channel 26.' It was good to be back.

Saturday 12th saw us close-hauled off Slyne Head, impressive, with black basalt cliffs and brilliant white lighthouse. WSW4, a lumpy sea, High Island, to port and into the far end of Inishbofin Harbour – good holding in mud. It was with some relief since the leading beacons (or were those dun-coloured marks really beacons?), seemed to lead us straight onto the mole head. There was barely a boat's length between it and rocks to port. With burning faces we celebrated our first day with gin and tonic and memories of a wild ride with full sail across Atlantic rollers. 50NM at 5.1Kn.

Sunday 13th. Not quite enough wind to hold the boom on the big swells. Spectacular surf bursting 100 feet on Inishkea. Force 8 swells in a Force 3 wind, through Eagle Island race – Erris Head, the big one today. It seemed a long way to Broadhaven, the tide was not quite right round the head. We were all feeling a bit shook-up, it was nice to get into smooth water. E sailed her like a witch, luffing into the approaching dark, just reaching Ballyglass anchorage without a tack, welcomed by a family of dolphins. A cold night, a warm bunk and the gravelly growl of the anchor chain as the tide turned. Landfalls seem forever, what a huge scale – this empty western fastness. 60NM at 4.7Kn.

Monday 14th. Sea wrack, the grey shapes of the Stags (inverted fangs in a gum of foam), and a cold F.5 from the north. No matter, a long stretch across the open water of Donegal Bay, reaching into the unknown, hissing and cutting the Atlantic swell. By noon it had cleared from the west, we could see Inish Murray distant to starboard and headed for Killibegs. It had an easy entrance and most facilities. We changed to Teelin because it would save an hour's westing tomorrow. The pilot is dismissive but it is OK, quite pretty but no facilities. 62.5NM at 5.7Kn.

Tuesday 15th. All ships, all ships, all ships told of a low, approaching from the northwest. It was a cool gunwale-under day. Whilst flopping around, a slack mainsheet lassoed my hearing aid. It went screaming into the drink. Black squalls came and went, a helicopter appeared to be rescuing climbers on the west coast of Aran. Ballagh Rock showed white, a brilliant setting sun saw us through the narrow rock-sided gut, to anchor in the steeply shoaling sides of Rutland Harbour – a dinghy stretch from Burton Port. Now, there's a place! – small, all you can want, the garage supermarket stays open late and, although it seems unlikely, three good restaurants – the French one is outstanding. 41NM at 5Kn.

Note: Ballagh Rock is now very conspicuously white (you cannot read the black). A confusion of orange channel markers is visible in the distance but leading marks, B.W. (front) and B.Y. (back), are not at all easy to locate. Look for what appears to be a white square – it is not the side of a white hut.

Wednesday 16th. Bloody Foreland was anything but. We sped on wings in a cream of wash in a blue circle fringed with building cumulus. The distant wet granite mountains gleamed icily in the rising sun. Evening found us feeling our way into Mulroy Bay. `Feeling', because the charts are wrong. Best water is now one cable to the north of High & Low Rocks with a turn to starboard afterwards, to approach the bar. Fanny Bay gives good shelter, has a fishing boatyard and is a short walk to Downings, an expanding holiday centre with all facilities. Pity such an ugly scatter of rubbishy dwellings should spoil the beautiful surroundings. 49NM at 6.5Kn.

Thursday 17th. Light to moderate, sunny, some engine to maintain our average. Have to watch tides now. My first view of Malin Head. Disappointing, no lighthouse. A new country, different people.

The only good thing about Port Rush is the quayside pontoon, but The Giants' Causeway is worth a visit. (A taxi for 3 with 3/4hr waiting cost £20.) Glacial basalt cooled very slowly to form hexagonal columns, some over 6m. 56NM at 5Kn.

Friday 18th. Perfect weather, incredible clarity – 50 miles or more. M calculates a visible area of 7800 square miles. There was Scotland, you could almost touch it!

For some reason we went to Port Ellen. It exists for the export of malt whisky, not for yachtsmen. Nowhere to go and a long row from an unattractive anchorage. *Passim* turns tightly to starboard so we were off, inside the islands and outside the rocks in a cold northwest F.3 to Craighouse, good shelter, and a pretty, small white and grey village with all you need including Jura Malt from the distillery and showers at the hotel. At 2100 we sat with our drams in the cockpit watching the sunset casting buttery clouds against the dark cones of the Paps of Jura. 55NM at 5.4Kn.

Saturday 19th. Up the narrowing sound, our first tussle with the overfalls. There were so many squiggles on our chart, all without consequence so far, that we had come to appreciate them as a design rather than information. Suddenly, we were moving sideways at 5 knots – our transits disintegrating. The current should sweep us between the rocks rather than onto them but we did not wait to find out. Our little engine with the big flywheel puffed us back, up Loch Craignish and into Ardfern – a very special harbour. An excellent chandlers, the facilities of a major yacht haven, pretty walks, excellent eating and a mooring by a natural island garden next to *Blue Doublet* (a Rustler 36, owned by HRH Princess Anne). Someone else knows where to go. 28NM at 5.5Kn.

Sunday 20th. Why leave? Only because the afternoon tide called and George Seaton offered to lead us with his Nicholson 38. 'I'll take you up the village street,' he said. He was almost as good as his word. I enjoyed it. Without my hearing aid I could not hear our depth alarm.

We were deposited in Loch Puilladobhrain, a perfect anchorage in soft black ooze. We went ashore looking for wild goats, some may think this foolish – and it was! All we found were midges. Gladly, they do not share our addiction to the sea.

A silent moonless night, billions of stars, Andromeda glowing milkily and the Northern Lights wheeling. 22NM at 9Kn (some tide!)

Monday 21st. Tides rule, so we were underway with the harbour bottom now on our foredeck at 0650 in a moderate northeasterly. Mostly smooth seas, grey green islands rearing to 2000 feet, and disoriented winds. The tide held long enough for us to make Tobermory. Easy entrance, visitors buoys, all facilities, comely town, some fishing, nice people. M and I were finally dragged from a rare old-fashioned chandlers. E had visited the distillery and arrived in happy mood for our short leg to Loch Droma Buidhe. Very beautiful, but deep. Two little bays on the E side are just shallow enough otherwise it is to the south end in rocky shale and mud. We dragged twice before digging in. 36.5NM at 4Kn.

Tuesday 22nd. NE F.3-4. Around the dreaded Ardnamurchan Point, we were headed northeast but we fooled the Gods by sailing north to Muck and Eigg. There is no brass at Muck but we had found our favourite island. Oh, to be Laird of this fertile pocket paradise! We wandered among the corn and sheep, horses and cows. Muck means Pig Island, so there were pink pigs and black pigs spread like obese bathers in their own nudist colony. I had not realised that pigs could smile. These were laughing.

We followed the one road for a mile or so. There was the farm, modest house and big outbuildings, tucked under a crag overlooking Port Mor, island studded and fringed by white sand beaches. We found stone cottages on wooded knolls. Only the bicycles stacked in the fuchsia hedges gave them away.

Rudha Chroissein where we anchored is having a new pier to match the school with its twin wind generators. I asked a pink-faced boy, 'how many pupils'. He said something that sounded like 'eight'. There is a home-made tea-room staffed by redoubtable Scottish grandmothers. The building is shiny with restoration, its thick hand-cut slates glinting gold with iron pyrites. There are signs of good husbandry everywhere.

We were slow away to Eigg, clipping inside the southeast corner through the shallows behind Castle Island and on, with a backing Force 5, past Mallaig's iron quays and into Loch Nevis. Both water and Catholic tradition run deep – perhaps Bonnie Prince Charlie hid here – anyway, a white marble angel guided us past some fairly obvious rocks to port to anchor close to a steep shelving beach in Inverie Bay. A cold, crisp night frozen with stars – we were almost level with Norway. 44NM at 5Kn.

Wednesday 23rd. This was the last day of our last sail. The sun rose red above the still water. Time for our 1967 Volvo Penta petrol sewing machine. We ticked up the Sound of Sleat until a fitful wind arrived at the narrows at Kyle Rhea, famous for 8 knots at springs. Accordingly we arrived near high water. There appeared to be a nonsense in *Macmillan's* current charts. They showed an arrow in our direction at the entrance, one against in the middle and another with us again at the exit. We produced our GPS to check our log speed and, sure enough – 3 knots with us, then 2 knots against and finally, 2 knots with us again. Neptune was prodding us.

There were pontoons each side of the kyle of Lochalsh just west of the town. We moored on the north side, met the new prospective owner and received instructions for entering Plockton Harbour 14 miles distant, where a new mooring, marked *Passim*, was waiting. We sailed on a close reach under the Skye Bridge and goosewinged in SW F.4 to our last port. Good shelter, utterly beautiful houses strung like rectangular beads along the waterfront. Cordalines, like palms, above the sandy edge.

Next day. Unloading a mountain of gear – one last circle in the dinghy, Highland rail to Inverness and sleeper to London. The North Western Edge must be one of the finest and least spoiled sailing waters of Europe. Why is it the best kept secret? I do not know. We had counted 17 sailing boats – less than 2 per day. Our log recorded 534NM in 10 days.

Passim is a composite 28 ft Twister. Elizabeth and Mike Davies had a half share. We now share a Rival 36.

UNDERNEATH THE ARCHES – FROM CLACHAN TO CONNEL

by Heather Howard

This is the Journal contribution for which the Dulcibella Prize was awarded.

The Loch Melfort meet was marvellous; it was such fun seeing all those lovely boats arriving and rafting up. We kept firmly to the end of the line, *Jubilate* being only little and we not wishing to be squashed. We managed to sample the hospitality of the fleet from end to end and back, before heading up to Melfort for the evening festivities. We had had a wonderful week before this, exploring the local anchorages in perfect weather, if rather little wind, but that was an improvement on Falmouth a few weeks earlier. Now it was time to move on and do something more adventurous.

We had been eyeing the Clachan Bridge, known locally as the Bridge over the Atlantic, which joins Seil Island to the mainland; both our pilot books were distinctly unenthusiastic about the feasibility of a passage through Clachan Sound and under the bridge, but we reckoned that it could be done, just, and it would certainly provide a handy short cut to the Firth of Lorne, avoiding the Cuan Sound, which the pilot books made uninviting to small boats such as ours. The Clachan Bridge is very beautiful, like so many pieces of practical engineering. It had a glorious steep arch built of local stone towards the end of the 18th century, but looked rather daunting when we first visited it, by car and at low tide, with a mere trickle of water among the rocks and thick weed. Beyond at the north end of the sound was a 2.4 metre dry shoal clearly visible where there is a disused slate quarry, which has caused much silting of the old channel. So we decided to return for another look at high water, armed with *Saecwen's* old leadline and my chest waders, Billy muttering Napoleon's dictum, 'Time spent in reconnaissance is seldom wasted,' with the added rider, 'This must be one of those rare occasions,' as we trudged the best part of a mile along a narrow, boggy path, knee-deep in rushes, reeds and bracken, to survey the shallows at the head of the

Under the Clachan Bridge, Jubilate sails the Atlantic.

Sound. The local seal, who was peacefully fishing there, was very surprised when I donned my chest waders and life-jacket, relieved my grumbling bearer of a large oar which he had carried through the jungle from the bridge, and took soundings over the last 100 yards of the channel. All seemed to be well. There was plenty of water, which threatened to invade my waders, and I could hardly stand up in the strong current, which starts flowing south an hour or so before high water. At the bridge we got a good reading with the leadline, which we calculated would give us sufficient room to pass through at high tide on the day when we intended to make the passage, though it would be prudent to lower both gaff and burgee to be sure of clearing the bridge. The trick is to work your tides so as to have enough water under you to clear the shoals, but not so much as to prevent passage under the bridge. We were aiming to go through half way between neaps and springs, which seemed to be ideal.

So off we set two days later with a lovely leading wind up Seil Sound and into Clachan Sound, where we proceeded with caution as the channel is narrow, with plenty of rocky shoals which have never been properly charted. We rested at a jetty half way up so as to get the last of the tide up to the bridge, where it had already begun to run south at a couple of knots by the time we arrived, which at least gave us the change to stop and turn back if we chickened out. All was well, however; our mast cleared the arch of the bridge by two feet or so, and with plate and rudder right up we chugged through on our 5 hp outboard without touching anything above or below us. Despite the strong current, we were soon in the pool at the head of the sound. Here we exchanged greetings with our seal friend before clearing the bar by the slate quarry and turning gratefully to port and into the enchanting little anchorage of Puilladobrhain (pronounced Pooldoran, and meaning Pool of the Otter in Gaelic), the perfect landfall on a perfect, clear, west coast summer's day. It was made even better by the sight of Robin Bryer hanging out his fenders on *Morven* to welcome us alongside. What peace! This must be one of Britain's loveliest anchorages, with shelter all round and not a building in sight, though there is a convenient footpath leading over the hill to the pub by the Clachan Bridge. After visiting this excellent place of refreshment, we rounded off a very happy day having supper with Robin on board *Morven*.

Our next objective was to get nearly to the head of Loch Etive, via the Sound of Kerrera and Dunstaffnage, spending a couple of nights on the way. Getting into Loch Etive involves going under the Connel Bridge; no problems about headroom for us, as there are 15 metres clearance at HW Springs, but the pilot books speak in dark tones of the Falls of Lora, just to the east of the bridge, and an alarming sight at most states of the tide. The channel is restricted by a submarine ledge on the north side, the centre part of which dries at half tide down, creating impressive rapids of white water on a full ebb. This causes violent eddies in the only navigable channel – that is for most yachtsmen, if not for the likes of my brother, Mike McMullen, who shot the rapids on a full spring ebb in *Three Cheers*. He reckoned he was doing about 20 knots over the land. (See Roving Commissions for 1975, '*Three Cheers* for the

Under the Connel Bridge, in the wake of Three Cheers.

Hebrides'). Slack water, or half an hour either side, is what the pilot books recommend as the ideal time to pass through, but with the caveat that slack water is almost non-existent, and that meteorological conditions can cause the time to vary by as much as 1.5 hours, with a bias towards being early, rather than late. Reality proved less dreadful than these predictions, and we passed through with no trouble, driven by our faithful outboard, but getting the sails up as soon as we were clear of the worst of the witches' cauldrons near the falls, to take advantage of a fine leading wind which accompanied us all the way up the loch to our destination. There are two lots of narrows after the Falls of Lora, at Kilmaronaig and Bonawe, with currents up to 5 knots, so it is advisable to work your tides correctly, and the tide elsewhere in the loch is powerful enough to give a small boat remarkable speed over the land. You pass the well known Inverawe Smokery at Taynuilt, and several fish farms, one of which had just sprung a leak and released a large number of hungry and rather stupid trout into the loch, greatly to the benefit of the local anglers, who were pulling them in like mackerel.

Loch Etive is extremely attractive all the way up, but north of Inverawe it becomes spectacularly beautiful, with the mountains around Glencoe closing in on both sides as you near the head, floodlit by the evening sun and only occasionally shrouded in low cloud. The main reason for our voyage to this lovely place was to visit my cousin William Ehrman (RCC), his wife Penny and their family, who have an attractive old stalking lodge as their holiday retreat. The lodge has no electricity, and is therefore blissfully free of TV and other banes of 'civilisation'. What a joy it was to see them as they chugged out in a little motorboat to greet us. *Jubilate* anchored alongside William's 17 foot Norfolk Oyster, making a pretty pair of traditional boats. William and his son Tom had just returned from a five day circumnavigation of Mull in their Oyster, landing on the Treshnish Isles and Iona, among many other places. When I asked William that evening to show me where they had been, he looked a bit sheepish as he took a beautifully clean new Martin Lawrence *Isle of Mull Pilot* from his bookcase, which he had forgotten to take with him, doing all his cruise on the chart alone. Quite an achievement, and it made our puny cruise look very unadventurous. Dinner by the soft light of oil lamps, and bed by candlelight. This was pure delight!

Next day on a fine moist morning, with cloud on the mountains and a good southeast wind to take us down the loch we took the last of the ebb under Connel bridge and into Dunstaffnage marina, where we began the business of unrigging *Jubilate* and getting her out of the water onto her trailer for the long journey south. By now the rain was pouring down and we felt even more blessed to have had two perfect weeks in such a wonderful cruising ground, and delighted to have done it in such a marvellous little boat as a Cornish Shrimper. You can take them anywhere!

THE SECOND FIDDLES
FORM A QUARTET

by Annabelle Ingram

It is often said that the Atlantic crossing in the trade winds to the Caribbean is merely a milk run, but to four Royal Cruising Club wives Christine
Lytle, Gill Price, Annette Ridout and myself it seemed a significant
challenge. Having long played second fiddles under our husband's batons,
Troubadour's 1999 crossing was the opportunity for us to be an independent quartet and to choose our own tunes.

We began our preparation by identifying the gaps in our knowledge and
experience. The diesel engine course although messy was great fun but
that for the long-range radio certificate was hard work. It lasted for four
days with the added horror of a stiff exam at the end. I enjoyed climbing
into liferafts on the sea survival course but as both Chris and I trained as
nurses, we felt we could forego the first aid training. Finally my exercise
trainer devised a 'keep-fit' program suitable for us to use on board.

In late May 1999 we had our first sail together on *Troubadour*. On a
rough, windy and overcast day we set sail from Newton Ferrers and had
a fast passage to Dartmouth and then on to Lymington with a night in
Studland. All went very well raising our confidence. A couple of months
later under the tutelage of Mike Pocock, we spent a day circumnavigating
the Isle of Wight. We learnt about the finer points of spinnaker handling
including the art of gybing the beast but I am afraid that although we
flew the spinnaker during the crossing, we always funked a gybe!

During September and October *Troubadour* was sailed down to Porto
Calero, Lanzarote first by Stuart and myself with friends and then from
Portugal by my eldest son, Peter, with a young crew.

By 12 November 1999 with all jobs completed, full water and fuel
tanks, the time seemed right for departure. Soon dolphins were playing
in the bow wave as we left in a light easterly F.3, an enchanting send-off.
With the smooth sea, we soon settled down and found our sea legs. But if
the crew was composed, the Autohelm ST80 instruments were not,

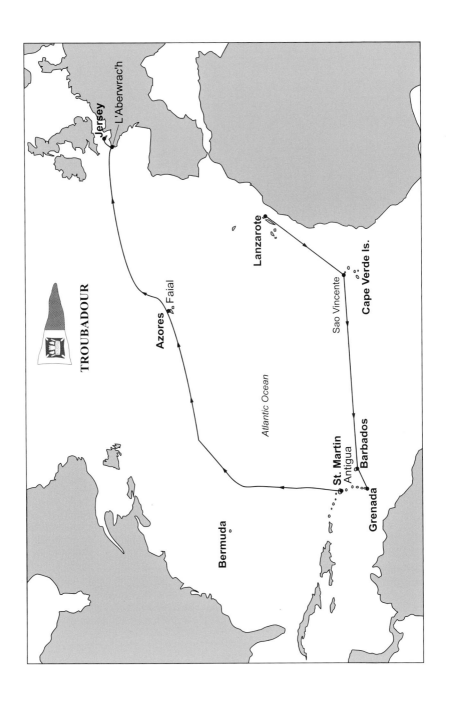

changing nautical miles into statute miles, metres into feet and switching the variation from west to east. We had an unpleasant feeling it had a mind of its own and was trying to show who was boss!

A week later we were at Sao Vincente and at 0800 on 22 November we were on passage to Barbados with a fine day and the wind east-northeast F.4. Our first night back at sea was wonderful with a brilliant full moon. Sitting on the cockpit coaming watching the water slide past lit by phosphorescence was a memory that will stay with me.

Initially the wind remained steady and the sun continued to shine from a sky with puffy trade wind clouds but it was not to last. The wind became light and for six days we had frustrating conditions. The slatting of sails drove us to try every conceivable sail combination to keep *Troubadour* moving. The large spinnaker helped but we were not confident enough to keep it flying at night. The remains of hurricane *Lenny* had drifted into the Atlantic to form a low-pressure area at 32°N 45°W; slow moving it blocked the Trades. It was clear from the SSB net that everyone was experiencing similar problems.

Days 6 and 7 were frustrating with almost dead calm conditions. We motored along keeping the speed down to five knots. The sun beat down, only the bimini gave a little shade in the cockpit as our tans grew steadily darker. Occasionally there was a strange popply effect on the surface of the water, you could see and hear it coming but we were mystified as to the cause. However, the calm did give me a chance to use my Reeds sewing machine and to catch up on some of my sewing tasks. As we moved west we twice put the clocks back at our happy hour to keep pace with the daylight.

Day 8 saw the wind return from the east, increasing slightly to keep *Troubadour* moving. It was warm and humid with a nine-tenths cloud cover; heavy showers washed the decks and cockpit clean of salt. During the night lightning lit the sky making us all anxious. There were numerous wind shifts but the breeze continued to increase slowly, reaching about 12 knots by midnight. We made quite good progress with the jibs twinned and the main furled. Gill received a forecast from New Orleans covering our area but it still showed the low to the north as the dominant feature. The next night heavy squalls set in from 0400 with loud thunder and vivid lightning crashing low, right overhead. The torrential rain reduced visibility to virtually zero and the wind gusted to above 30 knots. While Annette took the helm, the rest of us struggled to get the jibs rolled away, the reacher on its own roller kept getting jammed against the genoa. Finally we had it lowered onto the deck and bagged. All the while Annette was shouting at us to keep clear of the mast and rigging as she was terrified we were about to be struck by lightning! The main was hoisted with two reefs and *Troubadour* roared along at 9 knots, the sea was completely flattened by the rain. Gill unplugged the SSB aerial to keep it safe and the two spare GPS were put for safe keeping into the microwave, we hoped it would act as a Faraday cage! By the time all was sorted out, we were freezing. Dressed in soaking wet nighties and our hair plastered down, we must have looked a very odd sight.

The twenty-four hours of Sunday, 5 December (Day 14) were to be the worst of the entire trip. During my night watch a vicious squall passed through hitting us with no warning. The night was dark and moonless and visibility poor in the teaming rain. I made the mistake of taking the helm away from the Monitor's competent control in an attempt to keep *Troubadour* on course instead of letting it just follow the wind shifts. I could not then hold her in the rapidly increasing wind so as to lock the self-steering back in. The girls were immediately on deck and with their very able help the jib was rapidly rolled away and three reefs put in the main. Chris, now on the helm, somehow managed to keep *Troubadour* head to wind as we struggled. The day continued in similar fashion, humid, overcast and very wet. Squalls were everywhere and whenever we changed the sail configuration so did the wretched wind! This unpleasant day ended almost as badly as it began with Chris cutting her foot badly on a flipped up edge of the plastic floor covering. Almost immediately the floor was awash with blood and firm pressure was needed to control the bleeding. Stitching the wound was considered but Chris, not surprisingly, was not keen on the idea despite my enthusiasm. Adhesive steri-strips were applied and a firm bandage followed by a stiff brandy, purely for medicinal reasons! Another night of squalls and rain followed; the log at 0400 just says 'simply horrid!' We are all becoming very expert in shortening and increasing sail, reefs in and out in a trice and the running booms going up and down like a yo-yo!

On Day 15 we had a good sail with a steady trade wind and we saw Boobies for the first time. We were upset when we heard over the SSB that a crew member from another yacht had been lost overboard. We were too far away to be of assistance but it certainly brought home the necessity of wearing harnesses. It was only later in Grenada that we learnt of his amazing rescue after 17 hours in the sea.

The improvement in the wind did not last. Rain returned and, with the hatches all closed, it was like a sauna below. By the late afternoon the wind died and motoring was necessary to maintain any progress. These conditions continued the following night but then the sun appeared during Day 16 although the flat calm remained until the evening. The time was put to good use cleaning and tidying in preparation for our arrival in Barbados. A school of dolphins seen in the distance and beautiful frigate birds made us think that land was close, but it was not until 0400 on 9 December (Day 18) that Gill eventually picked out actual lights. It was all very exciting and we were on deck staring in awe as the land became more clearly defined in the gradually increasing daylight. The east-northeast breeze that had held all that night continued to give us a fine finish. There was one last heavy rain squall then, accompanied by more

Four wives: Gill Price, Christine Lytle, Annabelle Ingram and Annette Ridout.

dolphins that stayed with us for a long time playing in the bow and all around the boat, we closed with the island. We had left Lanzarote in the company of dolphins and they showed us the way in to Barbados.

By 0945 we had rounded both South and Needham Points and were sailing across Carlisle Bay to the deep-water harbour. Having received clearance to enter, we had to slot ourselves into a tiny gap in the angle between the south and west walls surrounded by an enormous cruise ship and a fake pirate ship. Crossing the Atlantic turned out to have been the easy bit! Chris and I went ashore, wearing our new *Troubadour* shirts and shorts, to clear customs and immigration. We quickly finished the formalities including signing a declaration stating we were free from smallpox, plague and rats! Getting out of our tight spot was a problem as the wind was blowing us hard on and there were no bollards to which we could tie warps so as to spring off. Eventually, with help from the pseudo-pirates, we managed to extricate ourselves. We were lucky to be unscathed, others were not so fortunate and this problem is a major deterrent to visiting Barbados. After re-fuelling, we finally dropped anchor in Carlisle Bay at 1430 after 2220 miles. We did feel proud of ourselves! It was entirely due to the terrific effort and support of the crew with their capability, cheerfulness and good temper the whole time that made it such a wonderful trip. I only hope that they feel the same way.

After the Millennium celebrations, Troubadour spent January and February cruising the Windwards and Leewards finally being left at the end of February in Falmouth Harbour, Antigua.

TROUBADOUR TRANS-ATLANTIC 2000

by Peter Ingram

This is the cruise for which the Cruising Club Bowl was awarded.

We left Antigua for St Martin at the sensible time of 1430 on 25 May. I felt it was time to get some miles under us and put the boat to the test. If there were any problems that would have to be sorted before the crossing, this would be the time to find out about them. We had done a little shopping for basic supplies, with the congenial help of Oliver Taxi, but were leaving the major provisioning until we arrived in St Martin. With an easterly F.4 we sailed gently out of Falmouth Harbour. As we rounded Cades Reef at the southwest corner of Antigua, I began to let Nick Martell settle into the boat. We gybed and set the full yankee on the pole while I offered careful instruction. By 2130 we were reaching at 8–9 knots and by 2230 we were taking in the first reef. All was well. We settled in quickly and, after the first of our many good meals afloat, I was happy to let Nick stand a watch alone. We passed Nevis and St. Kitts to port and by 0300 had St Barth's on the starboard beam.

At dawn we sailed into Simpson Bay, hearing dramatic stories of Robin's last departure from there on *Talina* hours before hurricane Lenny hit the island causing the loss of dozens of boats. We entered the lagoon through the lifting bridge at 1100. I had hoped that our time in the half-Dutch half-French island would be a relaxing holiday before the passage, but we worked permanently. We were already feeling like hardened sailors; sun-tanned, becoming leaner and unable to take our eyes off the lovely women that populate the island. However, I was then struck by one of the most difficult problems to solve while living aboard abroad. For the previous week we had been eating out well and as I offered my Visa card to pay for another fine meal it was rejected. 'Maxed-out', as they say. It was Friday evening and the UK bank holiday Monday followed so it would be Thursday before the situation could be resolved. The plan did not allow for delays like this. We had all our provisioning to do and fuel to buy. Luckily Nick volunteered his card and we made for the hypermarket. We did not hold back and amassed three trolleys worth, one of vegetables, one of dry foods and one of drink. A few basic sums relating to a projected passage time of 30 days and a discussion about the size of a human stomach suggested that three trolleys would be about right. The staff did not seem surprised with the quantities, but did offer three boys to pack the bags and a lift back to the boat. We scraped together the remains of our change to tip them.

Robin finally maxed-out his Visa card to buy six jerry cans and Nick cut the limit of his to fill them with diesel. We loaded the stores and charged out of the lagoon with seconds to spare before the bridge closed for the night. Anchoring for the last time in the turquoise Caribbean water we spent the afternoon stowing and organising, cleaning the fruit, adjusting ourselves to life without land and swimming. I took the opportunity to spend the last of the daylight drifting around the boat in the dinghy, checking *Troubadour's* trim and marvelling at the sight of a boat ready and willing to go anywhere we dared to point her. The others slept.

At 1505 on 28 May, after a lazy morning reading the Trans-Atlantic Crossing Guide, we weighed anchor. Sailing west-about the island and beating up the Anguilla Channel in squalls gusting to 30 knots we got some good practice at reefing. We rounded the eastern end of the low lying Scrub Island at 2155, thankful for the GPS as the charted light was extinguished, and bore away to head due north. As we picked up speed into the dark mystically deep Atlantic waters and left the civilised world behind, lightning storms surrounded us. I recalled Colin Mudie's visit to the Royal Zoological Society to enquire on the various sea monsters they might encounter, and felt remarkably unprepared. But, as the hours passed and we charged through the night, we soon appreciated that the only way home was onward.

We bowled toward the cautious waypoint at 30N 60W, and we settled into the comfort of the environment. Blissful days at 7 knots followed, flying the lightweight spinnaker and 160% drifter in entertaining conditions. After four days we began to swing east, passing 300 miles from Bermuda and still enjoying F.4 from the southeast, though the wind was now becoming more variable. At 2245 on 1 June, in south-southwest F.3, we submitted and started the engine for the first time (we had found that the towed generator was keeping us supplied with plenty of power so had not needed to run it for charging). By 1454 the following day, with the big blue spinnaker up, we were sailing at 7 knots. By 1935 the engine was on again and at 2203 the log recorded, '1008.9 miles, Lat 30° 09N, Long 59° 35W, course 055°M, wind south-south-west F.4. Sharpened pencil'! We were all beginning to see the funny side of ocean sailing.

We sighted Faial at dusk on 13 June and moored on the outer mole in Horta at 0340. The log trip distance was 2763 miles at an average speed over ground of 6.16 knots. We were satisfied to learn that other yachts, on the great circle course, had taken the same time and used much more fuel than we had.

Andrew Lytle caught up with us as planned at the Peter Café Sport. He had come fresh from university exams and quickly settled into the spirit of things. The town of Horta was very welcoming and we enjoyed our stay there though sightseeing was limited to half a day in a hire car, which I was told was fantastic.

We left on the afternoon of 17 June, pausing to check the compass in the bay before setting sail. The wind was northerly and we beat toward Graciosa, though it soon backed to west-southwest and began to increase. The nights were particularly dark and clear and the phosphorescence was astounding. We regularly saw dolphins and on several occasions enjoyed the rapturous sight of them leaping out of the face of the breaking waves we were surfing, leaving just the Fantasia style phosphorescent trail behind as they steamed off into the next wave. Nick could occasionally be heard whooping with the joy of it all from the bow.

On 21 June we altered to the direct course for Ushant. On the morning of 23 June we had the only breakage of the trip worth noting. The linear drive of our electric *autohelm* began to seize after an estimated ten days use since Antigua. We quickly dropped it off its tiller arm as it was seriously interfering with the steering and a strip-down the next day showed the thrust-bearing race to have worn. I filed it flat as a temporary repair and reassembled it with copious amounts of grease.

Andrew Lytle, Peter Ingram, Robin Slater and Nick Martell.

At 1310 on 25 June we sighted Ushant and found ourselves, after all this way, down-wind and down-tide of the point. We started the engine for the first time since Horta and motor-sailed for three hours to get ourselves into the Channel. We sailed into L'Aberwrac'h under the most beautiful sunset and dropped anchor up the river at 2220, 4325 miles from Antigua.

After a bottle or two of Champagne we quickly dropped the dinghy in, wondering whether we would be able to get dinner ashore. It was after midnight by the time we rapped on the windows of the Auberge du Point, up-river by the bridge, interrupting the staff from their ledgers and Pastis. We all took a step back as the waiter unbolted the door, looking at the startled bearded expressions on each other's faces. Being skipper, I thrust the youngest to the front to explain. Andrew threw his hands into the air and exclaimed something about 'Nous sommes desoleté – L'Atlantic!' They smiled happily, if wearily, as we left at 0400 and we were thankful that such food and service were available in the universe.

We unwound leisurely for a couple of days and sadly Nick left us at short notice for a rose-picking job in Oxfordshire. He had become a very able sailor and I was always thankful that we had him on board. We moved up channel through calms and fog, stopping for 24 hours at the Isle de Seic, before motoring on along the waypoints to Jersey. The fog cleared as we approached and we pondered on the relatively dull landfall ahead. I was already missing the ocean.

On 30 June at 1715 we made fast at the St Helier Marina. 4453 miles on the log, 26 days at sea and at the first of the Rolling Meets on time. My mother would never believe it! *Troubadour* had been superb throughout the trip and the sailing was an absolute joy. After all the planning I had failed to put in, all the lists I failed to write, all the books I had not read, and the original schedule (measured off the atlas along the edge of a cigarette paper) still clipped to the bulkhead, we had had the perfect trip. What's more, I felt that if the crew and the boat had had the time, we could have at a moment's notice turned her around and headed right back again. What a boat, what an ocean!

UP GREAT BLASKET AND HOME

by Henry Clay

Flycatcher is a near flush-decked Sparkman and Stephens design built by Jeremy Rogers as the Contessa 38 in 1973. Because of her previous exploits, whilst owned by John Roome, she is well known. Since buying her three years ago we have enjoyed being accosted by a French crew off Ushant, by strangers anywhere from remote anchorages to the crowded Solent, by colleagues at work and even by a Roome grandchild (who needed correction on telling me that *Flycatcher* was his Grandpa's boat!). It is a pleasure to meet so many friends of the boat. Like all owners I am biased, but they are, of course, absolutely right to admire her.

Family commitments of two jobs and four children confined our main cruise to a period of two weeks, though we did grab some additional days which extended our range and gave more time for exploring the southwest of Ireland. It was a family cruise with Edward (17) (joined by his rowing partner, Nick McSloy for the first part), Joanna (14) for the second part only and Bridget and Philippa (twins of 10).

On Monday 17 July we started from Lymington, where a faulty instrument was checked. From the entrance we beat slowly west carrying our tide most of the way to Lulworth to anchor for the evening. We had been joined early by a tired pigeon but assumed that it had flown off. Finding it, and the mess, under the dinghy stowed on deck proved our assumption to be wrong!

Up at 2300 Nick and I took the inside passage past Portland Bill but the wind died completely as we entered Lyme Bay, though Louise and Edward enjoyed a cracking two sail fetch after dawn. Late afternoon found us anchored off Cawsand until the tide turned in our favour. This ought to be a sailor's village. Its anchorage is sheltered from the prevailing wind and it is here that Nelson met Emma Hamilton whilst waiting off Plymouth. Be warned – its shortcoming is that no water is to be had. Edward and Nick scoured the village, finally being directed to a garden tap in the grounds of the hotel where they were chased from the premises by the proprietress.

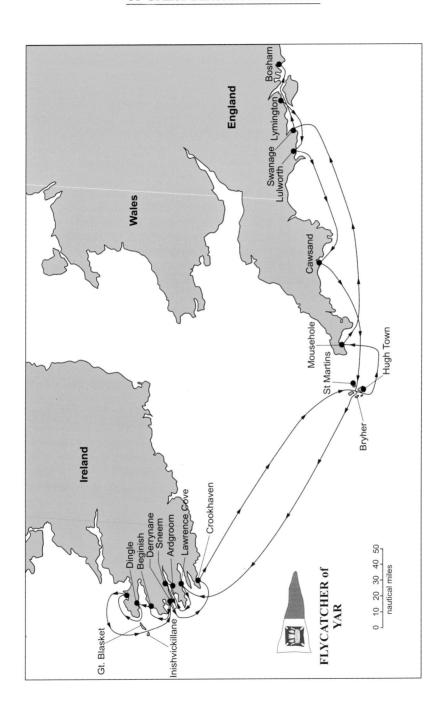

Ireland

Wales

England

Bosham
Lymington
Swanage
Lulworth

Cawsand

Mousehole
St Martins
Hugh Town
Bryher

Dingle
Beginish
Derrynane
Sneem
Ardgroom
Lawrence Cove
Crookhaven

Gt. Blasket
Inishvickillane

FLYCATCHER of
YAR

0 10 20 30 40 50
nautical miles

Away before midnight we fetched west from Rame Head against a fluky wind. After exercising the cruising chute and, occasionally, the engine, we arrived off the Scillies near high water. We took the passage through Crowe Sound and beat across the flats to anchor south of Bryher at 1850 on the 19th. After a peaceful night away from all others some of us rowed ashore early to explore Samson before sailing alongside the quay at New Grimsby for water and then to anchor outside Hangman's Island. Ashore Bridget and Philippa were keen to track down a school friend staying on the island. They duly left messages in the sand that, when we found the family, we discovered had been seen but steered clear of, unread, by a protective mother, lest they be obscene. The majority of the day was spent enjoying sun, swimming and exploring Tresco. Departing mid afternoon, we set the cruising chute until nightfall and chose a course which gave us options along the south coast of Ireland. The next morning was enlivened by a whale, as well as by an arresting double bang that we assume to have been caused by Concorde. By mid afternoon on 21 July we were in the lee of Clear Island and able to reach past the headlands to arrive in Lawrence Cove by 1940 – just in time for Louise to establish that the seafood restaurant could fit us in for a truly memorable meal looking across the cove. Our return over the weekend, by taxi, bus, ferry and train, is best forgotten.

Returning a little more than two weeks later, this time with all of the family, we found the boat had been well looked after by the Harringtons. Under way on 8 August through Beara Sound and inside Dursey Island we ran up the south side of the Kenmare River and anchored in a freshening breeze in Ardgroom, off Reenavade at 2045. Our night was partially disturbed by some vicious squalls.

After dinghy sailing and a walk we pottered across to Sneem in mid afternoon anchoring in the lee of Garinish where we renewed our acquaintance with a French couple with whom I had rescued a Laurent Giles design from dragging in the Scillies two years earlier. Dinghy sailing, exploration and some rock-climbing amused all, and a marvellous display of phosphorescence had Edward and Joanna rowing the dinghy in the dark to achieve a glowing bow-wave and puddles.

On 10 August we beat out of the river in bright sunshine to anchor in the bay at Deenish, one of the Hog Islands, inside the fish farm. Ashore, Joanna, Bridget and Philippa swam, Edward climbed whilst Louise and I walked and scrambled to the peak. Swimming back on board, we enjoyed an increasingly slow run to sail into Derrynane at 2000.

Next day Bridget and Philippa rowed around the anchorage but were too shy to accept an offer of fish. We, however, followed this up en famille to find a small French ply mini cruiser, complete with their house flag 'le pavillon du propriétaire' and a very piratically dressed skipper who offered us two sizeable fish, subsequently identified as pollack.

Ashore we searched without success for a bin for our rubbish, eventually being very grateful to the lifeguard who took it.

We beat out of the harbour to bear off north, finding it best to stay a little way off the coast to avoid the worst of the reflected swell (though not far enough to prevent Edward succumbing). Passing the entrances to Valentia we felt our way into an anchorage between Beginish and Lamb Island. It would be easy to go too far here onto the spit that connects the islands but keeping Doulus Head just open of Lamb Island provides a good line for anchoring in front of the beach. Ashore we wandered over Beginish looking into Valentia harbour and then returned to prepare and eat the fish.

The night was not entirely still with the growing ground swell reflecting into the anchorage, leading to complaints from Bridget. Next morning Louise and I rowed round the corner and into the Caher River to land on Church Island. There we found the remains of a beehive hut and a small building, rectangular in plan, with walls sloping inwards occupying much of the island above the high water mark.

We were forced to abandon sailing, becalmed and rolling, off Doulus Head so engined to Dingle, being met by the friendly harbour master, Johnny Murphy. He explained that the tourism industry was so dependent on Fungi the dolphin that not only was the dolphin that had met us a replacement for the original which died, but that another two were in training. Dingle has too many tourist shops and too many people for our taste but it did allow us to provision and to visit the excellent Currans butcher.

After this brief visit to civilisation we left in mid afternoon, anchoring off the beach at Great Blasket at 1745. Ashore in two trips we climbed a variety of routes with the main party reaching both the coll between the peaks and the cloud level. Returning to the tiny boat harbour we found great excitement as some four dozen sheep were being rounded up to be loaded into a RIB. We spent a long time watching this exercise that required five people, six dogs and a snorkeller who rescued those sheep that jumped into the sea. Prevented from getting afloat we waited for four trips by the RIB to the flatter island of Beginish (where the sheep were to fatten). The snorkeller, who swam to his RIB to give us a lift on board, turned out to be the operator of the ferry from Dunquin. He pointed out to us the considerable swell breaking on the rocks and cliffs opposite that he felt might prevent him operating the ferry the next day. Passing north of Beginish, we wondered how some of the storm-scattered Armada ships, short of water and provisions, had found their way through this channel. Committed by then to a night approach to Smerwick, we eventually felt our way into the bay to anchor in the south-west corner at 2300. A late supper was very welcome.

On Sunday we enjoyed a delicious breakfast of Currans' bacon and black pudding 'cake'. With the wind now strong from the southwest we chose to stay put. Louise assured us that we would find a fascinating eighth century oratory building 'just beyond that second headland'. Regrettably her sketch made from the chart provided no scale and did not identify landmarks so that after the third headland, with Bridget in particular complaining strongly, the girls agreed to return to play in the sand whilst Edward, Louise and I continued on. Eventually we approached Gallarus Castle and the oratory itself. Edward had been carrying two small bags of rubbish and here we finally found a camp-site with bins. Unfortunately he was accosted after depositing the bags by a threatening lady carrying a kitchen knife. Despite his explanation she insisted that he should pay a fee – something at which Edward balked so he found himself recovering the bags. After his earlier trouble in Cawsand, we began to wonder if it was Edward that provoked this reaction.

The oratory, in the shape of an upturned boat, was excellently preserved and the display was informative, but the example that we had viewed on Church Island was far more magical and atmospheric, if less complete. Despite getting a lift for a small part of the return journey both Edward and I felt that we might have better done some of the jobs on board, had we not been led astray.

Next morning with a strong westerly we reefed well down despite being assured by a ketch that had looked outside that we would soon be back. A tack to the north took us clear of the worst and we then lay close-hauled along the coast to pass Sybil Head some distance off. In improving weather, with the sun emerging, we headed south passing to the west of Great Blasket to pick up Charles Haughey's mooring in the lee of Inishvickillane. We all swam, observed from a distance by a large seal. Louise and I went to the shore though we were a little cautious about climbing the path to the top. Lunch was eaten at the mooring before we continued south and, after debating the alternatives, we sailed back into Derrynane for the night.

I was ashore early seeking milk and after a late breakfast Bridget enjoyed dinghy sailing in the harbour. Ashore, the girls swam from the beach before we ate a sandwich at Keatings, the village pub/hotel. Finally under way at 1520 we carried the tide west of Dursey Island. Off the Calf we were confused by a barge under tow, carrying very large rocks which in the swell looked like an additional island with a beacon, causing a rapid review of the chart! After rounding Mizen Head we anchored below the moorings in Crookhaven at 2200. The log records some complaints about the hour, but only from those who had been so difficult to get up in the morning.

Next morning the smallness of Ireland was confirmed when we met Mel Boyd, Chief Executive of the Commissioners of Irish Lights for whom I was undertaking consulting work at the time. He kindly entertained us to coffee, which led to our lunching ashore so it was 1400 before we took our departure towards England.

A CRUISE ON A RACING MACHINE

by Emma Laird

In 1885, Admiral de Horsey became an honorary member of what was then the Cruising Club. On learning of his election, he expressed his opinion that the objects of the Club should be encouraged, and that they were far worthier 'than that of most clubs, which unfortunately encourage the winning of prizes by racing machines sailing under a fictitious tonnage measurement'. Hillaire Belloc went even further: he was convinced that racing led to the devil. During the last two seasons, I have found myself on board one of these 'racing machines', built in the very year that de Horsey was denigrating the many yacht clubs that had already been established for the encouragement of racing. She was not the type of yacht that the original Cruising Club members would have approved of. Over a hundred years later, her restorer Alex Laird, myself and any friends we could muster have raced the Victorian gaff cutter *Partridge* for two seasons in the Mediterranean for the classic yacht circuit. I have even been able to pursuade some other RCC members to endure the evils of racing with us. However this year, with a big break between two regattas, we actually had time to turn what could have been just a delivery trip into more of a cruise than we had ever done before on *Partridge*. Our route took us from Antibes-Imperia to Elba-Argentario (where we took part in a regatta) and then to Portofino and back to San Remo, a total distance of approximately 450 miles.

On June 14, *Partridge* spent the night swinging to her anchor for the first time in over eighty years. That evening we sat on the beach and watched the sun go down behind what could have been straight out of the Victorian era; even the backdrop of the Italian sixteenth century citadel was in keeping, because over a hundred years ago British yachts like *Partridge* came to the Mediterranean to cruise and race. In those days though, it was the done thing to be there in the English winter since the Mediterranean summer was too hot and it was not fashionable to have a suntan. The historic image was broken only occasionally by *Partridge*

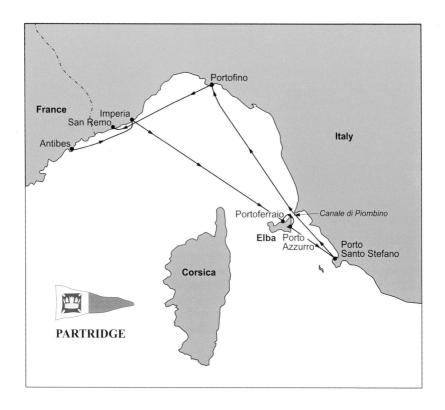

Portofino

France
Imperia
San Remo

Antibes

Italy

Portoferraio — Canale di Piombino

Elba Porto
Azzurro
Porto
Santo Stefano

Corsica

PARTRIDGE

nosediving over the enormous steep-sided modern ferry washes that were rolling across the entrance to the bay. We were in Cala Bagnaia in the Rada di Portoferraio on the beautful island of Elba.

It may seem surprising to many that we have not been more ambitious with cruising on *Partridge* especially as she has plenty of concessions to the modern age which have changed the style of cruising such a yacht immeasurably. She has a 40hp engine, twin propellers with hydraulic drive which make her very easy to handle under power, liferaft, EPIRB, and GPS. After all in the old days just a man and a boy would have handled larger and more complex craft and there are many examples of great voyages on yachts like *Partridge*. RCC member George Muhlhauser cruised a yacht not dissimilar to *Partridge* around the world in 1920 (the *Amaryllis* built in 1882), despite saying in his book that 'she is not my ideal cruiser'. In the racing fraternity, yachts were occasionally but not usually shipped between regattas; in 1885 a sister ship of *Partridge*, *Genesta*, crossed the Atlantic in a gale to challenge for the America's Cup and in 1886 another sister ship of *Partridge*, *Galatea*, crossed the Atlantic also to challenge for the America's Cup. *Galatea's* owners, Lieutenant and

Above: *Dodo's Delight rigged as a climbing hut.*
Below: *Partridge racing at Porto Santo Stefano, Italy.*
Previous Page: *Dodo's Delight under Sandersons Hope.*

Above: *Gollywobbler II arrives at Anacortes.*
Below: *Mayan village in Guatemala visted by Blue Sonata.*

Above: *John Gore-Grimes touches the Nordenskjold Glacier.*
Below: *Taraki anchored at Faja, Brava (Cabo Verdes).*

Mrs. Henn, were avid cruising enthusiasts rather than committed racers. They turned up with potted plants and a monkey on board. They agreed to put the plants ashore for the race but Mrs. Henn and the monkey stayed and thus she became the first woman to sail in an America's Cup race as well as being the first woman ever to cross the Atlantic on a racing yacht. She went on to cruise many thousands of miles on *Galatea* even after her husband died in 1894. I mention these particular examples because all of them, like *Partridge*, were straight-stemmed, narrow, deep-keeled, heavy displacement yachts with long counters, no cockpit, flush decks and tiller steering (though Muhlhauser did rig a wheel at some point during his voyage and the *Amaryllis* was a yawl not a cutter).

In the light of this, a trip across the Gulf of Genoa may seem like no great challenge – a matter of just one night at sea – but it was still not an undertaking that we could look upon lightly. All five of us on board were relatively inexperienced at handling such a vessel outside the safety of sheltered waters. Despite her concessions to the modern age, there is much about *Partridge* that is just as it would have been in the 1880s and while her style might have been second nature to the sailors of the nine-

Emma's grandmother is on the port quarter.

teenth century it was certainly not second nature to us. Her lack of cockpit is great for racing but leaves the deck 'wet as a half-tide rock' (*Corinthian Yachtsman's Handbook*). As in the 1880s, we sit on pouffes; in fact her deck layout is so authentic that she has paraffin navigation lights so as not to spoil the effect with electric wiring and her engine controls are hidden inside the binnacle box.

Also, by our standards we were undercrewed. We normally race with fifteen people and when thirty or forty yachts with enormous bowsprits are all hurtling towards the start line, the cry of 'helm's a lee' needs to be obeyed in a flash. At this point three sets of headsail sheets, two sets of running backstays, a sail area of 186 square metres and no winches at all leave not a single crew member unemployed. The racing staysail in a breeze can take up to six people to haul it in tight. With the 130 square metres spinnaker set, a gybe round a racing mark needs some 250 metres of rope to be handled. Thus, with just five people on board, our manoeuvres would have to be planned carefully, blocks and tackle would have to take the place of extra bodies and the jackyard topsail would stay firmly in its bag.

Most of the similar vessels in the Mediterranean, such as the 1896 cutter *Avel*, have a large mother ship, *Creole*, with washing machines, showers and full time cooks and stewardesses. The professional crew race *Avel* as an added extra to their job. In comparison we lived very roughly, we fed our crew from a paraffin stove (though it worked a treat –

Emma is nearest the starboard quarter of Partridge.

so we were not forced like Washington McCoy in his log of 1883 to drink cold tea or claret with a raw egg beaten into it when the stove would not work). We endured funny looks from passers-by when we took showers from a hose or emerged from this smart yacht with a bowl full of washing up to do on the quay. There is no sink because the final interior layout has not been decided and Alex did not want to let a seacock into the hull just yet. I should also mention at this point that she also has no real interior, she is open plan below, which is ideal for stopping sails down below during racing, and the heads are behind a curtain. The interior is interesting however because you can see the original timbers and the adze marks made by the craftsmen of 1885. We also do not run to jars of pickles and china teacups and long skirts, which I have seen in Victorian photographs.

Apart from the unstable weather, another very memorable feature of our time in the Gulf of Genoa was the wonderful reception that *Partridge* had wherever she went. This usually manifested itself in crowds of on-lookers and often in heavily discounted or free berths. We were often the centre of attention and one person said he had just read an article about the boat in *Yachting World* written by David Glenn RCC. Another man in a shop showed us a magazine with a picture of her on the front cover! Most notable, however were the few days we spent in Portofino. In June we had taken part in a regatta in Porto Santo Stefano, for which we were joined by Gillie Watson as my main sheet trimming partner. (We were beaten to second place by the Fife yacht *Tuiga*, whose extreme proportions would make Admiral de Horsey turn in his grave and make *Partridge* look like a neat little family cruiser). Gillie then stayed with us for the passage to Portofino, a really special place, one of the few places in the Mediterranean not to have a busy road spoiling the harbour front. The houses run in a manificent curve around the edge and the trees boast some prehistoric varieties. In a café we found a beautiful model of *Partridge*'s big sister, *Genesta*.

The most memorable thing about the whole summer however was the opportunity to sail *Partridge* without the stress of racing. We had probably one of the best sails we had ever had on board. This was from Portoferraio to Porto Azzurro. As we bore away into the Canale di Piombino, we took off down the east coast of the island of Elba in a northwesterly F.6 with a small jib, staysail and mainsail, which is still quite big even with three deep reefs. The sun shone, she surfed the waves as best a 28 ton deepkeeled boat can. We had the satisfaction of knowing it was just the five of us who were sailing her. We almost missed Porto Azzurro we were having such a good time. With regret we took down the sails but we did not have the forecast to risk continuing. So we then dropped the anchor in the most beautiful spot under the old prison at Barbarossa Beach and let *Partridge* swing quietly to her anchor for the second time in eighty years.

TRESPASSERS ON OSTROV VIKTORIYA

By John Gore-Grimes

Dmitry Shparo, the President of the Adventure Club of Moscow wrote to me on 5 July, 2000 to say, 'we understand that you are ready to pay $12,000 U.S. for getting permissions. You will transfer $3,000 U.S. in advance as wages for the employees who will prepare all of the documentation. The rest of $9,000 U.S. you will transfer to our bank account after you will get all permissions'.

This 'understanding' was entirely unilateral and I had not heard of the suggested fee of $12,000 U.S. prior to 5 July. I had tried to get a visa through the Russian Embassy in Dublin and through the Irish Embassy in Moscow but neither could help. With some misgivings and with a determined sense of desperation I responded to Dmitry's e-mail on 11 July by transferring $3,000 U.S. to the Bank of Nova Scotia Ontario, Canada – account holder, Dmitry Shparo.

Having failed to reach Franz Josef Land in 1988 and again in 1989, this year was to be my third and final attempt. In 1989 the late Tom Watson (C.C.A) had phoned his friend, Eduard Shevardnadze, and six visas issued instantly. 1989 was a bad ice year and we reached 77° 51' 44" N 55° 29' 32" E before being caught in the ice. The Shevardnadze visa was strictly limited to Hies Island on Franz Josef Land but we trespassed on Nova Zemlya for about 27 hours without meeting a single Russian.

In 1998 I did not trouble to apply for a visa because the ice charts made it clear that our objective was impossible. We pushed further North towards Franz Josef Land and reached 78° 22' 01" N 55° 24' 54" E. Our persistence left us trapped in the ice for five and a half days.

As the ice charts from the Norwegian Met Office reached me, in July of this year, it became clear that we could reach the southern tip of Franz Josef Land at Cape Flora. By the time we set sail on 21 July there were about 40 miles of 3/10ths ice to the south of the archipelago but it would take an estimated three and a half weeks to get there and in that time we could expect a further clearance. At the time of our departure we had no visa but while in Lerwick Dmitry's e-mail of 24 July was faxed to us. Mr. Yu. Bogaevski, The Deputy Chief of the General Headquarters Armed Forces has issued a refusal which reads 'Due to regime regulations the foreigners are not allowed to enter the area of the archipelago.' Our departure from Howth was at 1355 on 21 July, 2000, and after an uneventful trip on 5 August we entered Honningsvaag harbour. We tied up at 0740 and called to the Harbour Master's office where there was a pile of ice charts showing a fringe of 3/10th's ice to the south of Cape Flora. With a little persistence it was achievable. At the bottom of the pile was an e-mail from Dmitry:

'I have received a letter from the Director of Environment for Arctic Areas to say that he has no objection to your visit to Cape Flora on Franz Josef Land. The categorical refusal of Mr. Yu. Bogavski is still in force. I will try to have a meeting with Mr. Kvashin, the Chief of the General Headquarters Military Forces, and hand over our request once more. There is still hope. Let us wait for a couple more days'.

We had hoped to spend Saturday and Sunday in Honningsvaag and depart for Franz Josef Land as soon as the shopping had been completed on Monday. Our departure was delayed until 9 August, as Dmitry sent two further e-mails urging us to wait. The Nooden Bar is a good place to meet merchant seamen and fishermen and we told them of our problems with visas. The advice was clear and unanimous, 'Do not do it!'

They talked of the Vardo Radar Station and the bad relations which exist at the moment. Mr. Putin is not to be trusted and the likely outcome of attempting to land on Franz Josef Land was confiscation of the vessel, imprisonment in Murmansk Prison pending trial, a trial after Christmas and a fine of U.S.$50,000. I asked 'is that per person or does that include everybody'. Some said it was per person and others felt that it would be one fine to cover all of the crew. This was persuasive stuff which tempered our enthusiasm for Cape Flora.

The usual jobs were completed will full co-operation and good cheer by all of the crew. I would have to say that the crew in 2000 were certainly the strongest and most knowledgeable crew that I had sailed with and for good fun and harmony they ranked with the peace and enjoyment which I experienced in 1980 to Svalbard, 1982 to Greenland and 1998 to 78°N 55'E. It indicates there has been friction on many other voyages. Robert and I did several walks in the mountains behind Honningsvaag. Then it was time to go – visa or no visa.

The distance from Honningsvaag to Cape Flora is 640 miles. The course, once clear of Helnes on the east of Mageroy, is 042°. It was clear from what we had learned that the cold war still casts a shadow over Russian Territory north of the 80° parallel. We discussed the matter and concluded that we would be in serious trouble if we tried to defy the ban. We sent an e-mail to Dmitry telling him that we were still in the North

Cape and that we looked forward to hearing news from him. We sent an
e-mail home to say that we had failed to get visas and had abandoned our
attempt to reach Cape Flora. We had been defeated this year by politics
rather than by ice.

We steered a course of 042°. Something was still telling us to go to
Cape Flora. There were many fishing boats around us on 10 August.
The sea was calm with a slight swell and the fulmars glided around the
boat at times almost touching the sea surface with the tips of their wings.
The few Norwegian boats were easily recognisable. They were clean and
well maintained. The more numerous Russian boats were bigger and
were rusting badly. When we hailed the nearby boats on the VHF the
Norwegians replied in English but the Russians either did not reply or
sometimes merely said, 'No English'. There was much Russian chatter
on the airwaves.

11 August was a day of thick fog and slack winds. We were still headed
for Cape Flora when suddenly a smart fishing vessel appeared out of the
fog beside us. A smooth-talking, polite Russian called us on Ch16. We
then changed to Ch12. 'Hello', he said in a Russian/American accent.
'Hello, my friends. Where are you coming from?' The answer that he
wanted and probably knew already was 'Ireland' but I replied, 'the North
Cape'. 'Oh, I see', he said. 'How many persons onboard and where are
you going to?' 'Six', I replied, 'and we are bound for Nordausetland in
Svalbard'. 'Ah! I do not think you will get there. There is too much ice'.
'Yes', I agreed, 'but we might at least go to Hoppen and visit the Norwegians at the radio station there.' 'I know Hoppen well,' he said, 'but
you have a lot of east in your course which will not take you to Hoppen'.
I agreed but told him that as he could see we were a sailing boat and that
we could not sail directly into the northerly airs. Sometimes we would be
to the east of our track and sometimes to the west. 'Yes, yes,' he said, 'I
wish you a good watch and good sailing but please do not enter Russian
Territorial Waters'. I told him that we had no intention of doing so and
that he would soon see us with more west in our course. I wished him a
good watch and good fishing but we believed that the only 'fishing' done
on that vessel was 'fishing for information'.

That evening the wind arrived and it was a great joy to give the engine
a rest. Nick cooked a hearty dinner and in the peaceful silence we sum-
med up the days events. It was clear that the Russian vessel knew all
about us. It was bristling with aerials and had a very large radar scanner.
Two more genuine looking fishing boats closed in beside us but nothing
was heard on the VHF.

Speeds were slow on Thursday, sailing at between 4 and 4.5 knots, but
at least we were conserving fuel. During the afternoon we altered course
for 81°N 40°E to keep clear of the territorial waters of Franz Josef Land.
As I looked at the chart I spotted a small dot. It said Victoria Island
beside it. On checking the Arctic pilot we learned that the flag of the

USSR had been hoisted on Ostrov Viktoriya on 28 August 1933. I had an aeronautical chart showing the world above 80° and the island appeared clearly on it at 80° 09′ N 36° 43′ E. No one on board had ever heard of this island before 1600 on 11 August. During the evening we crossed 75°N. The VHF was still spluttering away in Russian and at midnight once again there were two large Russian trawlers on either side of us. Peter reported that they came dangerously close and that he had trouble avoiding them. There were five more Russian trawlers in sight during the next hour. We continued to sail on 12 August and the speed increased to 5 plus knots. The water temperature was plus 4°C and we were well able to make fresh water even at those low temperatures.

During the evening on 12 August we noted that the VHF had gone completely silent. The numerous Russian trawlers, which we had seen earlier, had vanished. Although the world did not know of it until 14 August and we did not hear of it until 15 August, 12 August was the day of an appalling tragedy for 118 Russian seamen and their families when the *Kursk* was disabled after a catastrophic explosion which sent it to the bottom of the Barents Sea.

Kieran's dinner that night again surprised us by its excellence. The fog rolled in and the wind disappeared. Visibility was down to one cable but we could still see the fulmars swooping out of the fog as they circled the boat. There were puffins about and, for the first time, we sighted little auks. The presence of these little birds is usually a sign that ice is not too

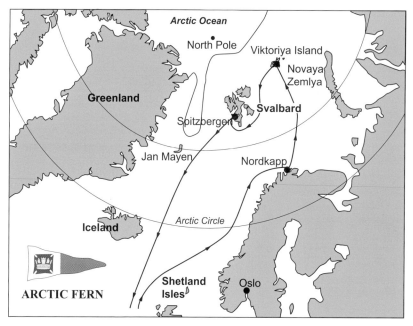

far away. The sea temperature at 79° 04′ N was +2°C. All of the ice signs were there but as we were to learn later, the ice front was still about 38 miles to the north of us. As we reached 36° E we steered due north. The ships GPS and the Loran C no longer functioned due to the low altitude of satellites at that latitude. We turned off the sat-phone and the VHF as we entered Russian Territorial Waters. We took our position by occasionally operating the Garmin hand-held GPS which still gave accurate readings. The ship's GPS has complex functions. It had a long list of way-points and of course it calculates the X.T.E. The Garmin had no way-points and nothing else to do except give a position. Perhaps this is why the hand-held GPS kept functioning. All transmitters and receivers were turned off with the exception of the occasional use of the hand-held GPS, for fear that they would betray our position.

There was a quiet anxiety aboard. At 0240 on Monday 14 August we sighted Ostrov Viktoriya. It looked like a large berg with snow and ice cliffs falling down to the sea. The water temperature was –0.2° C. As we got closer we could see the summit of the island which is 344 metres high. At the top there was a building with a round casagrane dish on it.

The island was due north of us and we headed for its centre. As we came to within four miles of it we scanned every bit of it to see if there was any sign of human habitation. We approached the south end where the sea was filled with walruses playing about with big clumsy splashes. They lifted their heads and fine tusks high out of the water to get a good look at us. They have smiling mouths and laughing eyes and they looked as if they were enjoying our visit.

The depth suddenly dropped and we moved away from the ice and snow of Ostrov Viktoriya to round a low point at its west end. We stood three cables off and as we went out to sea we noticed a complex of buildings, aerials, casagrane dishes, radar scanners, a possible runway for aircraft and some trucks and bulldozers. If the place was occupied, we knew that we were in deep trouble but using the binoculars we could see signs of wreckage and dereliction. Anyone who has been to a Russian base will know that there is much wreckage and dereliction around them. Robert carefully looked at a hut which seemed to have windows and a door. He trained the binoculars carefully on this hut to see if there was any sign of smoke or perhaps the shimmer of diesel fumes from the chimney. There was none. As we got a little closer he could make out that the windows and doors had been forced open by ice. This was good news. We anchored about half a cable off the snow and ice which hung above a small pebble beach. It seemed like a good place to land. Our hand-held GPS gave a position of 80° 09′ N, 36° 43′ E and the walruses played around us with amused curiosity. Our difficulty was to solve the problem of rowing ashore in a rubber dingy without getting a playful puncture from one or more of the walrus tusks. They swam around the boat and one nudged the hull with its tusks.

Reggie, Robert and I rowed ashore when the walruses departed to play their games in another part of the ocean. We were armed with a .375 rifle and a shotgun with cartridges fitted with heavy stainless steel shot. We took these ashore in case of polar bear attack. As we climbed up the snow and ice at the shore the terns screeched all around us and some swooped down within inches of our heads.

We walked through a lot of debris to get to the abandoned huts. Ice had come through the windows and doors. It covered the floor. In one room there were sofas and chairs and a library of about three-hundred books. The ice was two feet thick and since it was freezing, anything above it remained quite dry. Other huts contained transmitters, receivers, generators, decoding manuals and central heating plant. There was a large well-equipped kitchen and a large living area. The sleeping quarters were in nissen huts some distance away. Outside there were two old rusted bulldozers and an old truck. There was a defunct helicopter pad

Robert Pendleton at the summit of Ostrov Viktoriya.

and about forty 1000 gallon oil tanks. This station had been one of many which were set up to spy on the West and, later, on NATO activities along the Norwegian border. After the collapse of the Soviet Union both money and motivation ran out. This extraordinary place was a frozen museum of the cold war.

We walked over to a beach which had no snow on it. On the way we saw the unmistakable prints of polar bear paws. On the beach there were an estimated two hundred walruses grunting and steaming on the sandy gravel. The larger mammals were at the outside and the young were in a thoroughly protected fortress, in the middle. The polar bears had come to have a look but they would not challenge a fully grown walrus and had no means of getting close to the young. Apart from the two hundred walrus on the island we estimate that we would have seen at least another one hundred walruses at sea. Ostrov Viktoriya is a sizeable and important walrus colony of which very little is known. We were able to go right beside them. They did not feel threatened and were, in any case, too lazy to move. There were about fifty walruses lying close to the water and as we got near them they heaved their massive bodies into the sea. Movement on land is slow and cumbersome. A walrus in the water swims fast and moves with agility.

Reggie walked back to the dinghy to bring us ashore while Robert and I set off to climb to the top of the island. The pace was slow as we tested the ground in front of us in case of ice crevices. On our way a young polar bear jumped out of the snow and dashed over the brow of the hill. It moved so quickly that we did not have time to photograph it.

The summit of Ostrov Viktoriya seemed remote when we got there. There was a large container with a casagrane dish secured with wire stays on top of it. We descended with more confidence retracing our footsteps. In among the nissen hut dormitories we came upon the dead body of a full grown polar bear. It cannot have been dead for long because the skuas had not started to feed on it. In fact the poor bear would have made a bad meal for the skuas because there was hardly a pick of flesh on it. It looked as if it had died from starvation. To reach 80° 09′ N without ice is an unusual experience. Apart from the remote chance of picking out a young walrus there was nothing else to eat on the island. The seals had gone north to the ice edge. The prospects of survival for the young bear looked bleak.

It is now widely accepted that the polar ice-cap, which covers eighty percent of the Arctic Ocean, is retreating and this is very bad news for polar bears.

After a quick swim, we set off from Ostrov Viktoriya and steered 090° true E.

PETE

by Michael Gilkes

A little while ago Audrey was leaning on the rail of the *Explorer*, alongside an unquiet American, in Port Stanley harbour, Falkland Islands. The American turned to her and said, 'Gee, Audrey, what's that smell?'

She replied, 'That's peat!'

'Gee, who's Pete?'

One of the features of life in Islay used to be the aroma of peat in the streets of Port Ellen, Bowmore and indeed the majority of the small townships in the Hebrides. Sadly this is now rarely experienced. Whether this is as a consequence of affluence, or of the supremacy of other fossil fuels or of a reluctance to undertake the multiple labours involved in the gathering of peats, I am ill-equipped to discuss.

This preamble may appear irrelevant but it was these thoughts that came to mind when a fellow member, long versed in the ways and climate of the west coast of Scotland, confided in me that crew pressure – and of course it is always the crew – was leading him to consider whether the time might not have come for action to be taken with regard to some form of cabin heating.

I had been faced with similar mutterings some thirty years ago, after spending Easter day sheltering from the snow under the lee of Spurn Point, an episode which led to the never to be regretted acquisition of one of Pascal Atkey's *Pansy* charcoal stoves. So I was very willing to concede that I thought that his crew might have a point. I proceeded however to deploy all my persuasive powers to divert him from the options of diesel, gas or paraffin fuelled devices which nowadays seem to be the recommended answer. It is not that I have more than my usual prejudice about such gadgets but rather that they all have the disadvantage of producing water as a product of combustion when what is wanted is the production of dry heat and the promotion of warm dry air flow. These latter are attributes of solid fuel stoves and while there are many varieties

71

of these in the old chandlery catalogue (and vide *Dulcibella*) they are mostly obsolete and even the *Pansy* may now be unobtainable.

However, the construction of such a store is so simple that any sheet metal worker could easily reproduce one; fitting is straightforward. The stove pipe is a mere 1¼ inch diameter.

It has, however, one significant disadvantage. It was designed to burn charcoal (coke and coal are too hot) and it does this most efficiently. So much so that it is very difficult to slow down the rate of combustion or prevent a final flare up towards the end of a fill.

Many years ago, in an attempt to solve this problem, I bethought me of Islay and tried charging it with peat. The result was outstandingly successful.

Peat has a relatively low calorific value, produces very little smoke or ash. It also has the virtue of brightening up from apparent death when another piece is placed on cool embers.

A final breakthrough came when I discovered octagonal blocks, about 4 inches across, of compressed peat from Ireland. These ignite readily and glow away at an entirely controlled rate for hours per block; there is no risk of a sudden runaway. The blocks are dust free and can be stored in a locker or bag with no associated squalor. They appear to me readily available along the celtic fringe – and who would want to sail anywhere else! One final benefit may derive from using peat as a fuel: the gentle aroma is as specific for *mal de mer* as the proverbial sandy beach and palm tree. But one must be wary when beating to windward in poor visibility lest the scent from the stowed chimney pipe just forward of the helmsman (or woman) conveys a false impression of the proximity of land.

Conservationists and the politically correct may inveigh against the use of peat. They can be assured that, in Islay at least, it is a renewable resource!

COUNT ON ST KILDA

by Roddy Innes

On 9 August the heavies, who were also particularly keen to get to St Kilda, arrived; Robin Whiteside (alias 'Z') who had started the trip home from the West Indies last year, and John Simpson (alias 'the Bishop'), another one time submariner and musician who had moved on to 'higher' things, but never lost his sense of fun, and was now also recently retired.

By 1730 on 13 August we were nicely tucked inside the sound of Gighay and looking forward to a magical night. The forecast at 1754 was fair – fair for St Kilda. There was little wind, and after so many days of east or southeast winds, which could have made the anchorage there untenable, we felt that every hour might be crucial. So, with some misgivings, we weighed and crept out again and, in an oily calm, motored out through the Sound of Barra, which looked so harmless – but in anything of a swell could have been horrendous. Even as it was, we found a big uncomfortable swell at the western end, until well clear to the north west.

As the sun set we could just pick out the rocky heights of St Kilda, some 45 miles off, against the red after glow on the horizon. It was all going to happen! However, after dark, a light drizzle set in from the south and we had to motor sail all night. As dawn broke, the high, stark forms of the islands emerged, eerily large and threatening. The leading lights, once picked up, led us in, and at 0600 *Jessamy* anchored off the jetty in 30 feet, in company with a couple of MFV type vessels and a Frenchman, subsequently found to be there for the exceptional diving. We turned in.

By breakfast at 1000 the drizzle had stopped, and when we went ashore at 1130 it was brightening up. As advised, we sought out the warden, and chatted up some Scottish Nature researchers studying the wild life there. They were there, this week in particular, for the annual wild Soay sheep count. We started with a visit to the museum, in one of the restored crofts in the ruins of the 1860 High Street – an excellent

73

Village Bay with a couple of old sheep dogs.

background for anyone visiting the islands. We then climbed and roamed the heights above Village Bay taking photographs – the weather being much improved, though not quite sunny.

As we came down to the bounds of the old village – stone walls and enclosures everywhere – we became involved in the start of the round up for the annual sheep count. There were 1200 odd wild Soay sheep, all to be checked, tagged and DNA recorded. Apart from the professors, the sheep dogs/assistants were 15 undergraduate volunteers, mostly red headed lassies! Clearly the three extra old hands made all the difference, for the Village Bay flock were rounded up in record time. Well, lost sheep were the Bishop's business but this was most impressive!

It had been a very special and emotive day, and I think we were all moved by the history, the struggle for survival of the inhabitants, and the tragedy of the events leading up to the evacuation in 1930. We wished we could have stayed longer, and have subsequently read and learnt much more. The islands had historically been MacLeod country. Clearly the inhabitants had for centuries led a hard and unique way of life, but I was quietly relieved to read that the chiefs had generally been good land-lords.

That evening we went ashore again after supper to visit the 'shop' which the warden opened at 2100, for postcards, sweat shirts, books, etc, and, whilst waiting, to visit the most westerly pub in the British Isles, the aptly named Puff Inn; also, most pertinently, we wanted to contact friends on Pabbay, who were meant to be keeping a listening watch on their mobile, and who we hoped to meet up with the next morning. The best we could achieve was to leave another message. Back on board, we got our heads down for a couple of hours before sailing at 0100. A good southerly breeze overnight meant that we arrived between Pabbay and Shillay about 0800, somewhat ahead of schedule, and with no sign of life ashore. We had no large scale chart, and were not sure what or where we were looking for. The mobile had a good signal, but we could not raise or rouse our chums. The Pilot had nothing to say about Pabbay, but we were aware from the small scale chart that rocks extended off the southeast corner of the island, but not *that* far, as we struck the reef, and my heart fell through the bottom. I was below at the time looking at the chart, but fortunately it was calm and we were not going fast. We bore away and thankfully bumped our way off to the east, before feeling our way uneasily back west and anchoring about 3 cables to the south. Further calls on the mobile failed to get any response – subsequently found to be because of flat batteries ashore. As we waited the tide went out, and waves began to break over the offending far out-crop. I shall not return to Pabbay, ever.

At 1230 we weighed anchor, and headed for the western end of the Stanton Passage through the Sound of Harris. Again, I was very conscious how hairy this might be in low visibility or rough weather if one was not intimately familiar with it. As it was, it was low water, a clear day, most of the relevant rocks were visible, and it was no problem, but I was by now feeling a bit sensitive about my keel. If it is one thing to get to St Kilda, it is another to get back.

Jessamy is a Rustler 36, designed by Holman and Pye and built for me in 1990, in Penryn, Cornwall, near where 'the Bishop', with a daughter called Jessamie, was formerly a vicar.

2000 MILES FOR THE MILLENNIUM

by Michael and Julie Manzoni

This is the cruise for which the Founder's Cup was awarded.

We flew to Curacao at the beginning of February to join *Blue Sonata* where she had lain in the yard of ANSS for the previous nine months. From the three yards in Willemstad we had chosen the one recently taken over by two young Dutchmen, Geist and Pierre Verbeisen who make the very best of the limited facilities at their disposal and where repairs and provisions are readily available. We launched by mid February and sailed down to Spanish Water where we completed provisioning and awaited the arrival of our crew.

With five on board we set sail on 27 February in east-northeast wind of 20 knots which quickly rose to 24–27 knots as we pulled clear of Curacao running into open sea with swells of 6–8 feet. Comfortably reefed we were on a fast reach in typical Caribbean weather with a sparkling sun to be enjoyed by all – but sadly not so. Before long all the crew began to feel seasick and by late afternoon the watch system had collapsed leaving Julie, not feeling too good herself, preparing to share the watches with me through the night. Fortunately the sickness did not last long and they were all soon back in action. For a while we headed in the direction of Isla La Vache just off the coast of Haiti which is said to be one of the most attractive islands in the Caribbean, but on second thoughts we decided against it. Even for a brief stop we would have to spend at least two days checking in and out or take the risk of doing neither, which in a country of present political instability did not seem too wise. So as night approached with very little wind in the lee of the island we eased sheets to skirt the west end of Haiti. In contrast a few hours later we encountered the strength of the Windward Passage where the wind was blowing a good F.6. Close-hauled and well reefed we set about the last 100 miles of this leg of our cruise approaching Santiago de Cuba the following afternoon, four and a half days and 650 miles after leaving Curacao.

Like all those who have written of their cruising in Cuban waters we were absolutely enchanted by the friendly welcome we received from everyone we met. That included the army of officials who spent the best part of the first 24 hours checking us in.

First we were instructed to anchor just off the marina – no touching land without being properly vetted – whereupon a launch of fairly ancient vintage pulled alongside and five uniformed men clambered aboard with cheerful smiles and big boots. With our faltering Spanish we concluded that they must be the harbour master, the doctor, his technician who inspected the garbage, the guarda frontera and the mosquito hunter who crept stealthily up to each curtain in turn before whipping it aside the catch the intruders before they flew away. To be fair there is concern about Dengue fever in some parts of the Caribbean and Cuba boasts an excellent health record which they are determined to preserve.

With lots of Coke and Sprite, much laughter and endless forms duly stamped with the ship's stamp, they all welcomed us to Cuba as they took their leave each one shaking hands with each member of the crew – 25 handshakes. But there was little respite for a now weary crew wanting to prepare an evening meal. Soon the same vessel was seen manoeuvring alongside with four more inspectors, each carrying the customary brief-case politely seeking to come aboard. Customs first followed by Immigration, but the other two were a puzzle. It transpired that one was from the Ministry of Transport who issued a cruising permit for $30 and the other from the Ministry of Agriculture who inspected every food locker on the boat except the fridge. Fortunately we had decided not to bring fresh meat in the freezer on this voyage because there is no doubt that it would have been confiscated, but we were surprised that he wanted to destroy all the eggs on board too. Julie deftly side-stepped this by promising to make omelettes for supper and hard boil the remainder – a compromise accept-able to both parties but not the best use of three or four dozen eggs.

We were now free to move to the marina and go ashore and with help from the many officials and spectators alike we made fast alongside and settled down for the night.

As we were finishing breakfast the following morning we were taken aback to see two more uniformed men each with a lovely spaniel champ-ing at the bit asking to come aboard. The dogs were superbly trained to sniff their way through every corner of the boat, one looking for drugs and the other for explosives. As if that was not enough these canine visitors were followed by two more Customs employees and an interpreter who took at least two hours meticulously exploring every drawer and cupboard from bow to stern, insisting that Julie or I be with them all the time to ensure no malpractice. The various bundles of dollars hidden in socks or coffee tins raised a few eyebrows but thankfully were not illegal. There's no doubt that entering Cuba can be quite a performance which some people find irritating if not unbearable, but taking it in a relaxed

Chief Assistant to the Customs Officer.

way solved all the problems and provided a great deal of entertainment along the way.

The Nigel Calder and Simon Charles guide books have fairly daunting descriptions of the jetty but it has been improved since they wrote and there are new facilities ashore opened only in 1999 which were adequate for the short stay we enjoyed. We did not experience the oil and tar along the waterline threatened by the same authors but were amazed to see our decks developing a rash of little brown spots like a sudden outbreak of measles. However the Cubans know the pollution belching from their chemical plant and cement works nearby and all the hardware stores for less than a dollar have a product called Sulfadon (if memory serves me right) which will take away the offending stains.

After visiting Santiago which is interesting and the magnificent six-teenth century fort which guards the entrance to the harbour we sailed west, the first day to Chivirico and the second to Portillo, both tranquil protected lagoons where belted kingfishers fly and snowy egrets come in to roost while hawks circle the hillsides. We had permission to anchor but not to go ashore, the usual constraint where the bureaucratic presence is limited to Guarda Frontera only. So from Portillo, after obtaining some bread unofficially under cover of darkness, we opted for an overnight sail of approximately 100 miles well into the Golfo de Guacanayabo.

After a fairly rough passage in strong trade winds here was peace sublime. We spent the next ten days pottering about the islands generally in 6 to 20 feet of water, picking our way between the endless cays and coral reefs, swimming, snorkelling and lazing in the sun. We supplemented our home-made bread with so much lobster that we finally had to say, 'No more'. The world was our own as we covered about 160 miles, mostly under genoa alone, during which time we saw only three other yachts in the distance. Our companions were the fishermen who were always cheerful and friendly, willing at any time to exchange fish for whatever we had to offer. Rum was the favourite but beer, coke, soap, T-shirts, matches, anything was more than welcome.

In addition to shrimp, the principal catches appeared to be lobster and grouper which are caught by hand. Diving equipment is obviously too expensive and the divers operate with masks taking a hose pipe from the boat for air. They work for the state five days a week and return to the mainland for the other two days. One team of three or four boats had a primitive base camp on the beach, not much more than an old tarpaulin strung between the palm trees and an open fire for their evening meal, but the jewel in their crown was a small generator powering a large chest freezer incongruously sitting there on the sand. It provided us with yet more fish for supper and a most unusual photograph of a coral island.

Among many places we visited was the lagoon at Cincho Balas which has two very narrow entrances. Geoffrey Nockolds reported spending over six hours hard aground in the northern passage a few years ago so we opted for the south channel where the guide book simply said 'less than two metres' and advised following the groove cut in the bottom by the fishing boats. We adhered to the approach instructions implicitly, turning sharply to starboard a few metres clear of the steel post and were immensely relieved to see the groove which we managed to follow, although the depth meter flashed at 3ft and even 1.5ft at one point which did not help the nerves. Fortunately departure was assisted by the fishermen who guided us out. We handed over another case of beers with grateful thanks for this unexpected help and we set off for Zaza Alfuero and the next day to Casilda.

We were determined to visit the beautiful town of Trinidad de Cuba a few miles inland, now a World Heritage site with its elegant Spanish colonial buildings lining narrow cobbled streets, all kept spotlessly clean. The inhabitants welcome the tourists who provide a little extra income to supplement their meagre wages which are probably not more than $10 per month in many cases. We were ushered into their homes to admire their treasured possessions and take a coke or coffee to avoid any semblance of begging on their part. They are proud and charming people whose full potential is surely suppressed by the restrictive political regime.

Sad to leave Cuba with much still to look forward to, we arrived in Grand Cayman on 19 March where there is an excellent marina and plenty of safe anchorage in North Sound. A modern westernised island which makes a good place to change crew and take on provisions.

Home-made bread and lobster soon became the staple diet.

Although a number of large yachts are registered here and the island appears to be an active leisure-boat centre we found only limited facilities for chandlery and repair. Julie's discovery of a handful of ball bearings rolling around the deck had left no doubt about the reason for our genoa furling gear jamming during the crossing from Cuba and it was vital that it be repaired. Fortunately we were able to get new bearings shipped in from the States within three days and we found two charter skippers willing to give us a hand to take down the forestay and replace the bearing in the furling gear. Dismantling and re-assembling the bearing and the Norseman fitting was a first for all of us but it worked well for the rest of the trip.

The passage from Cayman to Belize was notable primarily for the difficulty we had trying to go slowly enough. We had decided to enter at San Pedro on Ambergris Cay in the north of the country where access can be gained by dodging a large rock in the middle of a narrow gap through the coral reef provided weather conditions permit. The entrance demands good light in addition to gentle seas and the problem was to time our departure for a 3 or 4 day passage to ensure arrival in the morning light. We got it wrong. The light winds soon gave way to strong easterlies which combined with the 1–2 knots northwest current to keep *Blue Sonata* bowling along too fast towards her destination. We tried main only, jib only, reefed jib with 12 rolls, even 15 rolls, then heaving-to for lunch but nothing could slow our progress sufficiently and we were obliged to heave-to at midnight on the third day about 5 miles east of the

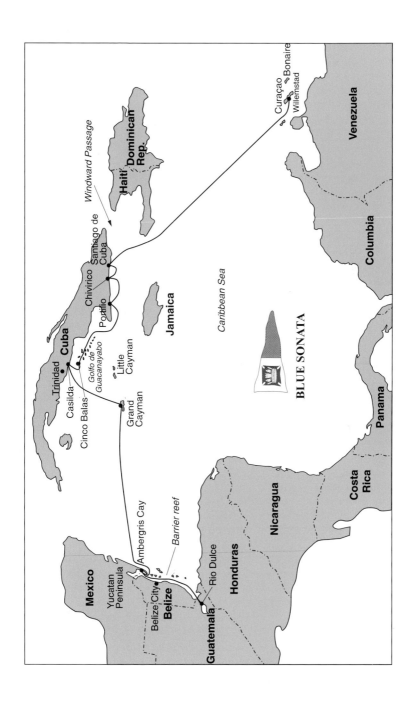

barrier reef. The wind was blowing 24–26 knots and it took some trial and error to find the best combination of reefed genoa and main. We finally settled down comfortably for four hours drifting north parallel to the reef, but it was surprising that during that time we covered the ground at the rate of about three knots. Obviously the combination of current and leeway must not be underestimated.

At dawn we approached the entrance to Ambergris Cay when it became clear that it would be extremely hazardous if not impossible to go through with the big waves crashing against the reef. Nothing for it but to continue south to the main channel entrance, well marked and approachable in any weather. Once inside the reef we took a cursory look at the unattractive landing facilities along the Belize City town front and decided to tuck ourselves in for the night in one of the off-lying mangrove cays.

The 30 miles north to check in at Ambergris Cay the following day turned out to be the most glorious sail we have experienced in the whole of the Caribbean as we piloted our way through the cays and shallows in the steady trade winds and the protected water behind the barrier reef. We arrived in the delightful village of San Pedro with its superb beach and fabulous colours of crystal clear water with only perhaps 15 or so boats anchored where there would be hundreds if Europe could provide a place to match it. In Belize there are hundreds of coral studded cays waiting to be explored. Picking our way between the islands and the coral provided some of the most fascinating pilotage we could wish for. Most of the cays are uninhabited and very small, some not more than two or three acres, and only occasionally did we find ourselves sharing the anchorage with another yacht.

Two weeks cruising in this indescribable area is clearly not enough but we made the most of the time we had in glorious weather – with one exception. Weather forecasts on the local net had warned of a front passing through so we chose a tiny protected lagoon between coral reef and mangrove but still had trouble. Fortunately Julie was not sleeping well and at about 0200 she realised it was time to call the crew to attention. The wind had veered through 180 degrees and was now blowing 25–30 knots from the northwest. We were not sure how good the holding was and lying so close to danger invisible in pitch darkness we were getting anxious. We quickly started to plot the last two decimal places of the lat. and long. readings from the GPS on an improvised grid and a pattern of our position swinging to and fro on the chain began to emerge. For a while we appeared to be holding. The second decimal point represents about 20 yards and since we were probably not more than 100 yards from the shore we could not afford to drift very far. Suddenly readings came up one and then two squares below the average of the previous ten minutes leaving no doubt that we had to move without delay. In night clothes and pouring rain, thank heaven for the warmth of the tropics, we weighed anchor and edged our way over the short distance to the other side of the lagoon where we re-anchored, this time on about 140ft of chain, seven or eight times the depth. Little room for a second anchor so we gambled on the extra length of chain being sufficient.

It was easier to say farewell to the magnificent sailing in Belize knowing that we shall be back again next year, perhaps also anticipating what was in store for us in Guatemala. Drawing 5 feet with the centreboard up we had no problems crossing the 6ft bar into Livingstone and were soon enthralled by this bustling town which has no road access and is served only by water. Checking in was a pleasant experience and at sunset we enjoyed a drink in the cockpit watching a hive of activity as the fishing fleet of well over 50 boats got underway motoring out for the night's fishing. At dawn, after a peaceful night we saw them returning in droves to be met by their families and friends who came out in dinghies, canoes, launches, boats of all kinds. And there were buyers too, some commercial and some private, all jostling for position to secure the best of the catch. Stirring scenes.

Then the Rio Dulce – that magnificent river up to 80 foot deep, edged by towering cliffs 300 feet high heavily covered by tropical growth. Motoring upstream was a whole new world from the open sea which had been left behind. We made one or two diversions to explore the tributaries where small Mayan Indian settlements can be found, mostly single-room thatched huts clinging to the river-bank, perhaps half a dozen or so making up the village with one slightly larger building for the church.

After crossing El Golfete, a lake 9 miles long and 2 to 3 miles wide, we arrived at Fronteras where the only road in the vicinity crosses the river on a high level bridge. We were amazed to see the extent of the holiday development on each bank for two miles or more on both sides of the bridge, again all serviced by water. Fast water taxis, private launches, speed boats, jet-skis, not to mention a fair number of yachts made the river like the M1 on a Friday evening. There were many private houses with their own jetty and boathouse tucked in alongside hotels, restaurants, workshops and marinas which have all sprung up in the last 20 years and look set to increase as more and more wealthy Guatemalans build holiday homes here.

A wide choice does not always make a decision easy and we took some time to decide where to leave *Blue Sonata* for the summer. We unfortunately suffered a break-in anchored just off Mario's marina while eating ashore and it was rumoured that there was a gang of thieves operating in that vicinity. Perhaps that influenced us, but in any case we like the protected water in Suzanna's Lagoon and despite its rickety piers and relative isolation we settled for that. For peace of mind we tied *Blue Sonata* to one of the marina huts as well as the pier before taking the six hour bus ride to Guatemala City and the long haul home via Mexico. It was the end of April and the end of 2000 wonderful millennium miles.

SOUTH AMERICA: SEA AND MOUNTAINS

by John Melling

This is the cruise for which the Romola Cup was awarded.

We left Plymouth on 22 June in *Taraki* and left Cape Verde for Brazil on 4 August. After a landfall at Fernando de Noronha on 18 August we beat up the river to Jacaré.

Early on 25 September we left Jacaré motoring down a peaceful river, but once out at sea it was an uncomfortable shock to the system to be beating south into a F.4–5 SSE wind for the next three days. On a beautiful sunny morning, after five days out, the high rise apartment blocks of suburban Salvador appeared glinting through the morning haze. The air was full of thousands of butterflies heading out to sea and the water had much floating plastic! An enthusiastic wave from a local fisherman was followed by a most unexpected bump then a grunt. *Taraki* had nudged a whale who swam alongside then rose behind. It was a humpback and a magnificent sight. We anchored off the Iate Clube de Bahia and were collected by the club launch and taken to the secretariat where with great charm we were given coffee and a pass to use their beautiful club for three days. We often ask ourselves where do we think a people's heart is and here it was on the beaches and in their music.

It was a short trip to Centro Nautico, the marina in downtown Salvador. Pelourinho the historic area is reached by the Lacerdo elevator. It is a vibrant and interesting place where we enjoyed restaurants serving moqueca dishes cooked with dende oil and coconut milk. Olodum music concerts are held every Sunday night in a large square, very crowded, very noisy and great fun.

We then went to explore the Rio Paraguaçu and the islands of Baía de Todos os Santos and the Baía do Aratu where there is another welcoming yacht club. For us the highlight was the Rio Paraguaçu, in particular the small town of Marigojipe. On Saturday mornings there is a market full of bustle and colour with many small stalls selling all manner of fruit,

Schooners at Salvador.

vegetables, meat, beans and spices. In the side streets there were carts and donkeys, which brought the produce from nearby farms. Everywhere we met friendliness especially at a bakery-cum-sucos bar which we visited frequently when in town. A short bus ride through interesting villages and countryside took us to Cachoeira, a pleasant old Portugese town.

After returning to Salvador we set sail for Morro São Paulo, a pretty seaside town, but too touristy for us, so after a day we left for Camamu and the Rio Maraú. This was to be another beat before arriving at the wide, shallow and poorly lit entrance in darkness. We had to decide whether to stay out all night or try and enter. We chose to enter using GPS and a recent Brazilian chart which showed a channel with many dog-legs and unlit buoys. Radar was of no help. Our spotlight never revealed any buoys, but after a nail-biting couple of hours we anchored off a small *pousada* at Campinho in perfect peace.

Next day we set off up river and anchored between thickly forested islands. When visiting Ilhas dos Tubarões we met an elderly man, who climbed one of the coconut palms and threw down two coconuts. We drank the freshest coconut milk ever. Further up river and now off the chart we wanted to anchor between islands covered with mangrove. It was high tide and we touched a bottom of very soft mud, but by jumping quickly into the dinghy with an anchor the situation was saved as we winched off. We now anchored in an idyllic spot. There was total peace

Locals sailing at Rio Paraguaçu.

and flat calm. Occasionally we saw fishermen in dugout canoes. Next morning I went off in the dinghy with a GPS to survey the islands and shore. The ebbing tide exposed muddy banks teeming with crabs with bright red claws. From here it was not far to Maraú. The administrative centre for the region. We stocked up with fruit, vegetables and bread before returning downstream to Barcello, a small and friendly hill top village with good views over the surrounding country.

On 7 November we returned down the channel we had entered in the dark. All the buoys had been removed so it was still GPS navigation whilst keeping a careful eye on the depth sounder. Once out in clear water we headed for the Canal dos Abrolhos and after two days anchored on the south side of Ilha de Santa Barbara. We had only been there a couple of hours when some naval chaps came over and suggested we move to the north side. This was good advice as a nasty cold front came through. The area is a maritime national park with restricted landing on the islands. Sãolo, a student oceanographer who was acting as a warden,

Dug-out canoes on Rio Maraù.

took us to Ilha Siriba where we were able to approach breeding boobies and tropic birds very closely. They seemed quite unconcerned.

Leaving Arquipeago dos Abrolhos with a light following breeze we could see a pod of whales in the distance. After two days there was a massive wind shift, great lightning display and we were once again beating until our arrival at Buzios. We did not land but next day continued round to Arriàl do Cabo, a diving centre and fishing port as well as a base for off-shore oil activities. From here it was a short hop to Praia do Farol, Cabo Frio before continuing on to Rio de Janeiro.

We had read many stories about problems when staying in marinas in Rio de Janeiro and decided to head for Clube Naval at Charitas near Niterói. Once again we were made most welcome and allowed to use their excellent facilities including swimming pool and restaurant. Suzy and Renato, two circumnavigators living on their boat, were especially helpful giving us much advice about anchorages in the Ilha Grande area and inviting us to a pre-Christmas party for yachts. We took a bus ride to Niterói then the ferry got us to Rio where we enjoyed some of the many art galleries and museums as well as a lunch time concert.

It was a long day's sail from Niterói to our next anchorage and we arrived after dark in an unlit bay at Praia dos Mangres, this time surrounded by hills, where radar was helpful. After arriving in an unknown place in the dark it is always exciting waking up next morning to see where you are. This time it was a new world, distant mountains, hills covered with tropical rainforest, sandy beaches, clear turquoise water and alone. Later in the day we walked across the island to its ocean side where there was a pristine sandy beach. It was miles long and there were only two other people. It was a short hop round a headland to the next bay where we anchored off Abraão, a very pleasant holiday resort where the only access is by ferry. Overlooking the village is Pico do Papagaio (Parrot Peak), a prominant granite outcrop at the top of a mountain. It is a climb of almost 1000m. We set off on our wedding anniversary and were rewarded with magnificent views after emerging from the rainforest onto the granite top.

After a couple of days at Angra dos Reis for shopping and clearing with the authorities. we continued cruising through the islands eventually arriving at the picturesque town of Parati. This was a little gem of Portugese colonial architecture with small cobbled streets, reputedly washed by tidal waters. After a few days at Saco Juruminim it was time to head for Ilha Itahanga and the Christmas meet. We arrived after a very pleasant sail anchoring in a small bay near a most interesting *pousada*. It had been the home and studio of a São Paulo architect and today it is a small art gallery providing the setting for a restaurant and our party. Next day yachts began to arrive, 25 eventually. One of the yachts, much to our surprise, was *Octopus*, a French yacht we had met in Gran Canaria.

It was now time to think about where we should spend Christmas and, after a return visit to Parati for last minute shopping, we headed for an anchorage at Ilha da Cotia. There were beautiful surroundings and a number of yachts. We all spent time on each other's boats and Manola, a Spaniard whose home is in Uruguay, joined us for Christmas dinner. This included a two year old Christmas pudding which Sally had lovingly kept for the occasion. Very charmingly Manola said it was one of the best Christmases he had had.

We moved on to visit various new anchorages including Pria Grande, Pouso, Ubatuba for shopping then on to Ilha Anchieta where we were to

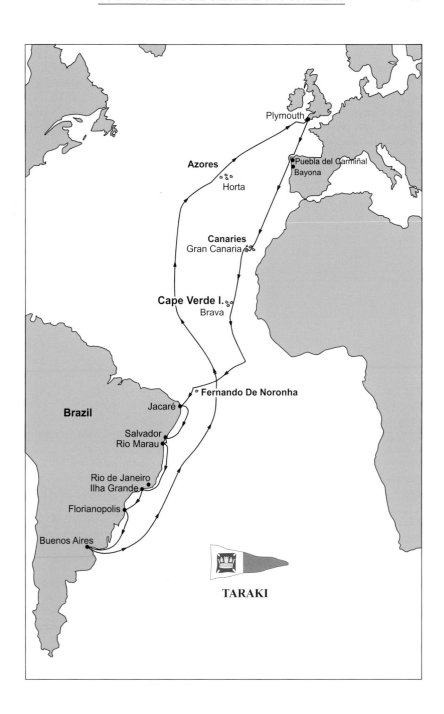

Plymouth

Azores

Horta

Puebla del Carmiñal
Bayona

Canaries
Gran Canaria

Cape Verde I.
Brava

Fernando De Noronha

Brazil

Jacaré

Salvador
Rio Marau

Rio de Janeiro
Ilha Grande

Florianopolis

Buenos Aires

TARAKI

see in the new Millennium. Firework displays competed with thunder, lightning and torrential rain. On 2 January we left a wonderful if rather windless cruising ground. There was heavy low cloud, rain and little wind for the next few days. It was going to be a very slow trip to Porto Belo where we anchored off rather than going into the marina. Originally it had been our intention to go to Florianopolis as our post was going there and we had to clear out from Brazil there, but detailed examination of the chart indicated too little water to risk a heavy deep draft yacht like *Taraki*. We went by bus, twice unfortuately as our post had not arrived. Eventually clearing out on 14 January we left Brazil bound for Uruguay.

With generally favourable winds and some very pleasant sailing we arrived off Punto del Este early in the morning with the sun shining on the skyscraper landscape. It did not attract us so we continued on to Piriapolis, investigated the new marina but decided to continue on to Colonia where we arrived just after midnight, seven and a half days after leaving Porto Belo.

Colonia is a step back in time, a pleasant place for relaxing. The anchorage gets very busy as it is popular with Argentinian yachtsmen both for holidays and weekends. Since leaving Jacaré we had met few cruising yachts and only one of them British; here there were none until a French single-hander and then a Swedish couple arrived. Miguel joined us for supper one evening and we were able to spend a little time with Silvija and Egon who were in a hurry to go to a nearby river where they could continue refitting peacefully. They had lost their mast some months earlier, were rescued by the Brazilian navy and had since built themselves a wooden replacement. They were most helpful in giving us information on where to stay in Argentina.

After a pleasant week in Colonia we went across the muddy waters of the Rio Plata to the Yacht Club of Argentina at Buenos Aires where there was a very friendly welcome and generous invitation to stay free for seven days with full use of the club's facilities. Patricia at the club was a great help to us with clearing in and out, probably the only downside to cruising in South America.

Our time in Buenos Aires was busy making final plans for trekking in Patagonia, getting air tickets to fly south and for Sally to return home. It was also a time for visiting friends and enjoying this pleasant city with its many restaurants and top class beef. We would have liked to leave *Taraki* here but it was not possible other than at a quite expensive marina and we needed somewhere for eight weeks. After a not very comfortable sail we arrived at La Plata and were welcomed by Edward Jones who suggested we should moor alongside his old wooden yacht *Hualun* at the Club de Regatas. We could not have found a more helpful chap. He looked after *Taraki* whilst we were away, introduced us to friends and family, was invaluable when dealing with the authorities and ferried us around in his ancient 2CV. The first ride was a bit nervous making as his car was partly tied together with string, the ignition was two bits of wire stuck together and he had no lights when we set off into the black of night. He could see the police from a long way off; a lovable rogue we thought. On 12 February we flew from Buenos Aires to Río Gallegos on the first leg of six weeks of wonderful trekking. It was fortunate that we had all our climbing and camping gear with us on *Taraki* so preparations were simple. We travelled by bus between various treks except for a flight from Punta Arenas to Puerto Montt. Our first trek took us to Parque Nacional Los Glaciares and around Monte Fitz Roy (Argentina), then south via Puerto Natales for a nine day circuit of the Torres del Paine (Chile). From Puerto Montt it was a bus to Osorno and then to the Parque Nacional Puyehue (Chile) and across a raw plateau of pumice formed by repeated eruptions of Volcan Puyehue, which we climbed on the way. It last erupted in 1960 but the crater is now covered by snow and ice. After returning to Osorno in a large truck we caught a bus back to Argentina to the fashionable tourist town of San Carlos de Bariloche in the heart of their lake district. It has many good restaurants and must be a haven for chocoholics with all its chocolate shops. Their summer season was almost over so it was quiet enabling us to stay at mountain *refugios* for our last two short treks into fine mountain country. With some sadness we left our mountain wandering to fly back to Buenos Aires.

Now back in La Plata *Taraki* was prepared for returning home. We had decided Sally would fly home to see the family including one new granddaughter and that I would return single-handed from La Plata to the Azores where Sally would rejoin me.

At 0900 on 6 April I cast off mooring lines and lifted the bow and stern anchors which had kept *Taraki* safely for the past two months and motored down channel out to the Río Plata. The sun was shining and there was a very light breeze. A gentle start to a long passage which was to take fifty days with a sailing distance of almost 6000 miles. This was happily much shorter than Tilman's frustrating trip in 1967 which took him eighty-six days from Montevideo.

On 2 June Sally arrived in Horta and we were delighted to be together again and to enjoy time on Faial before leaving for home. A slow but uneventful passage brought us back via the north of the Scillies due to contrary winds. We arrived off Penlee Point near midnight in thick fog and anchored in Cawsand Bay one year after leaving, having sailed 15,000 miles and having stayed at fifty-six different anchorages.

SCENES FROM A PACIFIC CRUISE

by Margaret and Graham Morfey

This is the cruise for which the Vice Commodore's Prize was awarded in recognition of the pilotage information supplied with the log.

Rescue in the Pacific

We left the Galapagos on 11 April bound for the Marquesas islands which were just under 3000 miles away. Our crew were Graham Morfey, Merryl Huxtable and Chris Haughton. Halfway there, at 1605 (2305 UTC) on 20 April at 7° 20' S, 110° 22' W, we had just concluded our regular chat on the SSB with friends on *Mustang* (another British yacht with a crew of four, Chris Green – skipper, Katie, Matt and Annie – a doctor). Being nearby we tried a call on VHF. There was no reply from *Mustang* but there was a strong signal, which we realised was a MAYDAY message from an Italian yacht *Elisio* which was taking in water. There were two people on board, the skipper Andrea and his wife Vanna. Their position put them only ten miles away downwind so that we expected to be with them before darkness. At each VHF call their position had altered and we suddenly realised that they were sailing away from us at 4 knots! They lowered sail and motored towards us, but it was 1830 and nearly dark before we saw them.

Elisio, a 9 metre sloop, was rolling in the big sea that was running (we had 30 knots of wind the previous day) but we could see her anti-fouling and she was not low in the water. Merryl volunteered to go to *Elisio* in the dinghy which we had inflated with a battery operated strobe light attached, but with the darkness and sea conditions this would have been too dangerous. We tried floating our dinghy down on a long line, but after several attempts we realised that this was not going to work and there was a risk of collision or a line around the prop. We dissuaded Andrea from entering his liferaft since trying to pick them up in the dark was not attractive. As *Elisio* was only taking on 10 litres of water per hour we agreed to sail with them while maintaining VHF contact.

At 1800 we had managed to talk to *Mustang* and said we might need their help; they agreed and slowed down to stay upwind of us. At 2300 when *Mustang* was 48 miles away, well to the South. We asked them to rendezvous with us. They were four very capable young people and they had on board a stable RIB which we hoped would be easier to control in the swell .

We had Inmarsat C which proved invaluable, allowing us to advise MRCC Falmouth simply and quickly and maintain regular communication with them. They subsequently advised other MRCC stations and appropriate authorities in Rome.

We did not get much sleep that night. Keeping close to *Elisio* required constant adjustments to the genoa and *Autohelm*. Merryl was regularly on the VHF to Andrea and on the SSB to other Italian yachts as requested by him. At dawn we were still close to *Elisio* as we both altered course to close with *Mustang* who appeared as a very welcome sight. By 0800 on 21 April, Good Friday, all three boats were together.

Although the seas had gone down and it was a beautiful day there was still a substantial swell and manoeuvring the yachts as they rolled was not easy. Chris of *Mustang* evolved a plan which was agreed by us and then relayed by Merryl to *Elisio*. The plan ensured that neither of the *Elisio* crew, who could have been in shock, was alone in the dinghy. It was not feasible for *Mustang* to launch their RIB and so our Avon was re-inflated. We and *Mustang* motored parallel and our dinghy line was passed to them. Matt, with a hand held VHF, boarded the dinghy. He was cast adrift and *Elisio* motored up to him. He boarded to inspect the damage which arose from an old repair to the keel. The keel plate was breaking free from the hull, water was entering and there was a risk that the whole structure could suddenly go.

Vanna with some personal possessions was helped into the dinghy by Matt. They drifted clear of *Elisio* and then it was our turn to motor up to the dinghy. The rolling made boarding difficult but soon Vanna and her possessions were safely aboard. The whole process was repeated for Andrea. Each move had to be relayed in French to *Elisio*, to Matt, *Mustang* and ourselves. Finally *Mustang* picked up Matt and the equipment that Andrea had salvaged in *Elisio's* small dinghy. It only remained for us to come up to *Mustang* and retrieve our dinghy complete with medicines provided by Annie for dealing with shock.

Andrea's last action had been to cut the sea-cock pipes and *Mustang* stood by for three hours to witness the scuttling while we set sail for the Marquesas with our extra crew. At 1110 (1810 UTC) we advised MRCC that the rescue had been completed. During the next twelve days Andrea and Vanna proved very pleasant companions, introduced an Italian flavour to the cooking and demonstrated a skill in catching fish which we could never emulate.

Flight of Time anchored off Hakahetau, island of Ua Pou, Marquesas.

Ua Pou

On 16 May we left Atuona for a quiet anchorage on the nearby island of Tahuata before sailing on to Ua Pou next day. We arrived at the main harbour of Hakahau at dusk and anchored overnight. Next morning we sailed around the northern cape and saw the amazing landscape from the northwest coast. Light clouds parted to show soaring pinnacles of rock above the thickly forested green mountains; there was even a rainbow crowning the scene. At the water's edge the village of Hakahetau lay among the trees around a church with a red steeple. Fishermen in their pirogues, canoes with outriggers, rose and fell in the heavy swell, waves crashed on the stony beach. We knew it would not be a comfortable anchorage, but the view of the island was irresistible and we decided to stay. We rowed around a rocky promontory at the north end of the beach to a concrete jetty. We got ashore only half wet, and moored the dinghy with a stern anchor. A large wooden double canoe lay on the beach, and several pirogues large and small. We found the church with the steeple; inside were carved pillars and beautiful wooden sculptures around the altar. Flowering shrubs were planted all around the church – hibiscus, frangipani, tiare, bougainvillea. Large velvety black butterflies with vivid blue spots drifted by. Under the shadier trees pigs were tethered. A stream ran through the village, and we crossed the bridge from the church to the main street and walked uphill. We found a house with a broad veranda shaded by large trees. A man on the veranda called us in to sit in the shade; he spoke good English and welcomed us, particularly when he heard we had come from a yacht. This was Etienne Hokaupoko, a retired schoolteacher who, with his wife Yvonne, hosts a kind of un-official club for all visiting yachtsmen. This was our first taste of true

Polynesian hospitality, which we were to experience many times in the months to come, but it was in Hakahetau that we learnt how kind and generous the Polynesians are. Etienne was a mine of information and an expert on the culture of the Marquesas islands. We talked about native crafts and languages, museums and other ways of preserving their traditions. Merryl, who works at the Victoria and Albert Museum, was interested in Etienne's plans to establish a museum on Ua Pou. Yvonne showed us the beautiful hats, jewellery and traditional dance costumes she had made from natural materials, and the tapa cloth which her son had decorated with Marquesan motifs. Hanging on the wall was a row of polished canoe paddles, also made by their son Adrien. Some had blades made in stripes of different coloured woods and were very handsome. Graham asked if he could buy one, and Merryl had one specially made to fit her by Adrien.

Etienne and Yvonne invited us to come back for supper that evening. Their son Adrien was there, a slender, handsome young man with beautiful patterns tattooed on his chest. We sat around the table and Etienne said grace. We each had a half coconut shell as a plate and there were forks, but everyone used fingers too. A wonderful spread of food covered the table, fried fish, chicken, salad, bread and a big bowl of poipoi made from breadfruit. Poipoi is a thick yellow creamy paste made by pounding freshly cooked breadfruit and mixing it with some fermented breadfruit. The fermented poipoi will keep for long periods and is one of the traditional foods of the Marquesas; however it is rather strong for most tastes. A jug of coconut cream stood on the table to add to the poipoi. We drank homemade fruit juice, and for dessert there was a bowl of pamplemousses peeled and cut in large chunks.

After our meal with Etienne and his family, Yvonne took us to the choir practice for the local Catholic church. In a large bare room, a few benches were lined up to face a wall where three blackboards were leaning. The first two boards had verses in Marquesan chalked on them, and a long haired girl was busily copying the Latin Credo onto the third. Three or four young men played guitars or ukeleles and most of the singers were women with a few older men in the back row. Children and dogs scampered in and out unheeded. We sat in the front row with Yvonne and her sister, both good singers. To see the other singers and musicians we had to peep surreptitiously over our shoulders . The sound from behind us was wonderful, it came and went in waves, as one or other of the singers felt the urge to give a lead and launch into a verse, the others chiming in and swelling the sound until they came to a difficult patch and the impetus faltered. There was no choirmaster or teacher; the whole affair was spontaneous, and no written music but lovely harmony. After a while we found we could follow the Marquesan text and join in when there was a strong wave of sound from behind.

A large moth flew in the open door, fluttered around and settled on the floor. A young dog picked it up carefully in his mouth, but then it got away and he looked quite perplexed, but bounded around the room after it. The singing continued without a pause. Now and then a naughty child was shooed away. The room could have been a kind of Sunday school; a beautiful painted model of the church stood in the corner, and a few simple drawings. A primitive Nativity scene showed a mother, father and baby in a room with a television set and a vase of flowers. After we had sung through all the Marquesan verses, a deep male voice at the back launched into the Credo. This sounded more European than the earlier songs, quite easy to follow, but I wished we had ended with the haunting Marquesan tunes lingering in our ears. We trooped out into the starry night between glossy bushes starred with sweet smelling tiare flowers.

Next day they were preparing a feast in the village. We went to look for an old man who needed aspirin, and learned that his wife was helping to prepare manioc. We picked our way through the breadfruit trees, purao trees dropping large yellow blooms, and a pistachio dripping juicy purple fruit. A winding stone path among hibiscus bushes brought us to an open air kitchen, where a young man was grating large peeled white manioc roots in a whirring electric machine. A young woman who understood our halting French showed us a large metal pot of the manioc roots set to boil over a wood fire. Beyond the kitchen area was a large oblong pit in the earth where they would make the *four Marquesan*, the earth oven filled with hot stones to cook food overnight. Two women were busy cutting up raw fish for *poisson cru*. Another woman showed us how they would take a large handful of the grated manioc, make parcels of it with two purao leaves and fill a dish with leaf parcels to boil. We think the feast is for Whitsunday tomorrow.

Ofu

We had anchored by the island of Ofu on the eastern side of the Vava'u group, and I came into the cockpit early next morning to look at the village. We were close to the shore, near two enormous banyan trees which cast a deep shade. Further along the beach two or three small boats were pulled up, and a small black pig wandered around them foraging for any fish which the fishermen might have dropped while unloading their catch from last night. Beyond the beach was the path which led through the village. We went ashore and were met by small children who helped to pull the dinghy up. We walked along the path in the shade of tall trees; small houses with exuberant gardens lay on one side, the sea on the other. An old dugout canoe with an outrigger lay on the beach under the banyan. Then we heard children singing and came to the schoolhouse, and beyond it the church. After we had looked inside the church and admired the enormous bell which hung in a separate tower, the children ran out of school to see us. We went and met the two teachers. Faka'anaua, the principal, was a middle aged lady who taught the younger children, and a serious young man taught the older ones. This was a Government school and although the teaching and the basic equipment is free, parents must pay for paper, pens and other materials. We had brought a gift of stationery; in the Polynesian way, they gave us leis made by the children from shells and drinking straws. Like most primary school teachers, they use great ingenuity in making their own wallcharts and teaching aids, but they need all the help they can get. Some of the reading books had been photocopied and stapled into coloured covers; new books were very few.

After playtime all the children went into one classroom and sang for us, in English, some of the Church Missionary Society's choruses which we remembered from our own childhood. One was 'I will make you fishers of men' which was very appropriate in a village which relies mainly on fishing for its livelihood. As the teacher pointed out, if the weather is bad and the catch is poor, everybody suffers. But they do have another source of income; Merryl had read that this village was well known for its expert weavers of pandanus mats. At the far end of the village we found a house with small children and piglets running around the garden, and a smiling woman sitting under a tree doing the laundry. Yes, she was the

Graham, Polynesian style.

weaver pictured in Merryl's book, and her sister and her mother wove mats too. They brought out two or three large mats and spread them on the grass. One had two layers, with a handsome dark and light checkered pattern on one side and the plain pale brown pandanus colour on the other. The pandanus leaves can be bleached to a pale cream, left with their natural colour or darkened with vegetable dyes. The browns can be very dark, almost black, and so the patterns are very striking. We went next door and saw some even more beautiful mats. Merryl bought one and we ordered another to be made and sent to us. They gave us three drinking nuts (young coconuts) and we strolled back to the dinghy with a crowd of barefoot children begging for sweets. An old lady had pulled the dugout canoe into the shallows and was washing it out.

After lunch we set out to cross the island and search for shells on the farther beach. Just as in England our settlements are organised around roads and cars, here it is the pig and his habits which dictate the layout of the village. Pigs will eat almost anything, and if it's growing they will dig it up. So gardens must be strongly fenced and gated; even on the beach there are pig-proof fences going right down into the water to stop the pigs wandering too far along the shore. The pigs shared their wide grassy spaces with chickens, dogs and a few horses. Tribes of striped and spotted piglets scampered among the palm trees.

We headed inland and left the village behind. Soon we came to a very stout pig-proof fence of corrugated iron with a sliding gate. Closing it firmly behind us, we walked through the forest to the peaceful and deserted beach on the other side. Sheltered from the wind, we looked out across a great calm stretch of water to scattered islands and reefs beyond. We beachcombed happily for shells for an hour or more. The forest overhung the beach in places, huge gnarled old trees with glossy leaves and white flowers. There were wading birds along the shore, songbirds in the forest. In the shallows were blue starfish, black sea cucumbers and spidery brittle stars. Regiments of whelks and winkles were on the move across the rocks, and hermit crabs seemed to have chosen the prettiest shells. We still collected plenty of empty spiral shells, cowries, all kinds of bivalves.

Striking back inland we found ourselves among haphazard plantations of manioc, bananas, taro, yams and other crops growing in rich profusion. This was the reason for the corrugated pig fence – pigs and plantations do not mix! We returned to the village and saw the pigs being fed, on coconuts of course. By now it was evening, and people were resting on the shore. One or two older people were bathing fully dressed in the cool sea. It was hot, thundery and oppressive. We went back to the boat for a cool drink, and watched the young people playing volleyball on shore. Dusk fell, and the evening chorus of crickets began. Lightning flickered in the southern sky, and by next morning it was time to seek a more sheltered anchorage in the old harbour behind Neiafu.

LIFE ABOARD *LUCINA*, CANARIES TO BARBADOS 1999

by Jeffrey O'Riordan

November 26 1999

We set twin head sails, though the easterly trades still seemed to be absent and our daily run had fallen to 93 miles. There were also engine problems – Peter P noticed the heat exchanger was moving around, due to the bolts getting loose over 20 years. It was quite a struggle to tighten them, and he emerged from the engine room very oily. The reading matter on board is high class:

Peter P: *Back Door to Byzantium*

Peter A: *The Venetian Empire*

Caryl: *Harry Potter vol 3*. Every so often she bursts out laughing as she reads.

Me: *Fermat's Last Theorem* – an excellent choice by Sal. Peter A commented about having forgotten about knowledge for its own sake!

November 27 1999

We sent the following message to RCC Northern Dinner via G3FWB on the SSB radio:

'Greetings from *Lucina*, 9 days out from Canaries, and 390 miles west of C. Verde. Delays working out last week's sun sights means we are dependent on GPS. No signs of scurvy. The Hams (the radio sort, not the edible type) compete to begin the day talking to mission control in the Dales.

In good radio contact with *Troubadour*, still 180 miles ahead, with 1480 miles to go to Barbados. Four Mummies enjoying themselves, sucking iced lollies. Today's message from *Troubadour* says they hope the men folk left at home are looking after themselves properly and cooking

Peter Price, Peter and Caryl Aitchison and Jeffrey O'Riordan.

well and they really miss them. We gather that Stewart, John and David are going North to get a square meal!

Sundance, Brown Bear and *Moonsong* all in the groove, drifting somewhere and heading west.

Have a nice evening and a good walk tomorrow – hope it's not too cold with you. Down here it's still quite warm!

Peter and Caryl A, Jeffrey O'R and Peter P'.

We have now been at sea 9 days and fresh food is getting limited. Some things are decaying. Bananas are over, the potatoes are all right. Butter stored on the hull was getting pretty soft – the water temperature must have risen.

DARWIN TO ASHKELON

by Ian Tew

The moon had just set, the Pole Star and Southern Cross were still visible. The object of my large detour to the north, seen at 6 miles on the radar, was Kadmat island. We had sailed from Darwin on 7 September 1999 to Sri Lanka via Indonesia, Thailand and the Nicobar Islands. On the last leg I had enjoyed the passage of a lifetime averaging 7.2 knots over 3953 miles. From Sri Lanka we had rounded the southern tip of India and headed NW.

A quarter of a century ago I had been off Kadmat in very different circumstances. The SW monsoon was blowing, the tug I commanded was towing a 50,000 ton storage tanker, one engine had packed up and could not be repaired at sea, and I had just received a message to go and salve a freezer ship aground on the windward side of Kadmat island. What to do! It was too deep to anchor in the lee of the island, so the next ten days was spent steaming up and down. The only way to reach the *Pacifico Everett* was across the lagoon but the entrance appeared closed by breakers. It was raining. Eventually I did enter the lagoon with a volunteer crew in the zed boat, it was a matter of waiting for a break in the surf and then full speed before the next roller broke. Getting out from the lagoon was slightly more difficult and on one day lepers from the colony helped us.

The ship was right up on the reef with great waves breaking over her. Her bottom was breached and she was finished. When I landed on the island to call on the Administrator, hordes of young people kept touching my bare arms. It turned out that for anyone under the age of 26, I was the first white man they had ever seen.

'What does it feel like to be Jesus Christ superstar?', asked one of my Filipino crew.

The local policemen were rowed out wearing full uniform, their boots highly polished, to inspect the tug. I was taken ashore with them, the rowers skilfully negotiating the way through the surf. The boat was carried up the beach with me still onboard so I would not get my feet

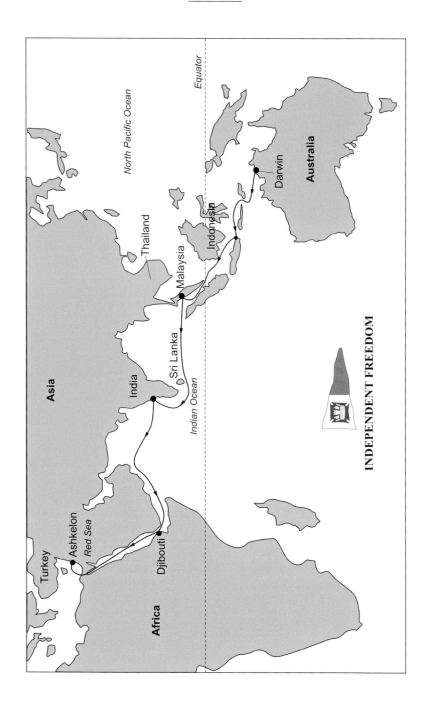

wet. A convivial evening was spent with the Administrator over a bottle of black label whisky I had brought ashore. When they rowed me back to the still steaming tug and tow, the rowers sang a song in praise of this white man who had come with a black monster. I wondered whether I had inadvertently entered H G Wells' 'time machine' and returned to the last century. The saga ended when the Selco tug *Salvanquish* turned up and took over my tow, the Swedish surveyor onboard declared the *Pacifico Everett* a total loss, and with the islanders help the crew were rescued. I took them to Cochin on board my tug the *Salvaliant* where the engine was repaired.

Back in the present *Independent Freedom* rounded the north end of the island where the lepers had helped and I saw what appeared to be the masts of the wreck. However they were not in the position of the wreck, marked on the chart and further south than I remembered. As I skirted the reef, a gentle swell breaking, it became apparent that the *Pacifico Everett* was no more and the 'masts' were in fact two substantial beacons marking a pass into the lagoon. They were not marked on the chart nor mentioned in the pilot book.

I altered course westwards for Arabia, my head filled with memories, another era, another lifetime.

And so began a week of perfect sailing. A fair wind at first but light so the reaching staysail was hoisted between the masts. The days were hot and sunny and the nights bright with the moon in a clear sky. Gradually the wind increased, the staysail was stowed and the day's runs increased from 71 to 168 miles when we had to reef.

Socotra was left 150 miles to port. There were reports of pirates in speed boats and just before we left Sri Lanka I had been told about an Australian yacht which had been pirated and a woman injured. There is also a warning in the latest Admiralty supplement to the *Red Sea and Gulf of Aden Pilot*. It warns of piracy and armed robbery in the south of the Red Sea, west and southeast of the Gulf of Aden against vessels of any size, especially at speeds of less than 12 knots. It really is quite outrageous that this scourge of the seas has been allowed to return. Halfway through the last century it was eradicated by concerted and firm action.

January 28 found *Independent Freedom* off the Yemeni coast and the courtesy ensign was hoisted. There was traffic about and we felt we were clear of any pirate danger. The wind had eased to F.3/4 and it was very pleasant coasting. In the evening Ra's Fartak and the hills beyond were bathed in the yellow sunset light, their outlines faint like an Impressionist painting. Dolphins were playing, their trails twisting and squirming snake-like glowing in the bioluminescence.

Aden was passed on 1 February and the anchor was let go off the Djibouti yacht club just after day break on the next day, 2449 miles covered in 21 days, only 3 days motoring.

Not much had changed. The place was as grubby as fifteen years ago and no less expensive. A chic air-conditioned shop with the perfumes of Paris looked incongruous in the main square with its hawkers and beggars and crumbling buildings. The French military presence is much reduced but there was a modern warship on the naval pier. Djibouti benefits from the loss of the Ethiopian ports to Eritrea and a couple of container cranes were being off loaded from a communist chinese heavy lift vessel. Armed guards force anyone on foot to pass the presidential residence on the far side of the road. French food is available, but at a price.

Our hull, filthy with long weed, was cleaned by Mustapha and his mate. The water tanks were filled by cans borrowed from *Tom* a French yacht that had been at Galle. *Havenga*, another French yacht, used his special fitting to fill our gas bottles from the large bottle I purchased ashore. I then donated the large bottle to the yacht club! Bunkers were taken from the *Total* filling station by the club although duty free was available in the port. Duty free cigarettes were purchased for use in the Suez canal when I obtained the clearance.

A week after arriving we moved out to the anchorage amongst the reefs off Ile Maskali and swam in the clear water. A very pleasant couple of days were spent preparing for the rigours of the beat up the Red Sea. I had visited the British Consul who was away but his secretary, whom I knew from my salvage days, was very helpful. The basic advice was, 'Don't stop!' Saudi Arabia discourages yachts, there was a war on between Eritrea and Ethiopia, Mig fighters had been reported over Massawa, and the twenty-five year war continues in Sudan. So we decided to make a passage direct to Suez, with a stop at Massawa unless a fair wind took us past!

The waters of Djibouti were finally left on 17 February when the yacht was sailed out of the anchorage. There was enough south in the wind to fetch Bas Bir past the ruins of Obock, and then to ease sheets and reach along the desolate barren cliffs of north Djibouti. There was a good breeze from the SE and the speed was a satisfactory 7 knots. The traffic lanes outside the Straits of Ban el Mandeb were crossed at right angles and course had to be altered to avoid a container ship flying light, the *Colombus Olivinos*.

I had a healthy respect for the prohibited zone round Perim island on the east side of the strait having been fired on by a machine gun when I passed too close in my tug *Salvanguard*. The wind had freshened but I was keen to clear the straits and we were running fast goosewinged. At 1830 it was gusting F.7 and Perim island was on our quarter. The foresail was lowered and *Independent Freedom* continued fast under the full main. She was still well balanced and easy on the helm.

2000 – sailing very fast indeed should reef!

2100 – Rough following sea rolling and yawing.

2130 – Wind increased and surfing up to 9 knots gusts force 8. Put in 3 reefs.

2200 – 2/8 cloud, fine, rough following breaking seas, still sailing very fast up to 7.5 knots, alter course 335° so as not to hit Al Mukha.

Sunday 13 February 0100 Cloudless, wind backing to south. Running very fast, breaking seas.

0200 – Very rough, gust 45 knots, big breakers.

0300 – Inadvertent gybe broke boom lashing bent rail.

0318 – Very rough gust 46 knots.

It seemed to moderate a little for a time and then increased and at 0712 there was a gust of 47 knots. Abu Ali was close to starboard, the seas a white mass, the tops of the waves blown off, breaking and leaping up the rocks. The lighthouse buildings looked a bit dilapidated.

Thirty years ago I was Second Officer on the *City of Poona* and we had stopped in answer to a flag signal and picked up a sick lighthouse keeper. Eighteen years ago I had salved the *Cape Greco* ex *City of Worcester* on which coincidentally I had served also as Second Officer. She was aground in the bay on the opposite side of the channel to the lighthouse and the accommodation was burnt out.

The wind moderated, or at least there were no more gusts over 40 knots, SSE F.7/8. However the sea increased and at noon the breaking seas were coming onboard. For the first time since New York, two and a half years ago, a breaking sea came in over the stern. A ship passed bound south shipping it green over the bows.

At tea time the Zubayr islands were in sight and the wind moderated. What a fantastic 24-hour run!

The wind continued far albeit light, the reefs were shaken out and Jabal Atair was passed the next morning although the light was not seen. At noon we passed the Pearly Gates entrance not to heaven but Gizan! I had salved the *Island Transporter* loaded with cement inside the Pearly Gates and had had to find a channel to extract her from the reefs. We had also found an abandoned ship aground on the reefs and salved her as well!

In the afternoon, although we were still running with a fair wind, the swell built up from the north which combined with that from the south and made for an uncomfortable time.

At 1800 the wind veered and went light. It continued round over the next few hours to NW and then NNW. The foresail was hoisted and the engine started to make progress through the meeting place of the north and south winds. It was calm for most of the next 36 hours. On the evening of 16 February the wind filled in from the NNW and it was a dead beat for the next 700 miles! The fair wind had carried us well past Massawa.

The wind was pretty steady out of the NNW with occasional variations to N or WNW and for the next ten days did not blow harder than F.7 nor less than F.3, mainly F.5/6. The main problem was the Red Sea, steep and short so the yacht had to be sailed fairly free. It was starboard tack at

night, port tack during the day and dinghy style tacking on any wind
shift. It was easy to go east and west the problem was to make a northing.
Ocean Passages of the World, sailing ship routes, recommends holding the
Arabian coast which is what we did. At night there was a bright moon
and the sun was out during the day although it slowly became colder as
we made our northing. In winds above F.5 we reefed, the yacht goes
better when not pressed. Although the days run sailed was usually about
90 miles she made good a steady 70 miles which I was pretty pleased
with, considering the seas.

On 17 February sailing towards the Saudi coast I was looking for
Qadd Humais reef with its sand islets. At noon when the yacht was in

Independent Freedom, whereof Ian Tew is Master under God.

their position, nothing was seen and the adrenaline was beginning to run. I found them 3½ miles ENE of their charted position. It was a beautiful day, sparkling blue water, white horses and a cobalt sky.

It was Michael's third birthday onboard the next day when the entrance to Jeddah was passed. The tack out to sea was made when Shib al Katir light bore NE by E, distance 3¼ miles. It was a full moon that night, rising minutes after the sun set so it was visible all night.

On Sunday afternoon the entrance to Yanbu was passed and for half an hour the water was smooth in the lee of Shib a Suflani which reminded us how rough it was once clear! In the evening the wind freshened to F.6/7 and it was very rough tacking between Shib a Sabah and the outer reef. I was glad when we were clear shortly after midnight.

Noon the next day found *Independent Freedom* tacking off the Saudi shore south of Ras Bardi with its factory belching smoke. The sea was much calmer 2 or 3 miles off shore and it was very pleasant.

No boats were seen until at 1740 we were accosted by two armed soldiers in a Boston type speed boat with a small cuddy. When they waved I waved back but when close to, one of them cocked his gun and pointed it at us. I realised we were in trouble. They shouted and indicated we should proceed directly into the wind. When I pointed to the sails and indicated we had to tack the one with the cocked gun aimed it at us. I luffed up into the wind, the sails flapping and eventually they got the message. For the first time in my life my mouth went completely dry and my tongue felt twice its usual size. Fear. Michael, who was below, wrote in the log, 'Those boys mean danger. Hope we will be OK'.

I pulled myself together and began to think. I did not think they would actually fire at us, but they might fire and hole the yacht. I was not doing anything wrong but it is foolish to argue with armed men who do not speak your language, and they were soldiers not sailors. I knew from the chart there were no anchorages along the immediate coast. It would shortly be dark. It seemed to me that if I could delay as long as possible reaching wherever they were taking us, they might become discouraged in the cold and dark or run out of fuel. The one thing I wanted to avoid was being taken ashore because once ashore I lost any control and was completely in their hands to face any charges that might be trumped up. I sailed as slowly as I dared tacking when told to. It became rougher the further offshore we went. We threw overboard in a weighted bag anything that might possibly be construed as offensive to the sensitive Saudi morals. The boat had no lights and it was becoming nice and cold.

We appeared to be heading for some bright lights on what we thought was a truck, but it was taking a satisfactorily long time.

Suddenly about two hours after dark the speedboat pulled up alongside and one of the soldiers said, 'Name, name'. I shone a torch on the name painted on the side. The soldier indicated in the torch light I should write it on paper.

Michael who was still below passed up paper and pencil. The soldier steering tried to come close enough so I could hand over the note. Eventually he made it and they shouted 'Go, Go!'

We went, reaching fast out to sea!

At 2300 Beacon 11 on Shib Shu Aybath bore north, distance 6 cables. The sheets were hardened and we were back on the wind. I kept 12 or more miles off the Saudi coast from now on!

There were no more excitements apart from having to tack and avoid a collision with a coaster despite illuminating his bridge with the searchlight. The further north we sailed, the stronger the wind tended to blow and it became colder.

Early on Thursday morning the wind backed and we were almost able to make the course for the straits of Gubal. It freshened and the sea became rough, but the wind later died and freed even more. What a break!

On Friday morning it was blowing north F.6/7. *Independent Freedom* was close reaching fast, the bright moonlight emphasising the very rough sea. At 0800 the sea moderated as the Sinai peninsula was approached. In the words of Adrian Hayter, 'the great barren mountains, giving a sense of timelessness as if they had outlived their own souls,' lay on the starboard side. Quite suddenly at 0845 the wind dropped. We could not believe our luck and turned on the engine and motored hard. The Pilot book warns of the strong winds and rough seas in the straits. We went through the inner channel in a calm, the sun shining on those brown barren mountains.

At tea time the engine was turned off and at 1730 two reefs were taken in each sail. The night was spent beating up the east shore for the Gulf of Suez amongst the oil fields with their platforms, pipes and flares. The radar was on to watch for anything without lights. The motor was used when the wind failed.

By morning it was blowing a gale and the third reef was taken in the main and foresail. It was very rough and cold. The traffic lanes were crossed and the west coast of the Gulf was closed. In shallow water with much reduced sea we beat up to the lee of the reef off Ras Ruahmi and anchored in 4.5 metres. There was no wind shelter but it was reasonably calm. Two fishing boats joined us in the anchorage. Anchor watches were set and a worrying night was spent with the shallow water alarm going off at intervals as the yacht yawed over a coral head. I might have preferred it dodging the oil paraphernalia and shipping, but I am not sure!

On Sunday morning it was only blowing F.6 so the anchor was raised and we beat up the coast, reef dodging in quite calm water. The wind moderated and it was motor sailing to Suez Bay.

We passed the canal and then reached Ashkelon. 8166 miles had been sailed since Darwin in 73 days at sea at an average speed of 4.7 knots, the engine used for just over 19½ days. 105 days were spent at anchor or in port.

FAIR AND FOUL WEATHER IN THE NORTHERN ISLES

by Katharine Thornhill

Two weeks in late July from Ardfern to Lerwick. *Sai See* had to be delivered to my parents in time for the most northerly point of the RCC Millennium Rolling Meet in Shetland in August. They were two weeks that could not have been more contrasting.

The first crew started the long drive from London to Glasgow in the rain, the train to Oban in Scottish drizzle and the taxi from Oban to Ardfern in glorious hot sunshine. We could not believe our luck, but there was no way this could last.

We had the most wonderful week. We saw so much of what the Western Isles have to offer. We stalked the puffins and guillemots on the Treshnish Islands, we sailed around Staffa and saw the wonderful basalt rocks. We tasted Talisker in Loch Harport and stocked up on a good selection of classic malts. We managed to land at the remarkable Shiant Islands with seriously dodgy holding and discovered a wonderfully peaceful anchorage on the east of Lewis called Loch Odharin which is beautiful once you pass the fish farms.

All this time we had beautiful sunshine and a lovely breeze. We managed to get every light weather sail up, sailing mainly up wind for the first half of the week, and then finding a following or reaching wind for the second half giving us the chance to get the spinnaker, the gennaker and the mizzen staysail up.

I do not think any of us could believe what a perfect week we had had. Scotland had been at its best and we had seen wonderful birds and scenery. Ido had discovered that he loved sailing and everyone agreed that they loved Scotland. What a contrasting week was in store for the next crew.

Clara, Ido and Thomas were replaced in Loch Inver by Peter Ingram, Luky Barrow (my cousin who is a familiar crew to *Sai See*) and her boyfriend Sean Lenar. We had to get to Shetland and the forecast was lousy;

northeasterly with a gale on the way. But there was no wind now and hot sunshine so we decided to leave and see how long it would last.

It was one of those magical days. The northeast wind started gently but quickly began to fill in. We had a tremendous sail heading northwards hard on the increasing wind still in sparkling and glorious sunshine. We had taken in two reefs within about an hour and the sail was only made more exciting when a school of dolphins came to see us and play in our bow wave. As if this was not enough Sean suddenly noticed that not far away there was a small group of breaching whales. We cannot be sure which type they were but they were leaping right out of the water, standing momentarily on their tails and then smashing back into the sea. I have never seen such a sight in Scotland.

But the weather was definitely deteriorating. Black clouds were rolling in from the north and the wind was getting steadily stronger, so we decided to anchor in Loch Laxford and wait and see what it was like in the morning. Worse, it blew and rained all day. Peter and I sorted out some electrics which meant that *Sai See's* interior was dismantled and everyone else had to vacate the boat and were forced to spend the day attempting to fish, befriending our neighbouring seals or wandering on the saturated hills. The next day did not seem to be much better but we left at midday, with the promise of a dying wind. How right the Met Office was.

We started off well, on the starboard tack heading northward, passed Cape Wrath and on a course that took us between North Rona and Sule Skerry. Unfortunately at 0322 Peter's log entry reads, 'Slow and in the wrong direction, grunt!'. Over the next six hours Lizzie and I made attempts to sail amongst bursts from the engine. By 0840 we had given up. The North Atlantic became like a mirror and we began to wonder if we would have enough diesel. For nearly 24 hours we motored continuously in a glassy calm fog with drizzle. A little different from the weather we had been hiding from just the day before.

Shetland however did not let us down and our landfall the following dawn could not have looked more dramatic. Swirls of mist and fog shrouded bright red jagged stacks and cliffs at the entrance of Ronas Voe on the northwest coast of the mainland. Everyone was on deck admiring the sights after such a seemingly long and frustrating passage.

We had to go to Ronas Voe as the pilot said it was the only place we could get diesel in the area and even there only in an emergency from the fish factory. This was indeed true. Somebody who worked in the factory had a wife who ran the shop three miles away. She seemed to think nothing of coming at a moment's notice to pick us up in her van, sell us the diesel and some fresh milk and drive us back. So nice to be back in Shetland. She even took our rubbish away with her. What service!

We motored around the corner in the fog to San Voe. It was not the day for a walk as the visibility was right down, so instead we set off to inspect the caves we had noticed in the entrance. We found a completely

Sai See anchored off the Rhamna Stacks.

unexpected selection of different caves. The one we had originally noticed at the entrance actually turned out to be a shallow one, but the colours were amazing; orange, pink, yellow and wonderful bronze. Not only that but it was also a breeding site for cormorants. Enormous fluffy chicks were perched precariously on what seemed to be a sheer piece of cliff. Unable to fly, they were sliding down the rock face and pathetically scrambling back up.

Other caves had tiny entrances, only about twice the width of the dinghy, but inside they opened out into great cathedrals. The roofs disappeared somewhere into the darkness, only the echo giving away their height. In the largest cave a gentle swell would occasionally make it through the entrance, pass underneath us and then ages later we could hear its low booming thunder breaking on the back wall. It was very dark and really quite eerie.

The following day saw slightly better visibility but still millpond calm. Peter decided he wanted to anchor for breakfast at the Ramna Stacks. They are a group of very exposed rocks off the northwest coast of the mainland. There is no shelter, no holding and a sunken rock just where you might otherwise want to anchor. We anchored with the tide streaming us away from any dangers and took it in turns to investigate around and through these rocks in the dinghy accompanied by a very inquisitive seal. We felt very privileged to have been able to do this. I do not believe that the weather and sea are very often calm enough to stop here. However, it turned out that it was not the first time *Sai See* had been there, only that time my father had climbed one of the stacks. Very annoying!

It was almost time to go back to Lerwick, and thankfully the weather gave us a lovely reach down the eastern side of the mainland on our last day. The visibility even gave us a break. Dad was waving on the quay when we arrived in Lerwick. We had had an amazing two weeks and it was all over too soon. We will be back for more next year.

THROUGH RUSSIA IN THE FOOTSTEPS OF THE VIKINGS

by Barry Woodhouse

On the Glorious First of June we departed for the second time from Vardo in Norway for Archangelsk. This time the weather was calm but cold. Noel Marshall complained on our second day that his cabin was 1°C warmer than his fridge and took up my previous offer of hot bunking in my cabin, with the added bonus of access to the Hammerfest duvet. After fog had lifted, the entrance to the White Sea came in sight. At first it looked as though there was another white cliffs of Dover in existence, but closer inspection showed it to be still more snow down to the high watermark. At the eastern side of the straits, the first of the fir trees, which were to accompany us to Kazan, made their appearance. The autopilot, which had been playing up, finally gave up the ghost and I took the wheel off to reinstall the old *Autohelm 3000*. So much for expensive technology!

Ominous black clouds welcomed us at the entrance to the River Dvina. Sailing under furled genoa we turned a corner to be welcomed by *Pomor*, a yacht from the Nord Yacht Club. On board was Sasha Lashenko, my guide and interpreter for the first and last part of my trip through Russia. *Pomor* escorted us for the 28 miles to Archangelsk. The riverbanks were lined with timber mills, factories, Elint trawlers and charming wooden houses reminiscent of the book, *The House on the River Dvina*. When we arrived at our berth in the Nord Yacht Club the greeting, 'Welcome to Russia,' from a very friendly border guard officer signalled the beginning of what was to be a most enjoyable sojourn in Archangelsk. Formalities over, vodka was brought out to celebrate our arrival. Most thoughtfully they departed early, to leave us to rest.

Our next destination was the Solovetsky Islands. I was slightly surprised to find that we had to clear customs and the border guards. We were soon on our way, however, bound for the Solovetsky Islands with Caroline Griffith, Noel's girlfriend, who had joined us.

Solovetsky Monastery.

The approach to Solovetsky was through a narrow passage. The monks had blockaded it with piles of stones in the water, to prevent attacks from the sea. What a magnificent sight the monastery made, as we got closer, with its onion domes, towers and a walled stronghold. We discovered later that it was a setting for total tragedy. From 1923 to 1939 this was a particularly brutal prison camp where 100,000 people were imprisoned, of whom only 50,000 survived. The thirty monks in residence provide purification from the horrors of those terrible years. Sasha and his girlfriend, Yanna, both felt the atmosphere strongly. I got into trouble with the monks as I filmed them on their weekly Sunday circumvention of the outside walls of the monastery. One is not allowed to photograph them and a monk detached himself, hissing at me, 'this is not a performance'. I have a marvelous video of the procession, high-pitched bells tinkling in the background; it was worth the rebuke.

Reluctantly we departed for Belomorsk. There was a good breeze with a flat calm sea and *Aenigma* slid through the water effortlessly under sail. Approaching Belomorsk, my binoculars failed to pick up the fairway buoys in the midnight twilight. There were none; the third time that I found navigation marks missing. A fishing boat passed us and, with relief, we knew we were on the right course. There was only a small channel with shallows on either side. The jetty had fallen apart and it was necessary to find a place without too many nails and rusty bolts protruding to damage *Aenigma's* side. The fisherman ahead of us kindly invited us alongside his boat.

12 June was an Independence Day holiday. Sasha commented that it was independence from themselves! A bearded SFB agent (son of KGB) visited us and declared that our documents were not in order. He said he

A lock on the White Sea Canal. Sasha and Yanna fending off.

would look into the matter; we were not to move from our berth. I had
visions of being returned to Norway.

The next day we were summoned to the harbourmaster's office, but
we were not allowed to motor *Aenigma* to the canal entrance. A taxi was
found with difficulty and three of us crammed ourselves into it. The
harbourmaster greeted us with a beaming smile, and proceeded to tell
us he had no papers to allow us into the White Sea Canal. During the
course of the conversation, which was going nowhere, the FSB agent
appeared. Alexander Galitski suggested that we were attached to the
Blue Onega rally to overcome the problem. 'Not a good idea. They would
be here for ages while Moscow made a decision. I think we should let
them through,' said the SFB agent. Thank goodness the harbourmaster
fell in with the scheme.

We were generously given a lift back to the boat in the FSB jeep. Two
very fit heavies accompanied us. A very warm send off by Mr. FSB with
a timely reminder that he controlled the area. 'Do not take any photos
until you are past the lifting bridge – it is a secret zone! Then take as
many as you wish to. Good luck.'

After entering the first lock, we waited till 1700 for the railway bridge
to lift. Then, with a great sense of relief, we started our trip through the
heart of Russia. Surrounded by fir and silver birch trees, we motored on
through a series of locks until the system closed for the night. As we
enjoyed 'sundowners' to celebrate our first day in the waterway system, a

net the length of the cockpit, made by Anna my wife, kept the mosquitoes out.

The next night, motoring through the northern twilight in an effort to regain our schedule, we gently ran aground. I was below and felt the boat come to a stop in the soft mud. Noel was looking through binoculars and directing Caroline, who was steering. Both were totally unaware that *Aenigma* was stuck in the mud or that they were well off the buoyed channel. The leading mark was close on our starboard. Thank goodness we were able to reverse back to the channel, as we saw only three ships in the whole of the White Sea Canal. The channel followed the old river on a tortuous route, making it difficult to see the buoys in the gloom. It seemed prudent to anchor for the night.

Lake Onega brought us the magnificent sight of Kizhi church, a world heritage monument. We were told by a bandit, to whom we declined to give an extortionate mooring fee, not to moor at the ferry terminal and we were moved on by the police from the place where we next made fast. Anchoring with the mosquitoes provided the answer. The problem of finding a place for the night plagued us for the length of Russia. There are few facilities for yachts.

I sadly said goodbye to Sasha and Yanna his girlfriend. My wife and Alexander Samoylov joined at Petrozavodsk. *Aenigma* made her way across Lake Onega, via an enchanting monastery with only three monks, to Vitegra. The water tank was replenished by bucket from the lake. A crane was found to lift the mast. We had to construct a cradle over *Aenigma*, to house the mast. The heat was terrible. It was in the 30s and,

Ruined church in the White Lake, Volga Balt canal.

while building the structure, many a glass of delicious Onega water was consumed to quench our thirst. The timber was bought from Victor Dmitriev, the director of the boat yard in Petrozavodsk. Thank goodness I had purchased the bolts and screws in Norway, as there are precious few to be found in Russia. We were doing well till the owner of the crane came. The lads were moonlighting, I discovered, and my bill was increased three fold.

The Volga Balt Canal, with its seven locks, passes through the White Lake where a ruined church stands in forlorn glory on the southern side, immersed by the flooding of the lake to make the canal. From here to Kazan the crew enjoyed the rich culture of the Golden Ring. Towns, churches, monasteries, Kremlins and museums make an incredibly picturesque portfolio of early Russian craftwork.

Kostroma, on the Volga river, was yet another difficult place to moor. As we made fast alongside the Gims (small ship inspectorate), the director lent over with a loud hailer, two meters above my head, ordering us away but offering no help as to where to berth. A floating accommodation barge, which I had spotted earlier, kindly provided us with a mooring. We discovered later, returning from an excellent meal, that it was a floating brothel!

We approached Nizhny Novgorod to find a floating bridge barring our way. *Aenigma* was sprayed with silver paint as we found out from the workmen above us that it would not open until 2200. My wife Anna made a meagre meal as the food supplies were almost finished. We had hoped to have a last supper ashore that evening with Noel, who was to leave us. After a magnificent red sunset, which was splendidly reflected in the Volga, the floating bridge opened. We made our way to the Railway Workers' Yacht Club. Alexander Samoylov (our Russia guide) thought it was a bad place to stay but, next morning, the Director of the club welcomed me with open arms, telling me *Aenigma* was berthed in exactly the same place that Miles Clark's *Wild Goose* had been in 1993.

With another change of crew, we sailed our way to Kazan through most attractive countryside on either bank, stopping at villages, monasteries, towns and our first and only stately home. This had been lived in by Stalin's daughter during the war. On the banks of the Volga stood many ruined churches. After we had passed under the Trans Siberian Railway Bridge, Kazan loomed ahead, looking very industrial. We stopped for fuel beside a boat carrying the works secretarial outing, clad in bikinis. With typical Russian generosity they filled our tanks with diesel and would not accept any payment.

The yacht club was run by Oleg Turin, who had sailed around the world. It was also very welcoming and Oleg took us under his wing. We had the official red carpet treatment, given by the city's sports minister. A tour was arranged around the attractive historic city and a trip to the most impressive Raifskij Monastery run by Abbot Vserolod. Over ten

years he had fulfilled his vision of restoring the buildings and setting up
an orphanage. Into our transport the Abbot had generously put five
bottles of their award winning water from the holy spring. With temperatures in the 30s over the following weeks, this was much appreciated.

Reluctantly, after another change of crew, Vladimir Ivankiv and I
headed southwards. The appearance of the first mosque, recently built
on the western bank of the Volga, reminded us that we were entering a
Muslim region. The Volga got even wider, ranging from five to fifteen
miles. The heat was intense, making holy water and lemon Fanta essential drinking. Vladimir was introduced to Campari and soda, which was
served as a 'sundowner', until it ran out.

As we arrived at the Tol'yatti Yacht Club, a large fleet was starting an
evening race. The director made us most welcome, taking us for an evening trip around the hometown of Lada cars. Leaving the next afternoon,
after a number of visits by curious Russians, I saw a boat depart the
marina after us, trying to catch us up under sail. We stopped and, when
he came alongside, the owner very generously gave us an oil painting of
his boat.

Next morning found us aground, trying to work our way out of the
mud banks on the side of the Volga that I had put us into for the night so
as to be clear of the shipping. We visited a seaplane manufacturer, working under canvas, with an experimental plane. On to Samara, where we
asked at the Electricity Yacht Club if we could moor there. 'No you will
be arrested,' was the reply from one gentleman. While we were making
our way to the next possible place, a fleet of boats from the yacht club
pursued *Aenigma* to tell us that, on the contrary, we were most welcome.

Approaching the Balakovo lock, we caught up with a yacht tacking in
the light evening breeze. They told us to follow them to the Nuclear
Electricity Yacht Club where a berth could be found for the night.
Realising that for *Aenigma,* under engine, it was pointless to shadow their
tacking at three knots, they passed over a twenty-one year old ex-
paratrooper to direct us to the yacht club. The night watchman kindly
agreed to our night's stay, on the understanding that we should leave
before 0730 as, he said, the yacht club director was a terrible man and he
would be fired. Our paratrooper, Sasha stayed for dinner. He wanted
whisky and a full tumbler was downed, Russian style. Vladimir and I
looked at each other then back at Sasha who, having dispatched this
foreign drink in one, wore a self-satisfied grin. Two seconds later the
reaction we had expected came. Sasha grabbed Vladimir's glass of Fanta
lemon to put out the fire building in his belly. He lived, but it was a close
call.

Two days later we arrived in Saratov as a regatta was in progress.
There was Alexander Bajev's yacht with the rest, awaiting the wind on
the city's waterfront. Vladimir had been trying to phone him for the last
few days but with no success. I asked if it was possible to stay the night

against the wall. A committee was formed but no progress made, as it appeared that it was against the city's regulations. I saw an enormous black cumulo-nimbus cloud build as they procrastinated. Suddenly there was wind. The fleet was to race. I thought it prudent to make for the yacht club off the chart, on an island.

Someone had thoughtfully drawn a map of the approach and, armed with this, I departed in haste. All too late. As *Aenigma* approached the longest bridge in Europe, a Force 12 hit us. The waves were terrible. I thought of rescuing the fishermen caught out in rubber dinghies but rejected the idea as I suspected they were safer where they were than having a yacht smash down on them. The discothèque ferry hastily returned to harbour. I knew that I had to avoid the shipping, as my navigation lights were not working. Steaming up and down, with lashing rain and a howling wind, I realised the bow line was now trailing in the water, waiting to foul our propeller. Vladimir bravely went forward to gather it, and the fenders, in.

I was not sure of my way into the yacht club. Suddenly, out of the gloom, I recognised Alexander's boat sail past us under jib. Following him, we found ourselves at the yacht club. I was caught broadside on, being blown towards the shore. Slowly *Aenigma* was brought head to wind, mooring ahead of Alexander. They had their main blown out. His propeller was off to reduce the drag for racing so he was unable to help rescue the other boats in difficulty. Eighteen boats were lost that day but

Rostov on Don.

no lives, thank goodness. Alexander, a businessman, took us under his wing and gave us a tour of his city.

Our arrival at Volzhskiy late in the afternoon left Vladimir and myself uneasy. There was something wrong with the atmosphere. I promised Vladimir I would leave as soon as the crew change was complete. We were delayed the next day on our sightseeing trip as the new crew was late getting up and then a bus caught fire, blocking our road to Volgograd. Unwisely I stayed another day. At 0320 the next morning I heard a raiding party running along the pontoons. I was struggling into my clothes as I saw the first man disappear down the companionway. A cry of 'Police' came from them. They banged on my door and I handed out my passport which, not surprisingly, produced little interest. As I came out of my cabin, a torch was shone in my eyes and a silenced pistol pointed menacingly at me. There was a bandit sitting on the companionway steps and another with a similar gun by the forward cabin. Tim Bruce an old school friend of mine, who had refused to come originally, on the advice of a Naval friend of his who considered the trip to be highly dangerous, was lying handcuffed on the saloon bunk, unusually quiet. I asked Sasha Lashenko, who had, thank goodness rejoined us, if he had seen their police ID cards. 'I do not think they have any' was his laconic reply. 'We want your money and we will not harm you. If you do not we will take you out into the centre of the lake' was how Sasha translated the bandits' opening statement. 'Where is your wallet?' ' In the aft cabin', I replied. Having divested it of all my dollars and roubles, the bandit courteously handed my credit cards back to me. 'These will be needed to get more money to buy fuel to get to Rostov.' Was he planning on another attack, or did he realise the hopeless problem of using credit cards in Russia?

All the males had their wallets similarly burgled. Then they changed their attention to the forward cabin, where the two women were living. With great courtesy, Bandit N°2 banged on the door of the cabin with his silenced pistol. Fi, a neighbour in England, came out and disgorged some money. The rest she had hidden. Then it was the turn of Ingeborg, a Norwegian, to come out of the cabin. By this time everything had been hidden. The bandits wanted to be on their way. 'Where are the keys to the bicycles?' Bandit N°1 asked. Luckily Noel had secured them to a post in the cabin. I handed them over quickly. We were all bundled into the aft cabin with instructions to stay there for an hour after they had left. I passed Sasha my mobile phone to call the emergency services. 'We have been robbed at gun point' Sasha said. 'Where are you?' 'At the yacht Club in Volzhskiy.' 'We only deal with emergencies in Volgograd.' The phone contact was severed with the outside world. Forty minutes later, as dawn broke, I ensured the coast was clear and Sasha radioed the lock keeper, who sent for the police.

One person was left on the boat while the rest went to the police station

A lock on the Volga Don canal, built by German captives.

to be interviewed. The only lavatory was the far end of a cellblock, with prisoners waving their hands through the bars. Late in the afternoon, after hours of interrogation, we departed through the lock and anchored *Aenigma* beyond Volgograd. I decided to have a night lookout, armed with mini flares, to ward off intruders.

As a scenic dawn broke, we motored *Aenigma* to the start of the Volga-Don canal. Mooring up against the Volga Fishery Protection barge, we were wonderfully entertained by its crew while waiting for a gap in the commercial shipping traffic to allow us, late in the afternoon, to enter the first lock in company with a Russian yacht, *Albatross*. We stayed together as far as Rostov. After the first lock we were spat on. At the next stones were thrown at *Aenigma*. Things got better after that for, as we waited for the third, a man and two girls parked their car, stripped off their clothes and treated us to a porn show. Once in the lock, we were offered gifts by the passing onlookers.

The skipper of *Albatross* was very saddened to hear our tales. 'Russia does not need this bad publicity,' he commented. To me it was a blip which would never overshadow the generosity and kindness that I had experienced. He realised we were tired and moored his boat on the inside for protection. Two nights later at anchor a nude man and woman boarded *Aenigma* by climbing up the anchor chain!

German prisoners of war built the locks on the Don. Many are in grandiose Roman architectural style, some even with statues. I was invited to visit one still complete with the original electrical installation from the fifties. The moulded ceilings were works of art in their own right, each topped off with an elaborate gold chandelier. The Don was delightful, meandering through green fields and villages We stopped to see a magnificent church in Starocherkassk, the old Cossack capital. We discovered, luckily before departure, that a small kitten had been pushed through the hatch over the forward heads in our absence.

Soon Rostov was upon us, with formalities which could have been avoided if the skipper of *Albatross* had not contacted the harbourmaster, who saw it as a chance to get passage fees from both our yachts. I thought for a moment we were going to have trouble with him, as he was not at all friendly. I had wanted to buy some charts from the office but, on Sasha's advice, I did not pursue this. I later borrowed a chart to plot the last part of my passage, from Azov into the Sea of Azov. Miles Clark in *Wild Goose* had similar problems with these harbour authorities.

Reluctantly, as we would have preferred to stay longer in this delightful city, *Aenigma* departed for Azov, where we had been told there would be problems with the customs and border guards. Just before Azov we turned off the river for a Yacht Club with a crane, as we wanted to step *Aenigma's* mast. We went aground for a quarter of an hour but luckily, and inexplicably, suddenly came free. The director of the club, who was ready waiting for us, offered to step the mast for $25.

The temperature kept rising as we worked. A searing 50°C was recorded on the thermometer and the tools had to be put into buckets of water to cool them. As the crimson sun went down, the last tool was re-stowed. A swim was in order and Sasha commented that, in any case, it was better to swim in the Don at night. 'Why? I asked. 'You cannot see what you are swimming amongst!' The next morning we reached Azov, expecting to refuel and re-victual for the trip to Yalta. I dropped Sasha ashore, as we had been told extortionate harbour dues were levied on people mooring in the commercial port. While standing off, awaiting him, the border guard boat forced us onto the quay, with much mirth. The next thing we knew, we had armed guards standing over us. It looked bad for our departure.

The customs allowed two ashore to buy goods but only after we had given them a copy of the shopping list. There was a cargo ship astern who kindly provided us with fuel and, as we were carrying the diesel cans from the engine room, I spotted some showers. They generously let the crew have a shower and wash their clothes. Late in the evening the customs and border guards came to clear us. They were quite charming and, formalities quickly over, we had a drink together to celebrate a successful trip through Russia. We said goodbye to Sasha and then moved to the quarantine area, ready for an early morning departure.

Aenigma slipped her mooring in the misty dawn, and motored to the mouth of the Don River. We found the Azov Sea brackish and covered in algae. As night fell, we were treated to a display of shooting stars, which lasted all evening. On the approach to Kerch we found that my strategy to keep to the Ukrainian side of the waterway paid off. Russian border guards stopped a ship that encroached into their territorial waters. Dolphins played under the bow and, as we got into the Black Sea, the engine was stopped for swimming.

We reached Yalta the next day. I had to stay in the commercial harbour as the border guard would not give me a temporary visa. An eighteen-year-old customs trainee-officer came to look at the boat and, although the TV camera trained on the boat worried her, she stayed to practise her English. On the second afternoon a very attractive blonde slid through the fencing and asked for a trip to Italy. At last we were off, but not without more bureaucratic problems including the need to organize and pay for a taxi for the border guards. Crossing the Black Sea was as terrible at sea level as it was at altitude when I flew my 747's across it. We encountered Force 8–9 gales, accompanied by dramatic lightning storms and, on the first night, the mainsail split.

It was a great relief to arrive at the entrance of the Bosporus where, by late afternoon, *Aenigma* was berthed at Atakoy Marina. It took four and a half hours to clear Customs, Immigration and the Harbour Authorities before we could make a sightseeing trip to the St Sophia Mosque. I was just thinking what a great achievement my trip was when, there on a banister high in the church, I spotted some Runic graffiti, dating from 900–1000AD and written by a Viking from the west coast of Norway: 'Halfdan was here.' It had all been done before, and without an engine!

TWO GRAND-DADS TO CAPE HORN

by Jeremy Burnett

On 30 August last year, my friend Ben Pester and I left Falmouth in his yacht *Marelle* bound south for Cape Horn.

Marelle is a 36ft teak McGruer sloop built in the sixties. The sum of the crew's ages is around 140. Preparation had taken more than eighteen months. As a concession to modernity we had bought a GPS and an EPIRB to supplement the several sextants (never used) and the VHF. Provisioning was planned and executed by our wives Susan and Adrie. Many lists came and went. As well as large quantities of corned beef, steak pies, tuna fish, and other necessities, we stowed a whole dry cured ham from Richard Woodall in Cumbria, who had been recommended to me by Paul Heiney, an expert in such matters. Through the good offices of Juliet Larcombe at the Royal Geographical Society we obtained supplies of Dutch tinned butter. The ham lasted until we were well down into the South Atlantic. When at one stage, due to unsuitable stowage, it got a bit maggoty, we washed it off and thereafter stowed it on deck where it endured all weathers and remained good to eat if a little salty.

The passage to Porto Santo in Madeira took ten days. The winds were largely favourable, and we were able to learn about living on board and test our cooking skills. A three hour watch system seemed to suit us well.

Porto Santo harbour while not beautiful was practical and not crowded. There is a fair walk to the town which is pleasant when you get there. We stayed for four days before sailing to Puerto de La Luz on Gran Canaria where we anchored off the beach in company with several other yachts of various nationalities. Ben had been here in 1953 with *Tern II* and reported that things had changed a bit. As planned a third crew member, Tomas from Barcelona came aboard.

Sailing again on the 24th we had a pretty unpleasant eight day passage to Porto Grande in the Cape Verdes. The weather was hot and humid and the sea rough for much of the time. The island of Sao Vicente is very arid and, although Porto Grande harbour is secure, it seems permanently windy. Supplies are not easy to obtain and the water is very dubious. However ashore there is an interesting cultural mix with some fine old buildings and cobbled streets. In the early part of the century the town used to have a cricket club. One evening we were invited to join a supper of *catsoupa* a local speciality that thankfully belies its name and consists mostly of fish and vegetables. Tomas had not enjoyed the trip down and it was decided that he would leave us here.

After leaving Porto Grande our main concern was in what longitude to cross the equator. All sailing directions counsel strongly against getting too far west. Our course therefore lay south. The northeast trades soon expired, cabin temperature was around 30°C. There were many flying fish. Slowly we were engulfed in the doldrums. This became a testing experience as we drifted around in little or no wind. The heat was oppressive and the slatting of the sails was hard to bear. From time to time heavy rain squalls passed by. When this occurred one stripped off and stood hopefully on deck soap in hand. Most of the time they seemed to pass ahead or astern, and one was left all soaped up with nowhere to go, as it were. We did some motoring but were anxious to conserve fuel for battery charging. On 20 October at 2°N. we began to feel the first of the southeast trades. Rio was now approximately 1900 miles off and Mar del Plata another 1000 further on so we had a long way to go. We crossed the equator on 22 October in 23°39W.

We now had some days of steady trade wind sailing clocking off 120 miles per day in warm and pleasant weather. We saw a couple of ships who agreed to report our position to Falmouth where the coastguard relayed this to our families. As we got closer to Brazil the weather became less pleasant, indeed cold and rough. Early one morning I was confused by some unusual lights. Eventually a tug closed with us and after illuminating us with a searchlight, politely informed us that they were seismic survey vessels and were towing cables nearly five miles long. There is a lot of this activity in this area.

Cabo Frio lived up to its name and we were soon in sweaters. The rest of the passage to Mar del Plata passed uneventfully. We saw our first albatross and enjoyed the night skies. I found the Southern Cross disappointing, but Orion remained a constant and spectacular friend. On 24 November we arrived at Mar del Plata 44 days out from the Cape Verdes.

Our pleasure on arrival was tempered by some lengthy immigration formalities. In spite of it being late in the evening, we were taken off to the *Prefectura* where we were kept for a couple of hours while much form filling went on. It was hard to remain awake as the immigration officer printed out seven copies of each form on quite the slowest printer I have ever seen. However once this was over we were free to enjoy a friendly welcome at the Yacht Club Argentino. This included a pontoon berth, showers, use of the clubhouse and much logistical help from members

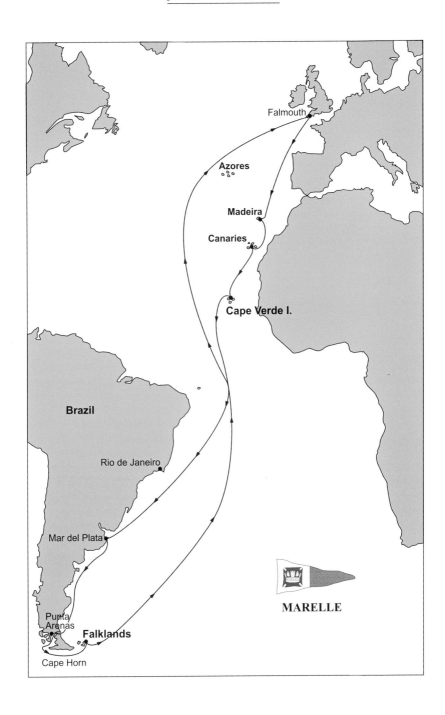

Falmouth

Azores

Madeira

Canaries

Cape Verde I.

Brazil

Rio de Janeiro

Mar del Plata

Punta Arenas

Falklands

Cape Horn

MARELLE

and a young man who attached himself to us. We were joined by Fraser Currie, a friend from Cornwall, and on 2 December we sailed for the Magellan Straits some 1000 miles to the south.

Two days out the barometer dropped like a stone and a violent storm blew up. The wind rose rapidly to southerly F.10. The seas were huge, and the noise incredible. We ran north under bare poles and after two days were back in Mar del Plata licking our wounds and filling in more forms.

Our second departure a week later was followed by a relatively uneventful passage to the straits. We stopped at two anchorages on the way, Puerto Santa Elena and Puerto Sara. In spite of the barren looking coast, this area is rich in wildlife and history. On shore we saw guanacos, like small smooth haired llamas, as well as rheas an ostrich type bird, black necked swans and steamer ducks. At sea the South Atlantic birds are magnificent, squadrons of magellenic penguins swim around while albatrosses, shearwaters and petrels glide effortlessly among the waves. This is also a breeding area for southern right whales. Great explorers passed this way, Drake, Davis, Cavendish, Darwin, Weddell, Tilman, to name but a few.

Shortly after Christmas we rounded Cape Virgins and headed into the straits. Romantic visions of the area were soon dashed. Strong winds, oil rigs and desolation all combined to give a distinctly unfriendly impression. Arriving at the first narrows in adverse conditions we were met by a Chilean Naval pilot boat and told to anchor in the lee of Punta Delgada. The next morning we could move on but 24 hours later after a violent night, we were forced to anchor again in Bahia Gregorio. We lay there for two days and celebrated the millennium with waves breaking over us.

Punta Arenas our next stop, is not recommended for yachts, and we came to understand why. When made fast alongside other yachts and fishing boats at a very exposed quay, the position rapidly becomes untenable if the wind goes to the south or east. Late one night during an enforced move, a masthead tang broke dumping the roller gear and its headsail in the water alongside, A depressing moment. We sought help from the local naval dockyard. Various possibilities were discussed over some time. Eventually two mountaineering engineers were found. In the still of an early morning they climbed the mast, drilled out the rivets and removed the fitting, They then had a new one made and fitted within a day. Once this was done our *zarpe* or permit to cruise was rapidly issued. In all the Chilean authorities could not have been more helpful, and we were impressed with the generally friendly atmosphere.

We left Punta Arenas on 5 January. and headed west down the wide reach towards Cape Froward, the southernmost point of the South American mainland. Here we turned south into the Magdalena Channel and began our journey through the spectacular Chilean *canales*. On all sides tree covered cliffs plunged steeply into the sea. To the east we saw our first glaciers, while high up there were snowfields. To the south the 7215 foot peaks of Mt Sarmiento were hidden in cloud.

Every day we stopped at a different anchorage, a small bay, cove, or inlet. Some had mountains and glaciers overhead, while others were more gentle with tree lined shores where wild fuchsias grow. There were many birds, steamer ducks, kelp geese, and others. Steamer ducks cannot fly but can flap their way across the water at a great rate. Over the mountains great raptors, possibly condors, circled.

To secure ourselves at night we laid out two anchors in tandem, as well as putting lines ashore to trees or rocks. This was to protect ourselves from the fierce catabatic squalls or *rachas* that accelerate down the mountainsides to achieve wind strengths outside our normal experience. We kept 100 meter lines in specially made bags on the deck and with Fraser doing most of the rowing we got pretty adept at deploying them rapidly. In Puerto Niemann, a landlocked bay at the west end of the Cockburn Channel we were initially unable to get lines ashore. In the late evening *rachas* struck with terrific force, and as the whole bay became a cauldron of white spray and foam we dragged backwards out of the anchorage. As the wind strength was probably well over 80 knots, we kept being knocked down, and it was a hard struggle to get the anchors up. I must admit to looking at the rapidly approaching beach astern and wondering where we could pitch a tent. However with the initially reluctant motor running hard and two on the windlass we were eventually able to re-anchor. We lay down to recover, only for the dose to be repeated a couple of hours later.

Moving on we turned to the southeast, and with the Pacific to starboard, we thankfully brought the wind on the beam. Our course then took us through the Brecknock, Ballanero, and Beagle channels. To the north are the high peaks of the Cordillera Darwin, glaciers from this run down into the sea. To the south of the Beagle channel, on Isla Navarino lies Puerto Williams the southernmost town in the world, a Chilean Naval base. Here they have converted part of an old ship, the *Micalvi*, into a yacht club. We lay alongside with others, including Eric Hiscock's old *Wanderer III* now owned by Dane Thies Matsen. At the club they serve delicious crab salad, and we enjoyed a local drink, *pisco sour*. There used to be lots of mussels as well, but the collection of these is now forbidden, due to the presence of *marea roja*, algae that makes them highly toxic.

To get to Cape Horn our course lay to the south across Bahia Nassau. We crossed at night, it was cold and rained very hard, but by morning we were among the islands to the north of the cape. It was bright and crisp as we threaded our way through and approached from the northwest. Turning east at around noon we were finally there off Cape Horn, our objective achieved. We had mixed feelings, glad to be there, but relieved also to think that we were now on the way home. We pressed on to the

Le Maire straits and out into the South Atlantic. Overfalls off Cabo San Diego gave us a worrying time. We got to Stanley on 11 February and stayed for four weeks. We moored in the Canache, the old careenage some three miles to the east of the town. Susan flew in for a visit, and I learnt that I had missed Adrie by a couple of weeks. She had come up from the Peninsula and South Georgia on a cruise ship. We made expeditions to see penguins and took on stores. As we were keen to increase our water and diesel capacity the skipper made an appeal on the local radio for containers. This brought in several cans for diesel, and the Army came up trumps with some jerry cans for water.

The daily walk to town got us pretty fit, and we enjoyed the excellent facilities at the Lighthouse seamen's centre run by Kiwi Mike Hughes and his Danish wife. Here there are showers, hot meals and easy chairs. We watched the Americas Cup on television. After a few days *The Alderman* with Richard Wakeford and crew sailed in. They had just completed a great voyage from New Zealand and the Antarctic peninsula. They immediately livened the place up with a party on board. On 8 March a window in the persistent northerlies presented itself and we sailed together. They were bound for Brazil, while we hoped to visit the Azores on the way home.

The passage north proved to be one of the hardest parts of the whole trip. We met a succession of gales and strong winds mostly from the north or northeast. On the plus side it did soon get warmer. It took us forty-four days to reach the equator, the doldrums treated us kindly and we were soon crossing the boisterous northeast trades. We got pushed so far to the west that we decided to miss the Azores and head straight for Falmouth. Supplies were boosted by a friendly German ship, but the weather north of the Azores was not helpful. It was therefore with some relief that on 4 June we sighted the Scillies, and after a spinnaker run down the wonderfully green and pleasant looking Cornish coast, sailed past Black Rock and into Falmouth.

We had been at sea for ninety days, and the whole voyage had taken nine months. Family and friends were there to meet us. It was great to be home.

BRIEF ENCOUNTER

by Colin Barry

On Monday 18 September, we were sailing north along the Spanish Mediterranean coast, starting from St Jose early in the day. We arrived at Garrucha in early afternoon and thinking that the weather conditions might be deteriorating we decided to moor there.

We therefore altered course and headed into Garrucha, which is sited some 56 miles from Almeria and is really the only secure stopping point on this particular part of the coast, without going on for another 20 miles.

On entry into Garrucha harbour we saw that the small marina was remarkably full and there was an RCC burgee on a yacht alongside the fuelling jetty. This proved to be *Physalian* with David Scott-Bayfield on board. Verbal and VHF communication quickly established that the marina was full. The locals were being uncooperative and it was clear that Scott-Bayfield's berth would itself be untenable in any kind of swell, due to the shape of the quay. He also told us that the authorities had tried to stop people anchoring at least until a big ship had left the harbour and that he wanted to move away from his berth in any case. We decided to anchor and size things up.

It was, at this stage, that my wife pointed out that our RCC burgee was firmly wrapped round the VHF aerial – how embarrassing. Pulling and shoving would not move it and obviously something needed to be done. Cally was not particularly keen on me putting my 13-stone bulk on the mast and very gallantly Scott came over and said he would either go up or put me up the mast. I managed to persuade him to put me up the mast and cleared matters up. Another brief conversation took place and Scott encouraged us, with our following wind, to move on to Aguilas. He proposed to wait as there was a strong headwind blowing against his intended southward passage.

We said goodbye and were on our way.

TRANSATLANTIC TALL SHIPS 2000

by Nicko Franks

I am one of the lucky RCC members who gets paid to go sailing. My job has the title of 'Ketch Manager' (or Ketchup Manager as some of our young crews call me) of the *Arethusa*, a 72ft wooden ketch owned by the Shaftesbury Homes and *Arethusa* charity. The charity operates homes for disadvantaged young people mainly in the southeast London area. It also used to run as one of its homes a large four masted barque berthed permanently at Lower Upnor opposite Chatham on the Medway. In the late seventies, this *Arethusa* was towed away to New York (where she still resides) and the present one was built to provide sail training for similar young people. Its role has since expanded and we now cruise almost continuously with different groups of young people. *Arethusa* has 18 berths. She has a salaried Skipper and First Mate, a young 'trainee' Bosun (currently a Barnardo's Boy), a couple of volunteer adult 'afterguard' and 12 or 13 young people. I work mainly ashore organising the programme, budget, provision of spares for defects, crew finding, and all the other myriad administrative tasks which go with keeping the boat running. The main perk of my job is that there is no salaried second skipper so I go sailing as the skipper when the resident one needs a break.

Every summer we are allowed to deviate from our main allocated task to participate in the Tall Ships races. These races began in 1956 and have become major spectacular events drawing huge crowds to the host ports to visit the ships in harbour and watch the starts and finishes. In the millennium year a major 'push' round the Atlantic was organised, starting from Southampton in April and finishing in Amsterdam in mid August. We in *Arethusa* split the race into five 'legs' in order to try to give as many different young people as possible a taste of the experience and we did indeed cycle through sixty-five of them using cheap charter flights to change over crews in Cadiz, Bermuda, Annapolis (Washington) and Halifax (Nova Scotia).

I was lucky enough to skipper Leg 3 (Bermuda – Annapolis) but this is the story of Transatlantic Leg 5 which I skippered from Halifax to Amsterdam.

I flew out to Halifax a couple of days earlier than the crew mainly to organise the serious victualling required for 17 hungry young people on the 3–4 week crossing. Our faithful chart corrector had been at our European Charts so they were accompanying me on the journey. I perhaps foolishly consigned them to Heavy Baggage and sure enough on arrival at Halifax there was no trace. They were eventually returned from Reykjavik but not until after I had navigated across the Atlantic, up the English Channel and into Ramsgate with one Atlantic routeing chart, Macmillan's and an old chart catalogue.

My young crew duly arrived and they did seem very young. The minimum age on the Tall Ships races is 15 and half the crew has to be under 25. We numbered five 16-year-olds and four 17-year-olds amongst our complement. We had only 24 hours to sort ourselves out and, despite my best efforts, *Arethusa* was boxed in alongside a pontoon with 2 other boats outboard so there was no chance of a 'shakedown' spin. What would have happened if I had sailed with a really bad 'sickie' does not bear thinking about.

Departures from ports on Tall Ships races always involve a spectacular 'Parade of Sail' before the start and Halifax was no exception. It was a glorious day and we paraded right round the large harbour with thousands of spectators lining the shore. There were also hundreds of beautifully disciplined spectator boats all kept at anchor by the Canadian police to avoid impeding the large un-manoeuvrable Class A Tall Ships – this is not always the case in European ports. We finished our Parade of Sail with a close pass of the Canadian Frigate *Athabaskan* in order to give three cheers to the Governor General who was embarked for the occasion. We also have a dreadful oikey 'ARE, ARE', chant for these occasions which I hope and pray no other RCC member will ever have to listen to.

Luckily we then at last had a couple of hours to introduce my very inexperienced young crew to tacking, gybeing and recovering a man overboard. Tall Ships race starts are staggered with the spectacular big vessels going first and us smaller craft (known as Class C boats) going later at 10 minute intervals. There were 10 in our class and I think we were second over the line which pleased us. The following few hours were gentle and pleasant but we did not sail very well as our new crew took time to settle in. Whilst the Tall Ships races are not contested with the same intensity as say the Round the World races, nevertheless a considerable interest is taken in the daily position reports. There is a weird and wonderful handicap system concocted by the race director but it has been built up over many years of experience with the same vessels competing and there are few 'drips'. Each race has a communications officer in one of the big Tall Ships and the whole fleet reports their positions in

Astrid & Zephyr
La Grande Greve
      Sark
   26 : 7 : 00

once a day initially on VHF and then on MF/HF as they spread out. The positions are fed into the race director's computer, the results are calculated and then these results are broadcast back to the fleet a couple of hours later. The next 5 days of our race were hard work as we beat to windward with the wind coming from exactly where we wanted to go. The square riggers make no ground in these conditions and even we began to forecast an October ETA. At least my crew were well settled in by now, no one was being sick and the 3 watches were working as teams together. On day 5 the wind veered quite suddenly through 90° and increased rapidly to a full gale. A nice Dutch girl happened to be steering at the time and she was wearing a self inflating life jacket which in the confusion of being caught aback, did indeed self inflate. The sight of this Michelin (wo-)man struggling to move behind the wheel would have been very funny if the situation had been less tense. However at least this gale was from the southwest and we started to move in the right direction. We flew along with No.3 jib up, the main firmly stowed away, and the mizzen deployed every now and then when the wind moderated slightly. Unfortunately during one of the lowering evolutions, a young female crew member got her wrist under the dropping boom and damaged it. I thanked my lucky stars that I had just at the last gasp managed to get a doctor for this leg and Lisa came into her own with her expert 'splinting' of the arm and her professional advice. She did have a radio conversation with another doctor, a Russian on the *Kruzenstern* and we elected to carry on. I think that probably without her advice, I would have turned back to land the patient. The happy end to this incident is that when the wrist was x-rayed on return to the UK, the hospital said that it probably had been broken but that it had been so well set that there was no discernible sign and it was a perfect mend.

The next 10 days after the gale moderated were fabulous as we tore along on a broad reach eating up the miles. We were doing over 200 miles a day and some of the 'big boys' were doing incredible mileages. The *Da Modzielzy*, a lovely Polish barque achieved a record 325 miles in one 24 hour run. I wish I could have seen her as the sight of a fully rigged ship averaging 13 knots with every sail set must have been truly magnificent.

The crew were now well together and really enjoying themselves. A blown-out mizzen staysail was the object of some intensive sail repairing as this is an important sail to set in a ketch off the wind. Food as ever loomed large in the daily routine. We carry no cook in order to get the young people to learn to cater for a big group and I have to say that we ate extremely well all the way across. Middle watch bread-making became the rule rather than the exception. In one magic hour on one day we were closed by a large whale, had a school of porpoises playing round the bow and sighted a turtle. We had a different Barnardo's Boy on each leg and this leg's Paul Fleming was sent completely ecstatic by dolphins which he had never seen before. He spent hours in the pulpit for'd shouting unintelligible Glaswegian curses at them and taking endless photos, the majority of which I suspect came out as plain blue sea.

We had some catching up to do after the first few days beating but at last we got our tactics right. The main body of the fleet (of 35) kept on or south of the Great Circle route and by heading well north we held onto a stronger wind for longer. It was really quite exciting as our daily position improved amongst the fleet and I wished I had gone even further north where a lovely old American schooner, the *Pride of Baltimore*, whom we gave a lot of time to, kept calling in positions still way ahead of us.

Anyway as we passed a race way point south of the Scillies, we were very excited to sight no less than 4 other boats from the fleet including 2 front runners from our class – amazing after 3000 miles of sailing. We were in third position in our class and heading for a prize as we ran up channel on a glorious afternoon past Start Point. The wind was easing and I had slight forebodings but we continued past Portland overnight and arrived off St Albans Head in the early dawn. The race finish was to be due south of St Catherine's Point as, although the finish port was Amsterdam, the race authorities did not want great big sailing ships duelling through the Straits of Dover with no engines on.

However disaster now struck as the wind died completely. The two faster boats in our class whom we had sighted at the Scillies had managed to ghost over the line before this happened but we remained 'glued to the spot' for nearly 20 hours. It was a hot, hot, day and so flat calm that we even all went swimming twice. The other mitigating factor was the close presence of the Russian Tall Ship *Mir* with the race communicator on board also engaged in the same desperate struggle to cross the line. Finally at about 0100 on the next day a zephyr picked us up and we finally ghosted over after 20 days 4 hours and 56 seconds. It was a lovely pink dawn with St Catherine's Point Light winking at us and the whole crew got up to 'dance and skylark'. Despite the final calm and fading out of the prize list to fifth in class, we had had a great voyage and all the young people seemed to have thoroughly enjoyed themselves and got a huge amount out of it. Although I had crossed the Atlantic many times in warships I had never done it under sail before and it was certainly a great experience for me also.

AN ANTARCTIC DREAM

by Richard Wakeford

This is the cruise for which the Claymore Cup was awarded. Bean Wollen was also awarded the Ladies' Cup for her part in this cruise.

The Drake Passage is the last barrier to the exciting sailing around the Antarctic Peninsular. The five of us aboard *The Alderman* were poised and eager to be moving off by the beginning of February 2000. We cleared out of Puerto Williams, Chile, and had a good crossing of the 'Drake Lake', as opposed to the feared 'Drake Shake'. Passing well west of the South Shetlands, we were disappointed that we had not seen any ice or whales, both supposedly abundant indicators of being near to the Antarctic Peninsula. The only sign had been the increasing number of layers of clothing we were wearing as the sea temperature dropped below two degrees Celsius. Then all of a sudden we were there. The high peaks of Smith Island to port appeared above the cloud some 50 miles away. Ahead through the clearing skies could be seen the coast of Brabant Island and then all expectations were met in a flood of new experiences: the first iceberg, blue against the white ice covered islands; the first penguins porpoising alongside the hull; a pair of humpback whales podding close inshore.

Even arriving from the huge scale of Chilean Patagonia, it took time to adjust to the size of our surroundings. In a dying wind we identified the Melchior Islands and motored in to the narrow creek surrounded by 75 foot high ice cliffs. The Melchiors are a common landfall and departure point for most of the charter fleet, so to find other yachts in the anchorage was not unexpected, but we were the fifth and space was getting scarce. However if we had arrived here alone I probably would not have stayed. The constant creaking of fissures opening in the compacted ice that towered above us was very disconcerting. Befriending Eric & Frederick from the French charter yacht *Croix Saint Paul II*, we gleaned as much as possible about where to go, the best anchorages, and where to

Off Cape Horn: Bean Wollen, Richard Wakeford, Harriet Faulkner and Tom
Falkus (in the foreground).

avoid. We stayed a whole day taking in the surroundings, trying a novel way of taking on water and giving the other boats a chance to disperse before we set off for a windless motor across the Gerlache Strait. The wind picked up as we approached Cuverville Island allowing us our first sail among bergy-bits. We dropped sail as we rounded the south of the island, and anchored stern-to to a penguin rookery. The comical gentoo penguins kept us amused for hours, though the smell was almost over-powering.

The following day, as we sailed around icebergs, we were constantly amazed and re-awoken to our surroundings. Paradise Harbour brought even more bergs in increasingly tortured shapes and seals sunning themselves on the floes. We motored in near calm with an ice watch fending off the smaller bits and directing the helm round the larger growlers. We arrived off an Argentine base and were invited ashore for a look around. The obvious anchorages were either inaccessible or full of ice, but there was a tenable spot directly in front of the base. Harriet (Harry) Faulkner (RCC), Bean Wollen (RCC), Hugh Naylor and Tom Falkus went ashore after fixing shore lines, while I stayed aboard, cautious of the increasing wind. The 'tour' was not up to much, but the view from the top of the steep climb and the toboggan ride down were so great that Tom ventured up twice. Aboard what little wind there was had backed and it was enough to carry ice from the nearby glacier down on to us. I was glad to

The Alderman in Paradise Harbour.

leave and, as we ventured back to Waterboat Point, we had the most extraordinary visit by a minke whale. As we gingerly motored through the ice, the whale began to swim very close to our stern, then along side. We all gave up steering, directing or fending to watch our own aquatic show, save Harry who was doing her best to keep us safe. The whale vented, broke the surface and often appeared to rub itself against the hull (though the bump could have been from an iceberg). As the wind cleared our path we sped up and the whale lost interest. Anchoring off a Chilean base, we did not use shore lines only for Hugh to wake us up at one in the morning with ice moving against the hull. We had dragged and in a cold wind with little visibility we tried to haul up 60 metres of chain and two heavy anchors. We re-anchored in much the same spot, and slept fitfully.

Waterboat Point is not an attractive spot and after the night's activities there was a reluctance to stay. As the rain eased, and after what we mistakenly took to be a slackening of the wind in the afternoon, we hauled up the anchors again and headed for Port Lockroy. We crossed Gerlache Strait constantly reducing canvas as the wind increased to gale force. With two crew on ice watch, one on the helm and the others warming hands and feet below deck, we were forced to rotate posts every fifteen minutes. We ended up running under bare poles down Neumeyer Channel, wearing ski goggles to protect us from the stinging hail. Dorian Bay was lost in a flurry of snow and as we rounded in to the lee of Wiencke Island we started the motor to carry us across to an anchorage outside Port Lockroy itself. We thankfully held with both anchors at the first attempt, then caught up with the local news. Eric aboard *Croix Saint Paul II* was anchored on a clay patch within the harbour. He offered the French method of securing a shore-line: 'Put the bows on the rocks and get one of the crew to step ashore. It does not do much for the paintwork but.......*Boff*'. We could all picture his classic Gallic shrug, but I was not going to ask for volunteers. Trevor on *Iron Bark II*, securely roped in all directions in Alice Creek, said that the wind had subsided sufficiently for him to dinghy himself ashore and that he could send a light messenger down wind to us. I was confident in the anchors and declined his help. Next Dave, one of two BAS workers at the British museum there, welcomed us to the Port. Finally we heard Kit Power aboard the cruise ship *Akademik Ioffie* trying to track us down and a mini-meet was arranged for the following day. The popularity of Port Lockroy would have been alarming in what we had thought to be the remotest place on earth, were it not for its friendly helpful overtones.

We moved inside the harbour the following morning, dried out, thanked the offerers of help and quickly took up Kit's offer of dinner aboard the ship – we had packed towels and wash things well before Penny had offered their shower. A total of nine members (full, associate & cadet) and two further crew disrupted life aboard the cruise ship until we were taken back by zodiac. A pleasant and warm day ashore followed and was capped by dinner ashore with the BAS workers, Dave and Rod. Rod remembered *Ardevora's* voyage, two years earlier, due to the presence of 'a pretty girl'. Pudding was provided by Trevor, a solo sailor who had over-wintered at Port Lockroy and who had only eight days previously dug out his shorelines. BAS rations, bottled wines and New Zealand dried (well frozen and well expired) crumble put our offerings of pop-corn and boxed wine to shame.

Reluctant to move on we spent a night in Dorian Bay. This had been Amyr Klink's winter anchorage aboard *Paratii*. It was after meeting him in Iceland on his way home from his Tilmanesque voyage that I first dreamed of sailing to the Peninsula. Reality had now surpassed Amyr's very animated descriptions of the Antarctic that had been with me for over eight years. On entering Dorian, Amyr's words that 'there is no purer or truer way to experience places than to touch them with the keel of a boat' came to mind as we ventured just too close to the moraine.

Reports of heavy ice and cruise ships being rescued by icebreakers tempered our desire to push for the Antarctic Circle and gave us longer to explore more sheltered waters. We chose to visit Arthur Harbour on Anvers Island, home to elephant seals, nesting giant petrels and the USA base of Palmer. We planned to anchor some way away from the base but called up to be polite. Next we knew we were invited to visit the base as there was another yacht due in the following day and we could accom-pany them on a site visit. Our arrival coincided with that of *Croix Saint Paul II* and we felt sure they would soon tire of us turning up like a bad penny, disrupting their tranquillity. We let them choose the best spot and pulled ourselves stern-to close by. Ashore we found a remarkable ice cave and an abundance of elephant seals and petrels. The diving skuas forced us to keep some distance from the petrels, while the smell of the bull elephant seals was enough of a deterrent to keep us away. We wel-comed the offer to make fast alongside the base the following day and had an enjoyable time ashore where we were made to feel at home. The delicious fresh cookies nearly enticed some to be permanent residents. With the wind increasing we roped ourselves in to the middle of Hero Inlet and that evening enjoyed a movable party of crews and guests across the two boats.

While the wind stayed in the north we were comfortable, but at 0530 the following morning the noise of ice on the hull had us up and assess-ing our options. The wind had backed and quickly filled the inlet. In dense brash ice we could only cast our lines clear and with difficulty motor in to clear water. Harry and Hugh went ashore to retrieve the lines and faced an early bombardment of skuas. We reluctantly said goodbye to the Americans and the offer of a party ashore that evening and headed south for the Lemaire Channel. The reward was a beautiful sail with clear blue skies and perfect visibility. Sailing through deep blue water with icebergs about has an air of the sublime, to the extent that I felt we

The Alderman and a leopard seal in Port Lockroy.

did not really belong there. Unfortunately the path through the channel looked blocked by ice, and even climbing the mast did not reveal a clear lead so we opted for the uncharted route outside Booth Island. This brought the benefit of a well proportioned iceberg with hole and our own 'Kodak Gap', followed by an eerie motor through an iceberg graveyard. The huge iridescent blocks of blue ice that towered over our masthead had been shaped by wind and sea into fanciful shapes. However we seemed to motor in to a cul-de-sac with our route blocked and our heading disoriented by the close proximity of the icebergs. We were forced to backtrack until Tom on the bow said a way was clear. Not until we had motored over the submerged saddle between two huge ice towers belonging to one berg, did I realise the predicament we were in. The engine was put in neutral and we held our breath as we drifted clear, trying hard not to imagine the consequences of a capsizing berg at that particular moment.

We anchored with picturesque views off Hovgaard Island and found *Iron Bark II* snug in the adjacent creek. The following dawn, very clear and wonderfully calm, enticed us to a leisurely day exploring around Pléneau Island. Hugh, Bean and Tom disappeared in one dinghy to climb and explore another anchorage. Harry and I opted for an artistic spell, producing dubious pastel and pencil sketches, before climbing the steep ice slope to the top of Pléneau. From the summit we had the most beautiful view in all directions and near to this vantage point the ice

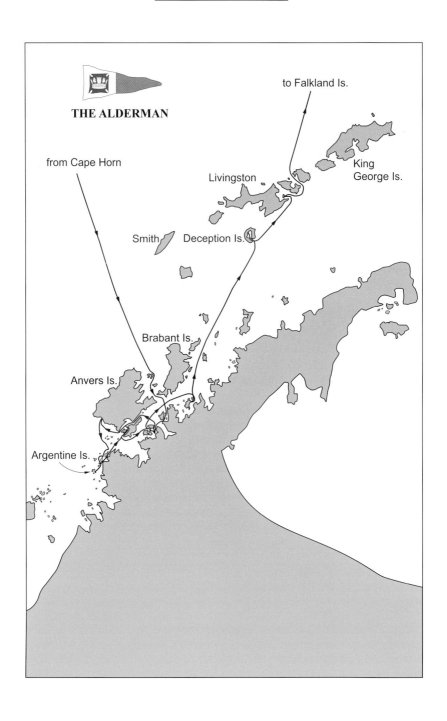

THE ALDERMAN

to Falkland Is.

from Cape Horn

Livingston

King George Is.

Smith

Deception Is.

Brabant Is.

Anvers Is.

Argentine Is.

conditions in the Peltier Channel could be seen. Looking north Mount Français, thirty miles away, stood icy white against the clear blue sky. Beneath us we could see penguins swimming through the clear water and jumping out to land upright on the rocks. There was not a breath of wind, the sea was flat and the many coloured icebergs glistened in the uninterrupted sun. It was a truly magical day but our relaxing was abruptly terminated. Harry jumping between rocks 'popped' her knee. The pain was obvious. We caught the attention of the others. Stretcher berth, rope and first aid kits were retrieved from *The Alderman*. Manhandling Harry across the rocks and ice then dragging her, in the stretcher, to the top of the ice slope we were forced to stop. An improvised 'comfortable' sling using oily trousers was added. We set up an anchor man with rope at the top and two others supporting the stretcher as Harry was lowered down. The analgesics were beginning to reduce the pain as Harry was carried to one of the dinghies and laid down as if part of a Viking burial. Not liking the implications and to ease the pain Harry sat up, prompting Hugh to wonder if the whole incident had been staged. Back alongside *The Alderman* we used a block and tackle from the boom and topping lift to swing the stretcher directly into the cockpit. From there, with much jarring, Harry was put in to a saloon berth with the lee cloth up to help immobilise her leg.

The Ukrainian base of Vernadsky in the Argentine Islands was only ten miles away and we knew there was a doctor there. We arrived the following morning, anchored and asked the doctor to come aboard. He then asked Harry ashore for an X-ray and his final verdict was that a half plaster cast should be bandaged to her leg to immobilise and protect the knee and proper medical attention sought. With the passage of a cold front we stayed another day giving Tom more opportunities to lose at pool and Bean several more opportunities to sample the home-brewed vodka available, alight if requested, in the friendly bar. Heading north we found that Circumcision Bay was full of ice, as reported to be for much of the time, and we opted to return directly to Port Lockroy. There we met the doctor from the cruise ship *Hanseatic* who thought treatment was quite urgent. We tried to leave for the South Shetlands, but were forced back by ice and wind. Then a day later the doctors from the *Akademik Boris Petrov* offered to take Harry back to Ushuaia for treatment there. We had a very rushed goodbye and suddenly found ourselves lacking part of our great, well tuned team.

Slightly subdued and beginning to suffer harbour rot we collected some dubious water and left for Waterboat Point. There, this time with shore lines, we entered into a crude sweep stake as to when the wind would change and fill the anchorage with ice. Hugh and I were within ten minutes, and at one thirty I woke the others to retrieve the lines, fend off ice and haul up the anchors. It was a miserable, cold night. We slowly motored through the ice dotted gloom with the bow watch becoming very cold while straining to see bergs. Dawn brought a fluky southerly that enabled us alternately to sail and motor to Enterprise Island where we made fast in the secure anchorage alongside the hull of a derelict whaling boat and slept. That evening *Pelagic*, with Emma Ellis (RCC) aboard, made fast outside for a reunion that had been arranged via Inmarsat. They left early after a late night and a rendition of 'The Alderman Blues' composed by Emma while we were cruising in New Zealand. We stayed for another beautiful clear calm day of water collecting, climbing and sketching, then left for Deception Island. The shortening days led to an overnight passage fortunately with wind but no ice.

The sight of the black and red mountains of Deception were a huge contrast to the ice covered land we had become accustomed to. We entered through Neptune's Bellows and anchored in a small inner basin at Telefon Bay. Unexpectedly we found the holding to be good but that the anchorage attracted every breath of wind and we yawed badly at anchor. On Tom's birthday we left the windy anchorage expecting not to be able to stop but found little wind in the volcano basin and took ourselves into Whalers Bay. We walked through the rising steam and were surprised by the level of development that had existed and by a half submerged tractor. This had been swamped by the devastating mud slide that terminated the BAS operations on Deception. In great style Bean produced a birthday cake as we reached with full sail towards Livingstone Island under cloudless skies and with the South Shetland mountains turning bluish as the sun set. For the first time in months we sat outside at dusk and toasted Tom's health.

Ashore the next day we were made very welcome by the seven Argentine personnel at the research base on Half Moon Island. Lunch and showers ashore, interspersed by visits to the chinstrap penguin and fur seal colonies, were repaid by drinks aboard that evening. The tense moment when it was discovered that one of our guests was aboard the submarine damaged and captured at South Georgia in the 1982 conflict passed quickly He eloquently wrote in the visitors book, 'Despues de 18 anos, eneventre a usteda Ingleses sin resentimiento. Veterano del ano 82'.

Leaving the following day for the Falklands the fog came down for the first time. Pushing a bit of tide through English Strait our last glimpse of Antarctica was a very murky Table Island, its sheer sides ice free. We had a good passage to Stanley with unexpected southeast and southwest winds until the last day. Harry meanwhile had been delayed in Ushuaia as she was not allowed to fly until the swelling had subsided. She arrived home the day before we left Antarctica, and three days later had surgery to remove a piece of damaged cartilage from her knee.

We were all Antarctic novices with dreams. After three and a half weeks in The Ice these dreams had been fulfilled and we had found the magic of Antarctica still intact.

CANAL VILLANELLE

"For the rain, it raineth every day".

With apologies to William Shakespeare and Dylan Thomas

As *Gem* glides gently along the canal's narrow way,
At Mem we leave the Baltic Sea in soft Northern light,
And the rain, it's plain, pours down every day.

Seven locks rise up to Berg under skies so grey;
Here Julie runs the warps up to the next in the flight,
As *Gem* glides gently along the canal's narrow way.

While his beer becomes diluted, Michael sees with dismay
That not all boats go gently into locks so tight,
And the rain, more rain, showers down every day.

"This Gota's got to get a bit of sun, one day",
Sighs Jack, who likes Swedish weather warm and bright,
As *Gem* glides gently along the canal's narrow way.

In Lake Viken, the high spot, Eve anchors in a bay,
Whilst the elegant *Diana* steams past and out of sight,
And the rain, our bane, drizzles down every day.

From Toreboda down to Sjotorp and the Gota's end, we pray
That we can pass all nineteen locks before the fall of night,
As *Gem* glides gently along the canal's narrow way,
And the rain, yet again, patters down every day.

Eve Bonham Cozens

In July, the Bonham Cozens family took their 40ft wooden cutter, *Gemervescence of London* (known as *"Gem"*), from the east coast of Sweden through the Gota canal, the Lakes (where they did some sailing) and the Trollhatan Canal to Gothenburg on the west coast, where she is now laid up. The transit took a leisurely two and a half weeks, and there were 64 locks rising from sea level to 92 metres and down again.

145

A DISLOCATED CRUISE

by Paul Heiney

It is rare these days for a member cruising European waters to make any kind of fundamental navigational discovery. The anchorages are well visited, the FPI astonishingly up to date, the charts usually correct, and the pilot books have never been better. So I consider myself fortunate to have rounded one of Europe's major headlands this year using a route I doubt any of you have attempted before. It is hardly a passage I would recommend, and I sincerely hope that few will follow in my wake, but I feel it should be recorded here for completeness. It might not be on a par with cleaving a new route through the North West passage, but I promise you it *is* a first.

I have rounded the infamous Norwegian headland, Stattlandet, by the inshore route. Statt is the most exposed point on the Atlantic coast of Norway and amongst Norwegian sailors it has a fearsome reputation. But since most of their navigation is done through their inner leads, or skjaergard, where the water is flat and protected for a thousand miles by a string of islands, it is easy to understand why having to round this headland would feel like being plucked from the cosy Solent and dropped into the raging Portland Race. Sometimes they round it in flotillas for safety, guided by a mother ship.

Our cruise started from Shetland where *Tinkatoo* had overwintered after completing the first half of our intended passage to the Lofoten Islands. As we cast off, the omens were not good. A couple of hours before sailing, the engine had pumped the contents of its sump into the bilge prompting mad car chases in search of gaskets. But more worrying was an aside in a conversation with a weather forecaster who, when discussing five days ahead, said, 'I see a system developing up there with *quite a lot of energy.*' Worrying, since it is five days at best from Lerwick to Lofoten. Already a dark threat was chasing us.

I could not have had a better crew to face it. Tom Stevens joined us (whose phlegmatic approach to cruising was recorded here last year) and Richard Woodman, maritime historian and recently retired from Trinity

House where he commanded their flagship, *Patricia*. As you might expect for a man whose job was to drop buoys in precisely the right spot, he navigates like a wizard. But more importantly on a longish passage, he has a swashbuckling tale to tell of nearly every navigational mark on the English coast. Cry 'Smiths Knoll!' and you will hear the story of relighting it in a storm with a soggy box of Swan Vestas. Mention the Humber lightship and you will hear how they wrapped its anchor chains round their own propeller in a hurricane, or better.

Sailing northwards, Shetland disappearing behind us in the mist, we joked about the 'system with quite a lot of energy in it.' I had pressed the forecaster. He had said it could be 'up to force seven', and so with the wind forecast abaft the beam and not even to gale force, we thought no more of it. Or pretended we did not.

Out of the shelter of land, the wind freshened from the southwest and we sped along on a rising sea flying genoa and mizzen only. After twenty four hours, spirits were still high. But by two days out we were less happy. The rhumb line took us through the Norwegian oilfields northwest of Bergen, and slowly we closed the Norwegian coast. The seas built, the cockpit filled several times, the crash of breakers on the cabin top sounded as if they might push in the windows. It was a full gale now and the seas were coming at us from all sides. More seriously, Tom's bunk looked as though a sodden Labrador had bedded down in it and he moaned that there was not one dry spot the entire length of his sleeping bag. We were cold, wet and miserable and not even a rousing tale of relieving the Bishop Rock lighthouse in a rowing boat could lift our spirits.

Slowly but surely, the odds started to stack up against our going any further north. If the promised energetic system had come through on time, we would still be a hundred miles or more from shelter, and the weather seemed already to be in a worsening mood. And so were we. The engine, I forgot to mention, had failed on leaving Lerwick, the smell of oil in the bilge had been joined by a distinct whiff of diesel, and every window in the boat had started to leak. The charts were on their way back to pulp, and the parallel ruler floated rather than glided across the chart table. So we turned our backs on an increasingly angry north Atlantic, and sailed slowly into flatter water. Sixty tiring hours out of Lerwick the bacon was sizzling in the pan, alongside in Aalesund.

Refreshed and uplifted by the clear bright sunshine, that afternoon we made a dash north to Molde, still believing Lofoten might be possible despite the ever shortening time that remained. A good tip when cruising Norway – there is free internet access in every public library and through it comes all the weather advice you could wish for. In the Molde library, it took just two clicks to reveal a bullseye of a depression heading our way, the isobars so close that at points they merged into one thick, sinister black line. We moved *Tinkatoo* into a thinly populated visitors' marina, and doubled the warps. In the absence of drink (strictly rationed by a skipper who knew the price of booze in Norway) the crew took their pleasure by repeatedly visiting the girl in the filling station who kept the key to the public lavatories. Such public facilities, I might add, have a brightness and cleanliness to them that I have never seen anywhere else in Europe. And the girls in charge of keys show similar virtues.

The Navtex flashed messages of impending maelstrom, but with the sun still high in the sky at 2200 and the breeze gentle, we doubted any of it could possibly happen. The first sign of its coming was the arrival on the quayside of an army of hefty Norwegian fishermen with serious looks on their faces. Heavy warps were dragged from fishing boats, breasts and springs doubled, fenders checked. 'Storm coming!' they shouted. We were not concerned for we had discovered a novel treat and were indulging in it – whale meat. 'Cook like beef!' said the woman in the Molde fish shop. Three minutes each side in the frying pan and you have a cross between a rump steak and liver with not a trace of blubber or the expected smell of fish, and dirt cheap too. In Norway, it is not a highly regarded food.

By 0200 the wind was up to full gale force with gusts that set the boat shuddering. This was the start of a storm which was to set oilrigs adrift and provide the record books with the lowest ever pressure recorded in this latitude in mid-summer. His sleep broken by the howling and crashing, the old labrador stirred in his bunk and poked his nose through the hatch to be met with horizontal rain. Woodman was already on shore, watching the warps, expecting chafe. With the engine still unreliable, adrift was the last thing we wished to be. Despite being twenty miles up a fjord in a harbour, the waves would have done justice to the open sea as they broke on a small breakwater to windward of us and sent spray high into the sky. The air was thick with salt. A cruise liner scuttled in and dropped her anchor briefly off the quay to land an injured passenger, then set off, butting her way into viscious waves before turning to face the open sea – which is where we would have been now if sense and good fortune had not prevailed.

It was a lousy June in Norway everyone agreed, and it showed no signs of improving. We admitted defeat and ruled out any further progress north. Instead, we would cruise south to Bergen, checking out the keeper of every public lavatory key along the route. Three days later, we were faced with the prospect of rounding the notorious Stattlandet.

We had spent a night in Kalveholm, anchored in a flat calm in a rocky lagoon, eating more whale, and thinking life was getting better. But by dawn, fierce gusts tumbled down the mountain sides and the anchor chain stretched out tight in front of us. Reefed, we sailed. Then we had our first katabatic experience which flung us on our side, the sea up the cabin top windows which was not where the designer, Kim Holman, ever intended the sea to be. 'We're tacking,' I said. 'You cannot. There's rocks!' said Woodman. 'Bearing away, then,' I suggested. 'More rocks,' came the reply. 'Ahead?' I dared ask. ' Rocks too,' was the reply. We crash gybed and started the engine for safety; one wrong move here and we would be trapped. But the engine stuttered and died. Minds concentrated, we threaded our way back into Kalveholm under sail and watched the stretched anchor chain singing once again in the gusts.

By teatime the wind was down, and with the advantage of the long summer nights here we decided to try for Stattvagen, a small, natural harbour on the very tip of Stattlandet thirty miles away. It would be a long, cold beat with the prospect of a tricky entrance, and so it proved to be as magnifying glass was taken to chart to try and spot the perches and transits which make the dog leg of an entrance safe to navigate. It was worth the effort. We felt we had anchored in the bowl of a volcano. Mountains rose steep on every side from a grassy foreshore. As we soon discovered, the wind will rise from calm to a gale-like blast in seconds, but go away just as quickly before attacking you from the opposite direction. But the edge-of-the-world sensation is worth the worrying.

We awoke the next morning to great news – sixteen gallons of diesel had cascaded into the bilge through a cracked fuel pipe. Apart from the mess we now had no fuel with which to make our exit, and the proximity of steep cliffs to the tricky entrance, coupled with the fluky and strong katabatic wind, would have made sailing distinctly risky. That afternoon, when the wind was down, I rowed ashore and met a cheery fisherman who said he would sell us diesel from his domestic heating tank. He told me to come back in half an hour.

From ashore, our boat looked so stunning in this inspiring anchorage that I decided to row back for my camera. This proved to be a great mistake. On climbing back down from the boat into the dinghy to row ashore once again, I felt the boarding step collapse under me and the Avon slip away. Soon I was hanging in the water, dangling by outstretched arms from the guard-rails. Why did not I let go? There were two able blokes on board to get me back, I was in oilskins and lifejacket. Foolishly, I hung there. Then my feet rose as the bouyancy in my boots took effect, and twisted my body round. At that point I did let go, but it was too late. 'I've dislocated my shoulder,' I shouted from the water. You have never seen a smile disappear so quickly from the faces of a crew.

They landed me like a cod, rolling me into the rubber dinghy and hoisting me aboard. But what to do now? I was in considerable pain. Our only option was the friendly fisherman ashore. How I climbed back into the dinghy, or managed the rocky scramble ashore I am not sure, but soon I was in a taxi bound for a local doctor. His surgery was a hundred painful hairpin bends away, and about 40 kilometres. I arrived, dripping, on his doorstep at about eight o'clock that night.

Clothes had to be removed, but not with scissors I insisted, mindful that these were a new set of *Mustos*. Instead, we went together into a shower cubicle to contain the water that was still filling my boots and pockets, and he started to pull at my seaboots, held tight by suction. He pulled hard. So hard that he slipped on the tiled floor and careered backwards crashing his skull into the cubicle door. For a moment it was debatable who of us was now the more severely injured.

Recovered, he gave me enough valium to calm a football crowd, and life improved. He lay me down, pulled and twisted my arm (no anaesthetic) and apologised for lack of a satisfactory result. He said I would have to go to hospital. 'How far?' I asked. 'Another sixty kilometres.' I suggested more valium. He tried harder. But even when putting his trainer-clad foot into my armpit and pulling like a man determined to win a tug of war (still no anaesthetic) he failed to make it click back into place. Three hours later, and with the meter on the taxi nudging three hundred and fifty pounds, I arrived at a small town hospital the location of which I had no clue.

Out of the midnight twilight an orthopaedic surgeon arrived, then an X-ray technician, an anaesthetist and a nurse. They sat me down and took details. Then the doctor looked me in the eye and said 'You realise you will have to *pay* for this?' That was when I really needed the valium.

Meanwhile, life onboard *Tinkatoo* was not without its thrills. My gallant crew had obtained the diesel, repaired the leak, bled the engine, and were heading out on a rough sea to round Stattlandet that night, bound for Maløy, the next major harbour south. It was, by all accounts, a long and wet beat and only when in windless shelter did they dare start the engine. It ran well, for an hour or so, but the sight of the Hurtigruten coastal ferry coming directly at it must have frightened it to death, for it failed with the ferry bows on in hardly a breath of wind. How we must all have craved valium that night.

I had the best night, lying in a luxurious hospital bed, and awoke to a stunning view down the length of some fjord or other, I have no idea which. The doctor checked me over and gave me the best medical advice I have ever received. 'Are you going back to your ship?' he asked gravely. I nodded, thinking he might forbid it. 'Then, once on board,' he said, 'go straight below and put a glass of whisky in your hand and drink slowly. Do not work, but shout all the time, telling your crew what they are doing wrong.' We chuckled. Then he presented the bill. It came to an astonishing eleven pounds sixty-five pence. Even the colossal taxi fare had vanished under a scheme where taxis used as ambulances charge a flat fare of seven pounds, even if they take you to the ends of the earth. I rang Libby. She declared Britain must leave Europe and instead join Norway, immediately!

Arm in a sling, I arrived that morning on the quayside at Maløy, my crew somewhat envious of my night in warm, dry sheets. Heroes that they were, despite their exhaustion they were up to their elbows in diesel, rebuilding the fuel system once again.

And I, of course, had rounded Stattlandet by the hitherto unexplored inshore route. I wish I could provide you with the precise pilotage details, but much of it remains a painful blur.

CROATIA HERE WE COME

by Peter and Gill Price

This is the cruise for which the Royal Cork Club Vase was awarded.

Lectron was made ready for sea after a winter ashore in Ginesta near Barcelona where we had been well looked after by Alfonso and his crew. Our master plan was a quick dash to Dubrovnik in Croatia, which was only about 15 cms port to port when viewed on our atlas, followed by some gentle cruising in the Adriatic. 1263 miles later having sailed via the south of Sardinia, Sicily and the Messina passage in varying weather conditions, including one full gale with breaking seas and a nasty moment with a patrol boat in the dark off the heal of Italy, we arrived in Croatia after 17 days including 8 night passages.

We made fast at Gruz to clear in and then went to the 'hole in the wall' for some Croatian money before going to the harbour authority. We paid a fee which gave us a 12 months permit. The immigration officer was brought to the boat within a few minutes. He quickly cleared and then informed us that we could take down the Yellow. We all looked at the blank space at the crosstrees and laughed. This was typical of the common sense and kindness shown everywhere. Then up river to the main ACI marina. We were tired after our 15 cm dash but elated to have arrived in Croatia.

From mid June to mid July we sailed north through the Croatian islands to Rovinj and on 16 July we started a night passage to Venice.

We had an easy crossing if rather a lot of motoring. Everyone was up for the dawn arrival. What excitement actually to arrive in Venice in one's own boat. Clear sun and everything looked wonderful. At 0940 we slipped into San Giorgio Maggiore marina where Gianpietro Zucchetta (RCC HFR) had managed to reserve us a place. It was lovely to meet him and his wife Milena after so many years of conversing by letter and Christmas cards. To add to the fun *Ardent Spirit* and the Beisers were there at the same time. The next few days were a whirl of kindness and

151

we felt like honoured guests. It was marvellous to be in the best spot in Venice with a ringside view yet separated from all the rushing traffic. The vaporetto took us to St Mark's Square as the first stop and we did Venice as one should, enjoying the many attractions including the excellent maritime museum. We had intended to leave on the 23rd but Gianpietro had one more surprise in store, with a wonderful ten hour sail in his beautiful ketch *Mattutina*. Down to the southern entrance of the lagoon and then out and back into the northern one enjoying all his electronic gadgets and being well fed all day by Milena.

24 July. Pat and Anne had now left us and in a cloud of red rain we departed at 0520. This time we remembered to hoist the Yellow as we entered Croatia again at Novigrad. Entry was simple as we had paid for the year. We had a good giggle at the concrete beaches which were very obvious here and are a feature of the Croatian seaside which does not have much sand. We moved on to Poreč where we enjoyed the Basilica with its Byzantine mosaics and the reconstruction of Roman mosaics. Much of the church had been restored but they were waiting for money from UNESCO to complete the project. We anchored in the bay rather than the crowded marina. Next morning was lovely again so Gill could swim before breakfast. We had a northerly wind to push us down to U. Artaturi (Lošinj) where we anchored between *Ardent Spirit* and *Baily of Howth*. For the second time we were asked by a charter boat to help them, this time a problem with their transmission system. Charter boats have few tools aboard and those in the know head straight for a British

Peter at the Krka Falls.

boat for help. This was a Slovenian boat and after a successful session they returned with a bottle of best Slovenian wine.

We stayed a day as Peter had mild food poisoning. Also the wind was blowing causing much drama and boats were dragging. Only 30 knots, a mini Bora, and by evening calm was restored. This was the opportunity to explore Mali Lošinj with its old tiled roofs (like Dubrovnik must have been before the troubles). A nice town and worth the visit. The next day we were up early to await the opening of the bridge so that we could squeeze through the Kanal and out to investigate the inlets on the southeast of Cres.

The MPG was used to help us drift south to the NW corner of Veli Orjule. Such beautiful clear water but only for a lunch stop. Later we picked up a mooring in Prolaz Zapuntel. This was where Peter Snow had touched a rock so we chose our buoy carefully. As we were told in the FPI, the restaurant on Molat was excellent and we had a lovely view across the passage with the boats peacefully on their moorings.

We had a gentle sail on the wind ghosting along into the narrow Prolaz Proversa to the south of Dugi Otok and then northwest into Luka Telašica. We moored in the innermost bay near *Ardent Spirit*, in one of the nicest anchorages we had visited. We dressed overall for the Queen Mother's 100th birthday which invited questions from passing boats. That evening we joined the Beisers and the crew from an American boat *Snowdance* for a pre-ordered lamb hotpot at Goran's restaurant. This

Dressed overall for the Queen Mother's hundredth birthday.

was one of the best meals we had since arriving in Croatia. Towards the end there was a curious noise and soon out of the dark came about 30 young men all dressed in black and white blowing cow horns and beating drums. They marched along the small jetty and we thought they would fall off the end like lemmings. However, back they came and played a curious tune accompanied by the gyrations of the leader. When they stopped the restaurant served them a huge bowl of seafood. It appeared that this was the opening night of the annual festivities at the nearby town of Sali. The horns were used by fishermen in the old days in lieu of radar. The next day we walked over the hill to Sali and back. In the evening there were to be donkey races there so we hired scooters and set off to watch the spectacle. Poor donkeys. It certainly was not a fast race but much fun was had by everyone and possibly even the donkeys.

Back on the mainland at Šibenik we found a fortified river entrance with a narrow channel through which most boats were motoring. We managed to sail past Šibenik up the Krka river to Skradin at one point being buzzed by a seaplane scooping up water to fight a local fire. Skradin marina was full but eventually a small boat left and somehow we wedged ourselves into an impossible place. 'Good skipper' said the sailor so we felt very pleased with ourselves. The village had a run down and unhappy atmosphere about it though the waterfront was bustling. That evening we had a meal ashore and sat with a Croatian family who were very friendly and kept us amused. We learnt that the reason the marina was full was that ACI were holding a festival the next evening.

We were up early to catch the 0800 ferry up to the falls at Skradinski Buk. When we arrived the place was empty and we had the beautiful park almost to ourselves. The falls were spectacular but must be even more so after heavy rain. We visited the water mill which was grinding corn and also banging lengths of wool with a huge wooden mallet to soften them before they were dyed. Paths wound through the trees above the falls, some on a wooden walkway above the running water rather like the Everglades in Florida but without the crocodiles. By the time we got to the bottom there were crowds of people bathing beneath the falls and the whole place was filling up by the minute. In the evening the marina staff prepared a table in the main square with free drink and some nibbles and a local group sang Croatian songs to the delight of the audience who were enthralled. The disco consisted of two competent musicians with guitar and keyboard who played tuneful music without too much bass to vibrate through everything. The church bells suddenly started to ring and we could see two youths banging the clappers by hand and making a most tuneful noise. They must have been exhausted by the time they climbed down the tower. Altogether a most enjoyable evening.

14 August. Had a good radio session with Paddy Carr approaching the Lizard, Jeffrey O'Riordan in the Caledonian Canal and Graham Hutt,

Italy
Slovenia
Trieste
Croatia
Venice
Rijeka
Porec
Krk
Rovinj
Senj
Pula
Cres
Rab
Pag
Lossinj
Olib
Zadar
Preko
Dugi Otok
Pasman
Kornat
Sibenik
Split
Ancona
Solta
Brac
Peljesac
Hvar
Vis
Bisevo
Korcula
Mljet
Lastovo
Dubrovnik
Italy
LECTRON
Palagruza

the editor of the North African Pilot, in Malta. What fun to be able to keep in touch via the airwaves. After more island anchorages it was time to moor in the ACI marina at Trogir with its lovely view across to the old town. Different again with high walled streets, clean and well inhabited. Peter took courage in both hands and waited for a haircut. The first two customers signalled a 1 or 2 and the trimmer soon shaved their heads almost bald. When it came to his turn he held up 10 fingers and after much hilarity lived to tell the tale. The following day found us in Split where we had arranged to leave the boat in the ACI marina for three weeks whilst we returned to the UK and the east coast section of the Rolling Meet.

On our return on 7 September we sailed to Viška Luka on the island of Vis where we anchored away from the town quay. We had great fun checking out the restaurants and found one which was reputed to be in Garibaldi's garden where we sat under palm trees to the sound of music. It was glorious chaos with one poor waiter rushing back and forth until he eventually called up reinforcements on his mobile phone. On arrival one said that they thought winter had come and they had been taken by surprise. The chaos was accompanied by a super meal so all was forgiven.

Next stop was the west side of the island at Komiža which was a real surprise with higgledy houses built of yellow stone all around the harbour, sheltering under the island hills. The harbour was nearly full that night so one would have to arrive early in mid summer.We walked ashore in the evening to the fishing museum in the old Venetian tower a mixture of old and new with a very enthusiastic minder.

Early next morning we set off in flat calm for the Blue Grotto on nearby O. Biševo. We had expected that we would have to jiggle around and take it in turns rather like the Skelligs in SW Ireland but we were in luck as the sea was flat calm and we managed to drop the hook in 14 metres. We entered the cave in the dinghy ducking our heads and thankful that there was no swell. As our eyes got accustomed to the dark we saw a passage ahead. We ventured further in and at the end found an incredible cave with bright blue water lit from the sun via an underwater hole in the rock and reflected upwards. It was a remarkable sight. Leaving in a light northwest wind we sailed gently east along the south coast of Vis watching yachts disappearing into tiny crevices as we picked one for ourselves for a sheltered night.

Entrance to the Blue Grotto.

14 September. Some sea splashed on deck as we sailed toward the island of Lastovo some 20 miles away, and oilies were unearthed for the first time for many weeks. We wound our way into the lovely enclosed harbour of Mali Lago and were on our own but with room for a fleet of boats. Although the bay is now surrounded by houses they were all lived in and there was a pleasant atmosphere. We walked to Ubli past yet another huge man-made cave big enough for a submarine. Indeed this island had only recently been reopened to the public having been a naval base. Ubli was quite the most run down and dreary place we had seen. Next time we will explore some more of the island.

The next few days saw us passing through Lumbada and Korčula marinas. There we compared notes with an English flotilla. Kept in port by bad weather they had just hopped onto a hydrofoil and gone to Dubrovnik for the day and been winetasting on Korčula.

After a night in Polače, we sailed between the wooded shores of Mljet and the barren Pelječac peninsular to the Stonski channel and up to Ston. A fascinating little walled town which was in the throes of being rebuilt after heavy damage in the 1992 war. It was then damaged again by an earthquake. It was here that the advance of the Serbians was stopped. It seemed appropriate as Ston and its neighbour Mali Ston were completely walled-in against ancient aggressors. The holding at Ston was very soft, smelly mud so we went downstream for the night to Kobaš where we were given free berthing at the restaurant jetty in exchange for a meal ashore. It is a family business with one brother doing the mooring, the second manages the restaurant and Mum does the cooking. Our last anchorage and a windy night was at Sudurad.

24th September. We were now in Dubrovnik where we laid up ashore accompanied by four other RCC boats.

It had been a wonderful holiday in a splendid cruising ground where everybody we met was helpful and cheerful. The weather was rarely too hot with cooling winds. A few 'pyjama' parties, to quote Guy Morgan, but otherwise a holiday to remember. We had covered 2205 miles and entered over 70 anchorages.

THE BRIDGE AT KHALKIS

by Bill and Hilary Keatinge

We will not remember Khalkis as peaceful. Easy enough as we came alongside the quay where we found three charter yachts en route to summer base. There is a bridge which spans a narrow gap with busy town traffic constantly crossing. The water level north and south of the bridge is different and the south going stream really rages through, 6–7 knots at springs. For fear of damage to bridge or craft the bridge only opens at slack water and usually in the depths of the night. It is impossible to predict the times of slack water, not even Aristotle could work that out, and today's port police were uncertain whether or when the bridge would open. Indeed the charter yachts had been there since the night before, but as the officials took our money we hoped they would actually allow us through. The cost of passage through is calculated on a very complicated formula which includes tonnage; our Part 1 Registration gives a British tonnage which is more than the actual manufacturer's figure and it cost us £32 which included the 75 per cent weekend surcharge. So we settled down to wait. Suddenly a maelstrom of tide race had us pinned against the quay with all our fenders needed on the rough wall. The wind went round in circles, sometimes pinning us on, sometimes blowing us off. It brought with it all the debris from the quay. The noise and disturbance were enervating. This lasted several hours.

As instructed we contacted the harbour police at 2150. 'Wait a quarter,' was the reply. Then just as we were resigning ourselves to a 0400 start, the south-going boats were told to get going at the double. We cast off only to be told to remain alongside as a ship was coming through. Too late we manoeuvred in the dark. The ship did indeed come through and then we were called to pass through immediately. The port policeman was resplendent in his immaculate white uniform with scrambled egg epaulets and VHF to hand. Saturday night crowds massed to enjoy his show. We roared through with the engine going flat out, but one of our group was left behind and was given two minutes to pass through. They

158

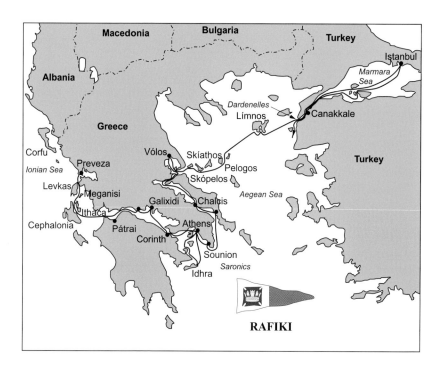

RAFIKI

just made it. We were exhausted as we dropped anchor three miles on at Nea Artaki (new harbour in the making).

Rafiki is an Aphrodite 42 foot ketch cousin of a Najad built in 1987. She was bought in Holland in 1992. The Keatinge's cruise started in Western Greece and ended near Antalya. They covered 2200 miles and visited 90 new harbours and anchorages.

A MENTAL MOUNTAIN

by David Mitchell

This is the cruise which won the Challenge Cup and the Goldsmith Exploration Award.

On 21st June 1999, Ondarina left Cairns, Australia, on a single-handed passage to Mexico via the outer rim of the North Pacific. This is an edited extract from 'A Bit of a Loop', the log of the 13,515 mile journey to San Francisco, California by way of the Solomon Islands, Papua New Guinea, the Philippines, Hong Kong, Japan and Canada.

I expected the passage from Hong Kong to Alaska to be a tough physical battle and was unprepared for the mental strain that frustration with the lack of progress, fog and fear would have on me.

Frustration

My first attempt to leave on 18 May ended with my scuttling back to avoid a typhoon and tropical depression. On 26 May, nearly four weeks after my planned departure date, the wind went into the southeast and I left. Three days later, *Ondarina* was tacking up the south coast of Taiwan on a flat sea and at a current assisted six knots. I could see matchstick people walking along the shore and what looked like a nuclear power station – with two reactors. The wind came and went but continued to head me. I motored whenever the speed fell below two knots as I was paranoid about being hit by a typhoon, which was a very real possibility and which was very worrying. On 3 June I effectively ran out of diesel, leaving forty litres for battery charging and emergency manoeuvring. The sun shone, I had plenty of books and there was the occasional low pass from a fighter for company. I was about two hundred miles east of Okinawa with six hundred miles to my corner off Honshu.

Low pressures that spin out of China, like clay pigeons at a team shoot, dominate the weather. I had great plans to use the excellent weather faxes from Tokyo and to duck and weave out of their way. But some systems travel at twenty-five knots whereas *Ondarina* was struggling to make four knots.

Knockdowns

On 6 June, the shank on the top swivel of the Profurl jib gear sheared and the sail came down, leaving the halyard at the masthead. But 'No worries' I thought as *Ondarina* carries twin jibs so I had a ready spare. Not for long, though. The gale struck on the night of 8 June. I handed the sails and lay ahull. She acted like the real lady she is, curtsying to the waves, but at 0630 a breaking wave caught her and over she went dipping her mast in the water. Fifteen minutes later, Neptune gave us his second barrel and over we went again. 'One more time and we'd better get moving', I thought.

Rigging problems

The explosive 'bang' of the bolts shearing woke me and I shot up the companionway not knowing what to expect. I found the jib flogging away to leeward, apparently anchored to the sheet deck-lead. I instinctively embraced the sail – on reflection, probably a nervous reflex. 'What the hell are you doing back here?' I wanted to know. I could feel the furling foil in the folds of the sailcloth. At the base was the furling drum. A quick trip to the bows and it was all too obvious what had been blown away and with it my last hope of making Alaska.

'What now?' I asked with foreboding and not a little shock. I've never lost a forestay. The first job was to secure the jib, which continued to flog away. The second was to plot a course to the nearest down wind port. The nearest port was Kagoshima on Kyushu Island, about 360 miles but into the Kiro current, and then a worrying 60 miles northeast leg into any northeast wind. 'Still,' I thought, 'we can worry about that when we get there.'

Masthead visit

We ran through the night in a strengthening northeast wind. I came on deck at first light to find some stitching in the main had gone, so down it came leaving *Ondarina* charging along at 4.5 knots through the fog and rain for two days under the trysail. At last, the wind died – I thought I would never want that – and I was able to climb the masthead to retrieve the broken halyard and secure the jib, which was starting to show signs of chafe where it rubbed against the cross trees. This was my first climb to the masthead under way and I cannot pretend that I looked forward to the task. Before setting off, I looked up and concentrated on the masthead. 'That's where you're going,' I said, hyping myself up. But a passing wave dumped me on the deck. 'Whoops, not a good start,' I laughed.

With a prayer to my guardian angel I set off and, after two trips up the mast, was mighty pleased to be back on the deck with 'a job well done' feel. Next task was the mainsail and by 1600 I had finished the hand stitching and it was ready for raising. Now, we could sail in any direction, the only problem was that we remained becalmed. I had another look at the chart and decided we had enough fuel to make for Kochi on the south side of Shikoku Island – 109 miles, course 324 degrees. I had no charts, but *Lonely Planet* has a useful street map and mentions 'ferries'

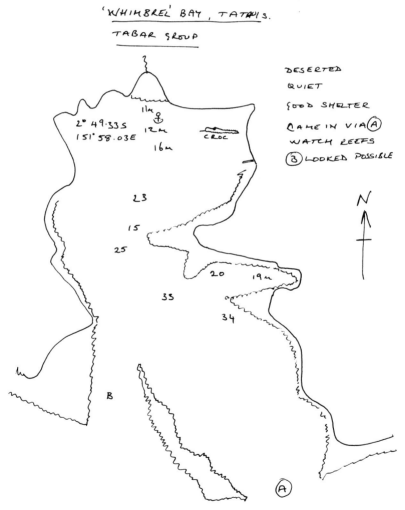

An example of David's Pilotage Information.

and 'port' which sounded encouraging. The road bridge shown crossing the river mouth was a dampener, but 'it must be high enough for the ferries,' I prayed - or was I begging? I started the engine and the next day motored under the soaring road bridge into the port looking for somewhere to park. Round the first bend and there to starboard lay a line of yachts. 'A marina!' What a relief!

Japanese hospitality

This was my first time in Japan and my first experience of their amazing generosity to visitors. I was in Kochi for a week.

I motored out on 21 June escorted by Horatio-San, in his 32ft, fast, blue hulled, sail boat, and some port office staff in their 40ft harbour launch. The sun shone and the southwest wind at 8 knots filled the spinnaker and pushed *Ondarina* along – on course for once. I used the Yanmar engine, whilst the fuel lasted, anxious to push on above 45 degrees north and 160 degrees east, where we should be out of the typhoon belt.

Avoiding action

I kept about 5 miles off the southern points on Shikoku and Honshu to avoid the internal coastal shipping and the fishing fleets further out. Twice I had to alter course to avoid being run down, in daylight. The vessel *Jin Hang* was so close that I could look through the open doors of the apparently deserted bridge.

Safety took a turn for the worse when the wind backed from southeast to east forcing *Ondarina* to tack through the shipping. By now it was a pitch-black night with a calm sea and we were making about four knots. The shipping travelled like the London buses on route 73; they came in a pack, and then there would be an empty pause, followed by another pack. I counted fifteen vessels around us at one moment. I weaved through them flashing my 500,000-candle torch on the sails. There was give and take on both sides and we emerged from the shipping lane unscathed.

First fog

Fog off Honshu did not help as I tried to pass through the Shima chain of volcanic islands that run south from Sagami-wan Bay. Currents between the islands run up to 4.5 knots. At 0815, three days out and by good fortune, we arrived at slack water and the ebb would carry us through. Four miles off, the islands of Nii and Udone appeared out of the fog. Grey-black cliffs, topped with treeless dark green, dropped shear into the surging waves. Fog swirled down gullies from the hidden hilltops. The scene looked like a backdrop for *The Tempest* rather than a glorious gateway into the North Pacific.

What a relief it was to alter course to 052°M and I felt we were off on the crossing, at last. The great circle route would take us in a parabolic arc up to the Aleutian Islands before appearing to drop down to Vancouver

Island 4112 miles to the east on a magnetic bearing of 110 degrees. (By then, the magnetic variation would be up to 22 degrees east).

More rigging problems

On the basis that something major breaks every two weeks on a passage, I was expecting quite a few breakages but had no idea where or when. I had done my best to prepare *Ondarina* and now it was a question of watching and waiting. I did not have long to wait.

21 June started gloriously with my first sighting of whales. They passed about fifty metres off the starboard beam, perhaps ten metres long, swimming slowly towards the Japanese whaling grounds, blowing as they went. I tried to tell them that swimming in that direction was not a smart move, but they did not listen.

At 1430, I noticed that one of the starboard shrouds had stranded at the top. To my horror, I found a port shroud had stranded also at the top with three, possibly four, snapped wires. This was far more serious. Thoughts raced through my mind.

'The rig's collapsing! You are going to lose the mast! It's over 3,800 miles to Canada! You'll never make it!'

I dropped the main and ran all unused halyards to the toe-rail on the outer edge of the deck to help take the strain. Then I went below to see the distance to the nearest port on Honshu. It was 146 miles due west. This was tempting, but there was a gale warning on the noon fax. I had what daughter Rebecca calls 'the cup that cures' (tea) and decided to sail on and think the problem through during the night.

Masthead revisited

0400 the next morning found me standing in the companionway with a clear plan. The bosun's chair was supported by a line round my neck, all necessary cordage – including pieces of serving twine – tied to the chair and tools stuffed into pockets. By 0900 I had finished. Everything had taken five hours and involved climbing the mast four times. My guardian angel looked down, calming the sea and guiding my hands. The log entry reads:

'I do not think there is anything else I can do. 3 lines to stbd [starboard], 4 to port. Main down [I was anticipating the gale], jib boomed out, trysail. Wind SxE. Course 055 at 4.5 knots – slow but safe, hopefully. 3,750tg [to go]. Celebrated with pancakes.'

Typhoons

The weather fax on 4 July showed typhoon Kirogi formed off the Philippines. The predicted wind at the centre was 65–75 knots (suggesting gusts of 130 knots and more) and the direction of travel was up the east side of Honshu. For the moment it was stationary but so was I. Our noon-to-noon run was a meagre 26 miles. The fax on the 5th showed a

tropical storm, Kai-Tak, on the west side of the Philippines and predicted to track behind Kirogi. I could do nothing but sweat and wait for a
better wind. I felt I was in one of those childhood dreams when you try to
run away from an unseen threat but your feet are glued to the ground.
But this was no dream; it was all very real. I knew exactly where the
threat was coming from.

At last, a favourable wind came in from the southeast and we fared
better with daily runs of 95, 129 and 141. We scuttled northeast and by
6 July our noon position was 46°N and 159°E. By now, Kai-Tak was a
full typhoon, but heading for Korea, and Kirogi, with winds of 80 knots,
was chasing us at 27 knots. But we were safe, as the cold water would kill
the typhoon (a typhoon lives on warm, moist air). That is not to say that
the strong winds disappear and there was no avoiding the predicted gale,
which covered a front of about eight hundred miles. It struck the next
night but this time we kept sailing.

'Stormy night. Trysail and reefed jib. O. going well @ 6–7 knots' reads
the log.'

The furling drum on the Profurl started to pull out of its casing on the
9th. My first thought was that the drum would collapse leaving me with
no means to reef and we still had 2592 miles to go. After a 'cup that
cures' I felt better. The furling gear continued to work but I was nervous
every time I reefed, dreading the day it jammed, fully open. It was going
to, and with over 1000 miles to go.

Debilitating cloak

I expected fog but not days on end when we lay shrouded in its damp,
dripping, debilitating cloak. What I did not expect was the psychological
impact that the weather would have on me. The fog created a sensory
deprivation that I was just not ready for. My world shrunk to five hundred metres, perhaps more, perhaps less but it was impossible to tell and
it really did not matter. All I could see was a gun-mettle sea merging,
somewhere, with the grey fog. It was like looking at a blank television
screen from the inside without the excitement of the white dot.

Sometimes I would hear the thump-thump of a vessel and once the
mournful blast of a foghorn every two minutes. A white, ocean-going
fishing boat appeared out of the fog running on a parallel course to
Ondarina until, after twenty minutes, another fog bank swallowed her
and we were on our own again.

Halfway across, I raised my glass and toasted the sea; it was symptom-
atic of the weather that Ondarina lay becalmed, in fog. Neptune must
have been out, or chose not to hear, as little changed.

Radio link

Every night, I would try to speak to Robbie (VK4YB) in Queensland,
Australia and give my position report, which he would e-mail to

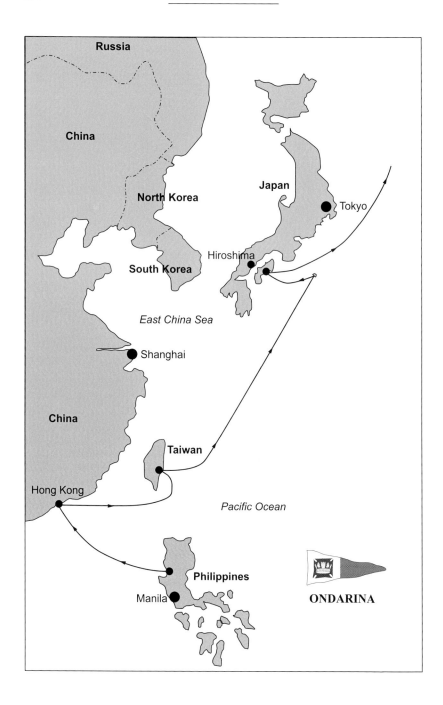

ONDARINA

Rebecca, and he would pass on any message that he had received. This was a tremendous boost to my moral. Nights that I failed to make contact were bad ones. At 146°E I lost touch with Robbie and made contact with Peter Thomas (VE7PT) on Vancouver Island. I first spoke to Peter in May 1998 on my way to the Marquesas. Peter had tracked me from Hong Kong as the three principal, private, Pacific, net controllers – Robbie in Australia, Tony (ZL1ATE) in New Zealand and Peter – speak to each other most days and pass on position reports for yachts heading into each other's area. Messages are relayed, as well. These shore-based controllers do a wonderful, selfless job for us yachties. Thank you.

Date line

At last we crossed the International Date Line, which was a geographical milestone. My memory is of the wind picking up, and whilst there were times of trysail and heavily reefed jib, the log shows that this was not always the case. In one five-day period, starting on 16 July, we covered a meagre 227 miles at an average speed of less than two knots.

Recognising fear

With 1051 miles to Vancouver Island, the furling jib finally jammed fully open. Normally, this would not be too dramatic as *Ondarina* can carry her 80sq.m (800sq.ft) jib in 25 knots of wind. But I had no wish to have anywhere near that wind strength with the rigging in its parlous state. Until the sea calmed down, there was no chance of my going aloft and so I had to sit, wait and pray for a calm. It was then, for the first time, I admitted what had been worrying me for so long and which I chose to bury under my 'stiff upper lip'. I was frightened. I've been frightened before, but, on reflection, these were passing moments. On this passage, I was frightened for days on end. Having admitted the fact, I felt so much better, and I still do. But, I had to look at the full jib for three days until the sea was smooth enough for me to climb to the masthead and sort out the problem.

Beautiful land

The wind had some cards to play and sent an easterly, so that, with fifty-eight miles to the entrance to the Juan Fuca Straight, *Ondarina* was beating to windward. A brief moment of joy was my second whale sighting. The whale blew so close that I smelt its fetid breath and altered course to avoid it. Needless to say, we were in fog again. The view of land as an elongated, black splodge on the yellow LCD radar screen, dampened the excitement of my first seeing Vancouver Island, at eight miles. The tide sluices in and out of the straight but, by good fortune, we hit the entrance as the tide started to flood and were carried forward. Then life took on a rosy picture.

'And not before time,' I told my guardian angel, Sarah.

The wind filled in from the west and we ran on out of the fog, at last, and into early morning, warming sunshine. Green, tree-covered hills, dotted with very English-sea-side houses appeared to port. Trees at last. Then a car and people out fishing in boats of all shapes and sizes. I sailed past wanting to yell, 'I've come from Japan,' but my English reserve held me in check. We, on the Canadian side of the straight, were in the sun. To starboard, in US water, the fog persisted and large ships would appear and disappear as they steamed past in the narrow shipping lane. Then, as I headed north around the southeast tip of the island, the snow capped peaks of the Olympic Mountains rose over the top of the fog and flashed in the sunshine.

'Now that,' I told Sarah, 'is a magic moment.'

Victoria is the first port of entry, and a fine town, but I was aiming for Sidney, twenty-three miles up the coast where there are repair yards. It is an entry port too. So I sailed past the high-rise blocks, the ferry terminals, the landing float planes, the immaculate looking golf course and yet more manicured sea-side-English gardens; squeezing between islands and their off lying, kelp-covered rocks through gaps which, to my unaccustomed eyes, appeared alarmingly narrow.

In the late afternoon, *Ondarina* stopped moving, at last, as I made her fast to the reporting dock in Port Sidney marina. From the Customs free telephone on the dock, I spoke to agent 15244-Anna, who cleared me into Canada. She sounded as enthusiastic about our trip as I did about my arrival. *Ondarina*, not to be left out of the number's game, was awarded 02181689 as her 'report number'. There was no stamping of passports, no inspection. What could have been easier? I rang Rebecca in Vancouver, went ashore for two showers – one was not long enough – then went out for supper and drank far too much wine but managed to find *Ondarina* where I collapsed into my rock steady bunk.

'Was not the arrival just too fantastic?' I asked. But there was no reply, just snores.

So ended the most testing crossing to date. I learnt so much: about myself, about the debilitating affects of the cold and fog, about *Ondarina*, about my guardian angel, Sarah, about the joy of living and the joy of arriving. All will come in handy when I return, as I will, to explore Japan, Korea, the Aleutian Islands, Alaska and British Columbia in the next three to five years. Before then, no doubt there will be more mental mountains but, I hope, none so high.

Ondarina is an Ohlson 35, GRP sloop, registered in 1972. David left England in 1996 on a single-handed circumnavigation that, he admits, has turned into a global wander. After Mexico, his plan is to complete the loop back to the Marquesas and be in New Zealand for Christmas 2001.

JESTER'S MILLENNIAL CRUISE

by Mike Richey

I have sometimes wondered, as I sail merrily into my dotage, whether the trouble is ultimately going to be not being able to hoist the sail, or just losing the thread, forgetting where one is going, and why. For the moment I will leave it at that but it does seem to me, as the years roll by, that it is now the mission that tends to be questioned rather than one's ability to fulfil it. That at any rate seems to have been one element in *Jester's* somewhat abortive single-handed millennial transatlantic race last summer.

In one form or another (for the original vessel, of which the present incumbent is a replica, was lost at sea in 1988) *Jester* has participated in every single-handed transatlantic race since the first in 1960. Blondie Hasler who originated the race also of course conceived the incomparably ergonomic *Jester* in which he sailed the first two races. The boat, basically a Folkboat, is 25ft on the waterline but the lower limit for the race was this year raised to 30ft. However, because of her long association with the race, the Royal Western Yacht Club of England invited the Jester Trust to enter the boat as a guest entry. It was understood that I would once again be skipper and, as was widely reported in the yachting press, would celebrate (or at least spend) my 83rd birthday in the course of the race. All of which added to the gaiety of nations and led to a number of unscheduled events such as a standing ovation at the skipper's meeting and boat-loads of spectators chanting Happy Birthday at the start.

Jester had never been sponsored but the expense of fitting a boat out for the transatlantic race is nowadays considerable and on this occasion somewhat more than funds would bear. Blondie after the war had become acutely aware of the damage to the environment from industrial methods of production and indeed as a way of life he went back to the land himself on his farm in Scotland. In these circumstances some of us felt it would not be inappropriate for an organisation such as Greenpeace to sponsor the boat and profit from the publicity. As a charity, Greenpeace is more accustomed to receiving than making donations but in the spirit intended by the trustees the supermarket chain Iceland, long a supporter of Greenpeace, undertook to pay all *Jester*'s expenses for the race on Greenpeace's behalf. They proved to be the most understanding and least demanding of sponsors.

In 1997 I sailed *Jester* back to England from Newport, Rhode Island and, although I have sailed the boat every year since, that was my last ocean crossing. But the ocean makes its own demands and there is no way of telling, short of experiment, whether another ocean passage would be tempting fate. In the event such problems as revealed themselves proved to be relatively minor. Sleep was perhaps something of an issue because one needs more of it; but in practice I found no difficulty in catnapping as hitherto when the occasion called for it. Quite extraneously, it interested me that the phenomenon which I (like so many single handers) have experienced over the years of waking spontaneously in the ocean to find a ship in the offing, occasionally on a collision course, was still in operation. During the passage on several occasions I found myself turning out in the early hours for no apparent reason to see, some distance off, a ship's lights. (That there may have been occasions when I did not turn out is of course equally tenable). I have always connected the phenomenon with the presence of people (unlike Bill King who put it down to the neutrino). Before the race I discussed the matter with Dr Claudio Stampi of the Chronobiology Research Institute in America who had distributed 'actiwatches' to monitor sleep and boat movement to some of the competitors. He was acquainted with the phenomenon and not surprised that I connected it with the presence of people. Wild animals, he told me (if I quote him correctly), are usually aware of the presence of others of their species.

With age one's agility inevitably declines but within the confined space of *Jester* I have found this of little consequence. Occasionally of course deck work will be called for, usually to perform some task that will not wait. When this happens in anything like heavy weather I have found that concentrating on the task in hand rather than on the chances of falling overboard puts me in the right frame of mind to which the body, presumably more relaxed, responds. The main physical deterioration seems to have been in my night vision which meant using the brightest of lights for chart work, often (until I bought a head-lamp in the Azores) a torch in the mouth. The sextant (now in any case obsolescent because of GPS) I found of limited use for the sun and moon and of no use for the stars. On deck too peripheral vision made scanning the horizon something of a formality. So much for old age.

Jester can in fact very largely be handled blindfold. On the night of 7 June, for example, four days after the start, we were hit by a vicious squall and I chose, for simplicity and comfort rather than safety, to heave the boat to. It was pitch dark with driving rain and none of the torches seemed up to the occasion. Facing the rope-box aft, I was able in a few minutes to reef the sail down to a single panel peaked up by the hauling parrel. With the whipstaff to weather, the boat would now remain virtually still in the water, fore-reaching a little and of course settling gently to leeward. I was soon able to turn in again and from my bunk monitor, by the sounds and movement, just what was happening on deck.

In 1968, my first solo race, I had attempted the trade wind route which Captain Beecher, an officer in the Admiralty Hydrographic Service, who wrote an admirable treatise on the North Atlantic in the closing years of the last century, deemed preferable to any other. 'If the time occupied in the passage might appear greater in consequence of the distance,' he wrote, 'it is really less as to the speed with which a vessel with sail from port to port'. Following his advice I arrived a predictable last (although more than half the fleet did not arrive at all) and was left wondering whether increasing the nominal distance from 3000 to 5000 miles could

Jester.

ever, even with an unweatherly boat like *Jester*, be justified by the increase
in speed from fair winds and a favourable current. I concluded that it
might for, although the passage took 57 days, we averaged 93 miles a day
in spite of agonizingly prolonged calms southwest of Bermuda. I have
since then taken longer than that by more conventional routes. Later in
correspondence Blondie doubted whether there would be more than one
year in five in which Jester would actually make a faster passage by the
southern route than any other. He was probably right but at the back of
my mind has always been the thought that with an unweatherly boat of
such modest dimensions the current might on occasions be the decisive
factor. This race seemed a suitable occasion to go south again and probably the last opportunity too. I discussed the odds with Robin Knox-
Johnston and on the morning of the start he brought me the noon positions of the Sail Training Fleet on its way from Cadiz to Bermuda, from
which I could interpolate the latitude of the Trades. The possibilities
looked encouraging, more particularly for the modified trade wind route
suggested by Tabarly which cuts the nominal distance down to some
4200 miles. Whatever the plan it is of course axiomatic that the most
constant feature of both winds and ocean currents in any part of the
world at any time of the year is their variability so that the interpretation
of the pilot chart to derive a route for a particular occasion is as arcane a
business as reading a horoscope.

Events from 15 June onwards bear all the marks of what the scientists
call chaos theory. Pre-heating with meths the burners on the paraffin
cooker, the boat took a lurch which spilt the meths and started a fairly
familiar blaze, generally of no consequence since it can be put out with
water. However, now the heat was such that the plastic pressure gauge
on the fuel tank melted, releasing a jet of lighted paraffin. I was able to
put the fire out but was from then on, until I could mend the gauge,
reduced to a diet of uncooked food. After a day or so I contrived to patch
the pipe up with heavy duty sail tape which seemed to work, but whether
securely enough to last the passage seemed doubtful. Somebody seemed
to be telling me something, for later that day I stepped into the control
hatch from aft and trod on and broke the blow torch, the only alternative
way of pre-heating the stove to meths. I measured the amount of meths
left and estimated it would last about ten days. I first wondered vaguely
whether I could stick to a southerly route by going to Porto Santo, but
the island was too far east, and anyway an improbable place to repair the
stove. I decided to divert to Punta Delgada in the Azores, then some 470
miles to windward. This effectively put paid to the idea of a trade wind
passage, and probably of a fast passage of any kind.

On 23 June a gentle northerly set in speeding us on our way. Life
seemed as pleasant as it could be. Towards noon a leviathan, a Fin whale
I think, perhaps twice the length of Jester, surfaced alongside seemingly
but a boat-hook's length away. The monster kept pace with us for about

20 minutes, very slowing diving with a rolling movement like a wheel, eyeing us (benignly I thought) each time its head surfaced. Years ago in *Jester* off the Grand Banks I had been charged by a killer whale and have since then preferred to keep these creatures at a respectful distance. But this encounter seemed so entirely peaceable that I wondered vaguely whether the fact that whaling has so long been abandoned in this part of the world could have had anything to do with it.

On the night of 26 June the lights of S.Miguel were visible and I made for Ponta do Arnel keeping south of the island. A spasmodic wind shadow and an upwelling of sorts that made the boat hobby-horse on one tack slowed things up and it took almost two days to beat up the short stretch of coast to Punta Delgada. I was somewhat fearful of getting swept south by the Azores current and so far as possible short-tacked inshore trying to get some rest on the offshore legs. This was a losing game and at one stage I must have passed clean out for I was awakened in complete darkness by what for some reason I took to be French voices all around. They were fishermen trying to alert me to the danger of running ashore, for I was almost within spitting distance of it. I had no idea where I was nor for how long I had been asleep, but there was enough wind to claw off. It was sheer exhaustion and I imagine at some stage the wind must have shifted. My alarm which might have saved the day seemed to have been on the blink. Later that day we reached our destination, the marina at Punta Delgada.

The chances of repairing the stove locally seemed dubious, although no doubt some lash-up might have been devised. But by great good fortune the skipper of an English yacht in the marina took an interest in my plight and was able to transfer the fuel gauge from his heater (which he hoped not to use for a year or so) to *Jester*'s stove. Thus, in principle, the problem had been solved and *Jester* could continue her passage westward. There had been no infringement of the rules and the boat was still in the race. But my own perception of the situation had changed considerably. Newport lay some 40 days or so away and by the time we got there the race (of which *Jester* was now an appendage) would long have been formally over. Of greater concern to me personally was that the boat would have to stay in Newport for the winter and this could be the last time I would sail her. Clearly such a time had to come but the thought that it already had caused me great angst. It was like the shoemaker and his last and I felt unprepared for it. However, there was little to be said for the only two viable alternatives that presented themselves. Sailing back to England with the boat in full repair seemed a feeble end to the adventure, and laying the boat up in the Azores in the height of summer could only be a counsel of despair. Thus, on 7 July, having waited an extra day to celebrate my birthday with friends ashore, *Jester* headed west again, before a fine northeasterly breeze that was to last for almost two weeks.

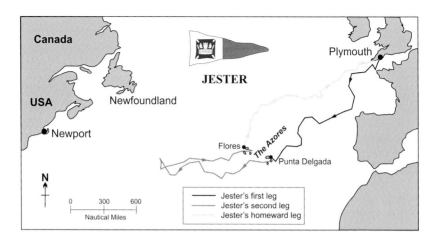

The ideal situation on what is generally called the intermediate route across the Atlantic, which approximates to the old low-power steamer route, is to keep well north of the Azores archipelago and reach something like 64°W before coming up to cross the Gulf Stream more or less at right angles. Starting from the islands such a course was not open to us but I hoped to keep clear of the worst of the easterly set by going even further south, down to something like 35°N rather than the more usual 38°. In the event, long before we reached anything like 60°W, the North Atlantic drift made itself felt and my efforts to find a more amicable regime further south were fruitless. The wind backed remorselessly and after several attempts to break out of the pattern on either tack, I decided to take stock once more. We were now about equidistant from Newport and Punta Delgada but so far as I could see only making up towards Nova Scotia would get us nearer America. It would be a long haul. Further, it was getting late in the year to arrive on the East Coast and would soon be getting late to leave the Azores for England if the September gales were to be avoided. On 24 July at about noon in about 36.5°N, 47.5°W I turned the boat around and headed downwind for S.Miguel. I had no regrets at the time but I soon became troubled about whether I was doing the right thing, whether I was not simply accepting failure. This was, I reflected, a consideration that would not have bothered me in my own boat.

I had set a course that made a generous allowance for the nominally south setting Azores current so prominently displayed nowadays on the Admiralty chart. I had no wish to be swept south of S.Miguel, perhaps unable to regain it. However, I was soon able to establish that we were in fact being set strongly to the west of north presumably in a large eddy as is known to occur from time to time. The sensible thing seemed to be to make for Flores which although further away from Plymouth was better placed to avoid being set into Biscay. At dawn on the 5th we lay off the tiny harbour of Lajes and later entered somewhat gingerly because I could see the wind would baffle inside the breakwater, as indeed it did. An alert American yachtsman in his skiff saw the situation and gave us help getting alongside the stone wharf where we lay, as is the custom, well off with plenty of scope. *Asgard II*, the Irish sail training vessel, came in during our stay and some of its young crew were able to give me a hand storing ship. On 9 August we set sail for Plymouth. Freed from the constraints of a race and from time to time struck by the sheer magnificence of the ocean I spent some time reflecting on what it was that attracted me to a life of often excruciating discomfort in this particular craft in an oceanic environment. I could find no answer, but I was sure I would die the happier for it.

In the early hours of 21 August we were struck by a squall that hit like a thunderbolt. It was the introduction to a period of strong winds that lasted the best part of three days, most of which we spent hove to, occasionally with the hurricane hatch in. We seemed chained to the spot and at one stage I tried running before the gale but did not like the feel of it. On the third day the glass started to rise and in due course the wind moderated. Remembering the prelude to a roll-over many years before when the wind dropped after a storm leaving uncontrollable seas, I hesitated a while before setting sail. Soon we were on course for the Channel and a week later the familiar landmarks appeared, the Bishop standing proud and then the Lizard, the southernmost point of England and historic Channel landfall. There was a gale warning in force and I dreaded the thought of a further period hove-to or wasting time seeking shelter. With a following wind and as much sail as seemed prudent we ran all night, weaving our way through the fishing fleet and other hazards, and just made Plymouth Sound before the gale. Shortly after noon on 1 September *Jester* took up the berth in Mayflower Marina she had left three months and incalculable nautical miles before.

Jester is a modified Scandinavian Folkboat, 25ft over-all, designed by H. G. (Blondie) Hasler with superstructure that gives full enclosure so that the boat can be handled and all deckwork carried out from a central control hatch; a rotatable canvas dodger enables the crew to keep a lookout with his face in the open but protected from rain and spray. The boat is steered manually by means of a vertical whipstaff connected to a quadrant on the rudder head. The sail is a fully battened Chinese lug of 243sq.ft slung on an unstayed hollow spruce mast. There is no engine.

The original boat, built by Harry Feltham in Portsmouth in 1953, was acquired by Michael Richey in 1964 and lost at sea in the course of the 1988 transatlantic race. A replica, but cold moulded instead of planked (construction by Colin Mudie), was built in 1992 for the Jester Trust by the Aldeburgh Boat Company.

CRUISING THE ISLES

by Mary Thornhill

These are the cruises for which the Sea Laughter Trophy was awarded.

This Summer was a learning experience for me and several crews. My season began in Greece in April and finished in Scotland in mid September, unfortunately with a large gap in between.

The plan was to sail *Sai See* in the West of Scotland for four weeks with me as skipper, four untrained crews and Daniel Max as first mate. For this undertaking I thought I needed some practice on someone else's boat and Daniel needed to be trained to be my second in command. At Easter we chartered a yacht for a week in Greece to give Daniel a chance to sort out which rope does what and to give my skippering skills some practice.

The week was thoroughly successful and served its purpose well. We had a lovely cruise on an Oceanis 311, *Kastros*, with not too much heat, starting near Athens and sailing south around the islands Aigina, Poros and Hydra and back to Athens. We did have the odd nightmare on the way such as the unfamiliar mooring habits of the Mediterranean. I am a North British waters sailor and am used to a boat which is difficult to manoeuvre under engine, so the idea of having to anchor and then reverse into a berth terrified me. However it was not as difficult as it seemed and by the end of the week we were fairly good.

The other problem was the ferries that were continuously buzzing around the islands, especially the Flying Dolphins (Hydrofoils), or as we nicknamed them 'wasps'. After being very nearly run down by one in the fog we decided they were definitely foe not friend.

Otherwise the cruise went on without serious problems, and *Kastros* was very easy to sail with just the two of us. The islands that we visited were enchanting, especially Hydra where the donkeys kept us amused for hours. It is an island without cars and the only form of transport is very old and weary ponies and donkeys. After watching these poor unfortunate animals carrying enormous loads off the ferry we learnt it is possible for a donkey to be loaded up with a huge air conditioning unit, but the poor thing is unable to manage two eight foot palm trees which had to be sent back to the mainland.

We were extremely lazy about cooking and ate out every night except one. The food was excellent although the menus were mostly very similar and sometimes fairly limited. We were also shocked about the price of fish in restaurants. I expected this to be the cruise that I learnt to like fish, but we could never afford it, which I found surprising considering we were always in fishing villages.

At the end of the week we both felt much more confident about sailing *Sai See* in August and Daniel had become a competent first mate. We were extremely sad that the holiday had come to an end and I hope we will come back to the same part of the world with more people very soon. The contrast between the tourism and the complete remoteness of the Greek Islands was wonderful and I would definitely like to explore further. We found it very satisfying to have such a great cruise in a new area of the world.

Then in August I had the challenge of sailing *Sai See* through the Caledonian Canal and around the west coast of Scotland for four weeks. After an excellent cruise with my parents round the Shetland and Orkney Isles they left me in Inverness with three new crew members, Clare, Olly and Gavin. We had just under a week to go through the canal and fresh water locks and get to Fort William to pick up our next crew; plenty of time. The first night away we anchored in Loch Ness just below Urquhart Castle with our stern made fast to the shore, which reminded me strongly of Greece! It is a very strange feeling to sit on a yacht in the middle of Scotland, it was absolutely enchanting. When visiting the castle, Clare and I were appalled to find that we were rapidly turning into our parents, reading all the signs and we actually bought a book about the castle's history.

The depth of Loch Ness lulls you into a false sense of security. We managed to go aground briefly when tacking too close to the shore, but we are pretending it was just Nessy coming to inspect us. The weather in the canal was very temperamental and we spent our entire time getting in and out of our oilskins. The crew soon learnt it was amusing to watch me getting soaking wet from the safety of the sprayhood.

Going through the canal was definitely a worthwhile experience and is extremely beautiful. We had a great time with a mixture of sailing and scrambling up cliffs holding onto heather. There was plenty of wind so the only complaint was the number of locks which got tricky with a hangover.

Gavin and Olly left in Corpach, the Fort William end of the canal, and Clare and I were joined by Tim and Daniel. It was now time to find out whether Daniel remembered anything from Greece. After a nightmare day restocking and cleaning we headed off down Loch Linnhe for the Isle of Mull. There was absolutely no wind, but we made it to Loch

Claire Nicol and Mary Thornhill.

Spelve for Tim and Daniel's first night on board. We then had a great cruise up through the Sound of Mull, out to Muck, Rhum and Eigg before returning to Tobermory.

The week was definitely the wildlife cruise. Tim was excited about everything from seagulls to dolphins, which was brilliant, but he was not going to be happy unless he saw a whale. This wish definitely looked as if it was not going to come true until the last sail of the week. Drifting between Ardnamurchan Point and Tobermory under spinaker and mizzen staysail, I suddenly noticed a minke whale on our starboard bow. Everyone began jumping around like mad things while I tried to keep the spinnaker filled. We had heard somewhere that whales liked loud bass so we turned up the Portishead album on the CD player. This rumour indeed appears to be true as the whale stayed with us for over an hour. After this amazing experience we decided to crack open our last bottle of champagne while drifting slowly into Tobermory as the sun set.

Tim and Clare left us here and Daniel and I restocked the boat and mended leaking pipes while waiting for the next crew, Sarah and Ben. We had four crew changes in all, the logistics of which were a nightmare. They all seemed to arrive roughly on time although we had one person miss a boat connection and two people miss train connections!

The plan for the following week was to cruise down the islands west of Mull. There was not a lot of wind all week, but this meant that we were able to anchor and land at more interesting places than is usually possible. It was ideal as Ben had only ever sailed dinghies and Sarah was a complete novice. On the second day we were able to stop at Staffa for lunch and explore Fingal's Cave, which is one of the most remarkable places I have ever been to. We took the dinghy into the cave, which made some of the crew extremely nervous. After sitting in the cockpit watching the huge crowd that managed to squeeze onto each tripper boat, we decided to look for somewhere more secluded. We found our way into Cragaig Bay on Ulva for the night. Another boat arrived in the anchorage after dark, which I was disappointed about as I thought I had finally found an anchorage to ourselves.

There was a gale warning, so after exploring Iona Cathedral and Tinker's Hole we set off for the safety of Puilladobhrain to sit it out. After a night of worrying whether the anchor was going to drag we had yet another day when there was almost no wind.

We had managed almost to run out of water, so had to fill up the next day. Loch Feochan was the closest place, and after we had negotiated the tricky and very shallow entrance we made fast alongside the small pontoon with not much water under our keel. There is a water hose which comes right down to the pontoon, so filling up is easier there than at a lot of places on the West Coast.

The following day light winds were forecast, but after lunch it blew up to over 30 knots. This was certainly unexpected and was not even on the evening forecast. The strong winds could not have been better timed as it was Sarah and Ben's last sail and we were finally able to show them what sailing is really like.

They left us the next day in Kerrera and Daniel and I waited for our final crew to arrive. Olly was coming back for another week of fun and was being joined by another friend Pete.

The forecast was much more threatening for our last week. We headed to Loch Tarbert, Jura, and anchored in the first narrows where we found the Lindsays on *Corryvrechan*. They advised us to be in a safe place by Thursday night and taking this into account we headed for the shelter of Loch Sween. Tayvallich was our first port of call and was far from my favourite place by the time we left. There are so many moorings that it is impossible to anchor with enough chain for strong winds.

At 0500 in the morning the anchor dragged. We saw 34 knots of wind register on the wind machine and thought that this maybe was not the place to be. After trying to anchor again several times, we decided it would be a better idea to go round to the Fairy Isles. As we rounded the corner the wind dropped from 30 knots to 10 knots which was both bizarre and very welcome. Later on that day we had an excellent sail and returned to the Fairy Isles in the evening.

We decided to head to Ardfern a day early as the forecast was still pretty threatening. Tacking out of Loch Sween with the wind funnelling up against us took a great deal longer than we expected and we ended up arriving at Ardfern in the dark which was certainly an interesting experience. The unattractive forecast never materialised the next day so we went out for a day sail before returning for a final celebration at the Galley of Lorne, the extremely welcoming local restaurant and pub.

WALTER SCOTT'S ROVING COMMISSION

by Bruce Weir

The passage of time has not been kind to the literary reputation of Sir Walter Scott. While he was living, there were no reservations about his genius. His poems and his novels were best sellers both in Europe and America and no library of a nineteenth or early twentieth century house was complete without a handsomely bound set of his works. His influence on the development of the novel is unquestioned and today he has many admirers who appreciate the power of his prose writing and his grasp of the grand historical theme. But to others Scott is regarded as long-winded, his writing in the Scots vernacular difficult to follow, and reading his poems and novels is considered a chore rather than a pleasure. Although nothing can be ruled out in the RCC, one can hazard a guess that a book by Sir Walter Scott is unlikely to be found on the cabin bookshelf of a member's yacht.

Nevertheless there is one work by Scott which deserves to be in every yacht library. This is 'Northern Lights or a voyage in the Lighthouse Yacht to Nova Zembla and the Lord knows where in the summer of 1814'. The author was invited to join the Commissioners of Northern Lights on a voyage round the coast of Scotland. The cruise started at Leith and ended at Greenock six weeks later. The Yacht proceeded up the east coast and northwards to Lerwick. From there she turned south visiting Fair Isle and Orkney before rounding Cape Wrath and heading down the Minch. Calls were made at places in Skye and Mull before crossing to the north coast of Ireland and finally into the Firth of Clyde. Throughout the cruise Walter Scott kept a journal.

From researches, it appears that the 'Lighthouse Yacht' was cutter rigged with dimensions of $58 \times 18 \times 10$ feet and had been built in 1807. She carried six guns and ten men. In addition to Scott the party consisted of four sheriffs who were lighthouse commissioners. The official chief of the expedition was Robert Stevenson. This remarkable man was responsible for the stupendous civil engineering achievement of estab-

Revenue Cutter. Fresh Breeze.

The Lighthouse Yacht was often mistaken for a Revenue Cutter.
© National Maritime Museum, London.

lishing three years previously a lighthouse on the Bell Rock off the Firth of Tay. Scott held him in high regard. 'We have the celebrated engineer Stevenson along with us. I delight in these professional men of talent; they always give some new lights by the peculiarity of their habits and studies, so different from people who are rounded, and smoothed, and ground down for conversation, and who can say all that every person says and nothing more'.

The voyage took place in momentous times. Napoleon had been exiled to Elba three months previously and by the end of the trip the Congress of Vienna was about to begin. Of more relevance Great Britain and the United States were at war, and American men of war under Commodore Rogers were enterprisingly (some would say impudently) cruising in British waters and taking prizes. Hence the six guns with which the Lighthouse Yacht was equipped. The risk was regarded as so real that a sloop of war was sent by the Admiralty, as Scott mentions, 'to cruise in the dangerous points of our tour and sweep the sea of the Yankee Privateers who sometimes annoy our northern latitudes'.

By the early nineteenth century there was considerable maritime activity round the Scottish coast. The Royal Navy had been vigilant in these waters since at least Jacobite times. There was trading between the Clyde and the Americas, and between the Forth and the Tay and Europe. The whaling ships to and from Greenland called at Orkney and Shetland to pick up crews and supplies. Fishing fleets ranged far and wide. Off Fair Isle, Scott noticed two Gravesend smacks fishing and made the wry comment (evocative of a certain Scottish feeling then and now): 'Lord, what a long draught London makes!' The frequency of shipwrecks had become a matter of public concern. Since the establishment of the Northern Lighthouse Board in 1786 a start had been made to light the coast. The approaches to the Firths of Clyde and Forth were reasonably well lit but there were only three lighthouses in the vicinity of Orkney, namely, Pentland Skerries, Start Point and North Ronaldsay; a solitary lighthouse in the Minch on Scalpay; and none at all in Shetland waters. It was the purpose of Robert Stevenson and the Commissioners on this voyage to inspect existing lighthouses and to reconnoitre sites for future development.

If the coasts were poorly lit the navigator in those times was able to rely on well drawn and reasonably accurate charts. Due to the pioneering work of Murdoch Mackenzie in the eighteenth century, the west coast of Britain and the coasts of Ireland and of Orkney had been charted. His work was added to and improved upon by the East India hydrographer James Huddart later in the century, and Murdo Downie produced good charts of the east coast of Scotland in the 1790s. The master of the Lighthouse Yacht would in all probability have had these charts on board. Although Scott was a landsman and not conversant with the niceties of navigation, reading his account one does not receive the impression of uncertainty or difficulty in pilotage, and considering the places the ship visited – the intricate tidal channels of the Orkney Isles, the perilous Pentland Firth, the rock strewn coasts of Harris and Mull and especially the dangerous and little known waters round Skerryvore – it appears that the master, Mr Wilson, was able to navigate with skill and confidence.

Walter Scott was no ordinary traveller. He had already achieved wide literary fame through his romantic narrative poems – *The Lay of the Last Minstrel*, *Marmion* and *The Lady of the Lake*, and his first novel, *Waverley*, had been published three weeks previously, albeit anonymously. He was a man of prodigious intellect. He had a phenomenal memory and an insatiable curiosity about people and places. He was the most companionable of shipmates and, as Robert Stevenson records in an account written some years later, 'he had the happy talent of being on easy terms with all around him. When it was convenient he often took a seat in the forecastle and entered into familiar conversation with the watch below.' His journal of the cruise is a fascinating, vivid, and detailed account of the social conditions of the places which the Lighthouse Yacht visited. He enjoyed himself immensely and was ready for anything. It was 'a sunny portion of my life. We had constant exertion, a succession of wild uncommon scenery, good humour on board and objects of animation and interest when we went ashore.' The reader will find that his energy and high spirits shine irresistibly through the pages of the journal.

A Revenue Cutter getting underway. © *National Maritime Museum, London.*

The Yacht sailed from Leith on 29 July 1814. She proceeded up the east coast with landings at the Isle of May and Bell Rock. Land at Girdle Ness was explored with a view to building a lighthouse to guard the entrance to Aberdeen harbour. Struggling across the Moray Firth in light airs, the wind strengthened as they passed Orkney and Fair Isle. Scott noted in his daily journal, 'The breeze increases – weather may be called rough; worse and worse after we are in our berths, nothing but booming, trampling and whizzing of waves about our ears, and ever and anon, as we fall sleep, our ribs come in contact with those of the vessel'. Robert Stevenson records that what greatly surprised him during this uncomfortable period was the different state of the feelings of the passengers. 'In the berth of Sir Walter and Mr Erskine a constant joking with much laughter was kept up; while in the after cabin very excited enquiries were made as to the state of the voyage and safety of the vessel when she plunged from the crest of a wave into the trough of the sea. The making "all snug" became a saying with the cabin party throughout the voyage.' On arriving at Lerwick a lively scene unfolded. Five whaling vessels from Greenland had arrived and the streets were full of drunken sailors. Apparently the Shetlanders had been paid off on their arrival home. Scott noted that with their pay they made a point of treating their English mess-mates, 'who get drunk of course and are very riotous. The Zetlanders themselves do <u>not</u> get drunk, but go straight home to their houses and reserve their hilarity for the winter season, when they spend their wages in dancing and drinking.'

The Yacht spent some days in Shetland waters and while Stevenson examined possible sites for future lights, Walter Scott and the rest of the party remained ashore sightseeing. Then they set off for Sumburgh Head and Scott observed: 'A frightful tide runs here, called Sumburgh Rost'. The wind increased as they approached this formidable headland and the ship was made 'SNUG – a sure sign that the passengers will not be so. The omen was but true – a terrible combustion on board among plates and dishes, glasses, writing desks etc., etc.; not a wink of sleep.' They then proceeded to Fair Isle where they anchored. Scott gives a vivid description of the way of life of the 250 inhabitants, 'Visit the Town, a wretched assemblage of the basest huts, dirty without and still dirtier within; pigs, fowls, cows, men, women and children all living promiscuously under the same roof and in the same room – the brood-sow making (among the more opulent) a distinguished inhabitant of the mansion.' The people knitted stockings and sweaters which they bartered with passing ships. They regretted the American war and mentioned 'the happy days when they could get from an American trader a bottle of peach brandy or rum in exchange for a pair of worsted stockings or a dozen of eggs'. Scott recalls that the Duke of Medina Sidonia, Commander in Chief of the Spanish Armada, was stranded on Fair Isle after losing his vessel. Always alive to historical events, he let himself go with a passage of sonorous prose worthy of Dr Samuel Johnson. 'Independently of the moral consideration that, from the pitch of power in which he stood a few days before, the proudest peer of the proudest nation in Europe found himself dependent on the jealous and scanty charity of these secluded islanders, it is scarce possible not to reflect with compassion on the change of situation from the palaces of Estramadura to the hamlet of the Fair Isle.'

The Lighthouse Yacht then sailed for the Orkney Isles where they inspected the recently erected lighthouse at Start Point, Sanday. Wrecks were frequent in that area and in the past all the houses had benefited from time to time from flotsam and jetsam washed ashore. Stevenson in conversation with a local farmer happened to remark upon the poor quality of his boat's sails. 'If it had been His (i.e. God's) will that you hadna built sae many lighthouses hereabout,' answered the Orcadian with great composure, 'I would have had new sails last winter'. Leaving Sanday they found themselves in a rost ('I hate that word') off Start Point and they then observed carcasses of 265 whales which had stranded on the shore nearby. Having escaped from this tide race they then proceeded into the sheltered waters of the islands. Scott commented that the sea was now moderate. 'But, oh gods and men! what misfortunes have travellers to record! Just as the quiet of the elements had reconciled us to the thought of dinner, we learn that an unlucky sea has found its way into the galley during the last infernal combustion, when the lee-side and bolt-sprit were constantly under water; so our soup is poisoned with salt water – our cod and haddocks, which cost nine pence this blessed morning and would have been worth a couple of guineas in London, are soused in their primitive element – the curry is undone – and all gone to the devil!'

After this disaster they anchored off Stronsay. Then they visited Kirkwall and after that entered Scapa Flow through Holm Sound using the same narrow passage as did U.47 on her way to sink H.M.S. Royal Oak one hundred and twenty five years later. Thereafter they ventured into the Pentland Firth. Here Scott made a careful account of the hazards of this channel. Although it was a fine day the sea was 'boiling in its fury' and he watched 'a large vessel battling with this heavy current and, though with all her canvas set and breeze, getting more and more involved.' It was the intention that the Lighthouse Yacht should go to Thurso on the mainland side, but the wind failed and they had to put back to St Margaret's Hope. The next day they managed to reach and land on Pentland Skerries and visit the lighthouse (finished in 1794) before going to Stromness. To work the tides in these waters and effect a landing on the Skerries in this vessel must have been a remarkable feat of navigation and Scott observed that 'we executed very cleverly a task of considerable difficulty and even danger'. From Stromness they went west visiting the Smoo Caves in Sutherland and landed just east of Cape Wrath in order to mark out a spot for a lighthouse (completed in 1828). They rounded the Cape and crossed the North Minch in bad weather to Scalpay thereafter visiting Rodel in Harris. Standing over to Skye they anchored off Dunvegan Castle, the seat of the Chief of the Clan Macleod where Scott was hospitably received and slept soundly for a change in the comfort of a bed despite being in the haunted apartment of the Castle. From Dunvegan, on Macleod's recommendation, they sailed to Loch Scavaig, that forbidding stretch of water encircled by the savage range of the Cuillins. The party landed and visited Loch Coruisk and anyone who has visited this place will readily recognise it from the colourful description given by Walter Scott. They next called at Eigg where they visited the cave where in the sixteenth century 200 Macdonalds were massacred by marauding MacLeods. The floor of the cave at the time of their visit was strewn with the bones of men, women and children and Scott retrieved and took on board the skull of what seemed to be a young woman. This act aroused the superstitious fears of the ship's company and was later to land Scott in some trouble.

On Saturday 27 August, four weeks after the start of the cruise, the Lighthouse Yacht again encountered bad weather. Scott describes what happened in memorable language. 'The wind, to which we resigned ourselves, proves exceedingly tyrannical and blows squally the whole night which, with the swell of the Atlantic now unbroken by any islands to windward, proves a means of great combustion in the cabin. The dishes and glasses in the steward's cupboards become locomotive – portmanteaus and writing desks are more active than necessary, it is scarce possible to keep one's self within bed and impossible to stand upright if you rise. Having crept upon deck about four in the morning, I find we are beating to windward off the Isle of Tiree, with the determination on the part of Mr Stevenson that his constituents should visit a reef of rocks called Skerryvore, where he thought it would be essential to have a lighthouse. Loud remonstrances on the part of the Commissioners who, one and all, declared they will subscribe to his opinion – whatever it may be – rather than continue this infernal buffeting. Quiet perseverance on the part of Mr Stevenson and great kicking, bouncing and squabbling upon that of the Yacht, who seems to like the idea of Skerryvore as little as the Commissioners.'

The reef came in sight and Scott describes it as a long ridge of rocks on which the tide broke 'in a most tremendous style'. They managed to land, got soaked to the skin 'took possession of the rock in the name of the Commissioners and generously bestowed our own great names on its crags and creeks'. One has to admire the spirit of Scott, a middle-aged man crippled with a permanent limp resulting from childhood polio, in scrambling about such a desolate place.

They then ran before the wind to the sound of Iona. The ruins of Iona Abbey were duly inspected. Following the visit they went to Staffa where they were able to land and visit Fingal's Cave. The weather for the first time in the cruise now became settled. The Yacht went north about round Mull to Oban, thence outside Islay, and held across to Donegal. At this point the ship's armament was made ready as an American privateer was reported to be in the vicinity. The lighthouse on Inishtrahull was visited. 'A fishing boat comes off with four or five stout lads, without neckerchiefs or hats and the best of whose joint garments selected would hardly equip an Edinburgh beggar.' Trouble was experienced with the tides in the vicinity of this island and with some difficulty they attained the mouth of Lough Foyle in the hope of visiting Londonderry. Having entered the Lough the Yacht was becalmed and plans to visit that city were abandoned. She then headed east calling at Portrush, Dunluce Castle and finally these indefatigable tourists landed at the Giant's Causeway. Here they learnt that the alleged privateer was no more than 'a gentleman's pleasure vessel' (one wonders who this could possibly have been). Passing through Rathlin Sound, the Yacht crossed the North Channel and a visit was made to the lighthouse established in 1788 at the Mull of Kintyre. Plans were made to proceed next to the coast of Galloway. However, the rumours and counter-rumours concerning the American naval activity crystallised into reliable information that two American privateers, the 'Peacock' of 22 guns and the 'Prince of Neuchatel' of 8 guns, were cruising in the vicinity and had made many captures. So a decision was made to proceed straight to the Clyde. The Commissioners visited Pladda Lighthouse (completed in 1790) and then the ship had a hard sail to Lamlash. By this time Scott's thoughts were turning to home. The vessel had to make her way upwind by short tacks, 'which made a most disagreeable night; as, between the noise of the wind and the sea, the clattering of ropes and sails above and of the moveables below and the eternal *'ready about'*, which was repeated every ten minutes when the vessel was about to tack, with the lurch and clamour which succeeds, sleep was much out of the question. We are not now in the least sick, but want of sleep is uncomfortable and I have no agreeable reflections to amuse my waking hours, except the hope of again re-joining my family.' The wind diminished by daybreak and slowly the ship made her way in the Firth of Clyde, ultimately becoming becalmed off Cumbrae. The captain told Scott that the crew blamed him for this state of affairs on account of his removing the skull from the cave at Eigg. The ship lay motionless all night and then in light airs next day they reached Greenock.

Scott's account ends: 'Took an early dinner and embarked in the steam-boat for Glasgow.' This ship was probably the *Comet* with which Henry Bell had commenced the first commercial steamship service in Europe in 1812. This vessel proceeded at eight knots 'with a smoothness of motion which probably resembles flying'. The party had been cheered by the ship's company when they disembarked from the Yacht. What Scott does not mention, but is recounted by Stevenson, is that the postmaster at Greenock personally delivered the mail 'to the man who had so often delighted his evening fireside'. When the steam boat left, the ships in the harbour dressed overall 'such was the celebrity and popularity of the man'.

Here we leave Scott travelling in the mode of a new age and a changing world. On arriving in Edinburgh, he learned from his publisher that two editions of *Waverley*, comprising 3,000 copies had been sold and a third edition would have to be printed. He was about to reach a pinnacle of fame and fortune.

The journal was published in Lockhart's Memoirs of the Life of Sir Walter Scott some years later. Robert Louis Stevenson, grandson of Robert Stevenson, while living in Samoa in 1892 wrote on Scott's journal: 'One thing I beg of my readers, that they will take down the fourth volume of Lockhart and read over again the 'Voyage in the Light-house Yacht to Nova Zembla and the Lord knows where', one of the most delightful passages in one of the most delightful of books.'

Lockhart's Life of Sir Walter Scott was last published in the U.K. in 1964 and is no longer in print. It is available in the U.S.A., having been pub-lished by A.M.S. Press in 1982. A paperback edition of the Voyage was published in 1982 by Byway Books, Hawick but is also out of print. One copy has been placed in the library.

RUM, PIRATES & A CASTAWAY

by Geoffrey Nockolds

Curacao is a pleasant place to fit out. Most things are available in the shops but expensive. What is not available can be flown in from the States. Sue and I left Antillian Slipway Services, run by two friendly Dutchmen, on 13 December and explored several anchorages up the coast before a 45 mile shakedown sail to Aruba prior to setting off for Cartagena about 400 miles down wind.

On 17 December the log records, '1530 wind shifted dead aft, blowing harder, yankee would not fill, generator line fouled, yankee furling line fouled, handed main. 1650 – all back to normal. Days run 168 miles'. We arrived off Cartagena at 2300 on 19 December and, after having tried to find the short cut through the Boca Grande boat passage, went on through the main well lit Boca Chica entrance in the south to anchor off the Club Nautico.

Cartagena is a large natural harbour formed by the bay of Cartagena to the east and Isla Tierra Bomba to the west. The Boca Grande entrance was blocked up after 1586 when Francis Drake sailed through it, anchored his fleet of 27 ships inside, landed his army at night and took the city by surprise. Henry Morgan with some French, sacked the city again in 1697 with a much bigger force, but Admiral Vernon tried the same thing about fifty years later, with the biggest force of all and was repelled. He had been so confident of success he had had coins struck to commemorate the event!

On Christmas Eve my sister Rosemary, who has lived in Colombia, joined us for three weeks and we sailed to the Rosario Islands 25 miles southwest of Cartagena. All we had was a photocopy of a rather inaccurate chart published by the Club Nautico, but it was a lot better than nothing. Inspite of, or perhaps because of it, we hit a coral patch going into the anchorage south of Isla Fiesta; but this was hardly surprising, because while two chaps in a *cayuco* were trying to guide us through the tiny windy entrance ahead, another was alongside trying to sell us

Above: *Judy Lomax and Jim Reeves at Flatey, N.Iceland.*
Below: *James Nixon and David Lomax in the thermal springs at Reykjanes.*

Above: *The Beagle Channel looking west.*
Below: *Marelle in Caleta Olla off the Beagle Channel.*

Above: *First Lady in Laguna Grande.*
Below: *The Alderman at the Argentine Islands, Antarctica.*

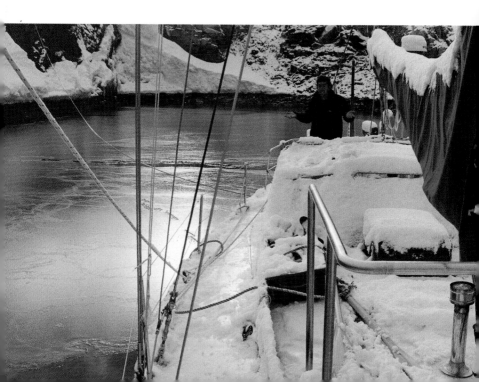

Above: *The Minquiers Meet, drawn by Penny Power.*
Below: *Leaving the Deben Meet (Julia Twyman).*

lobsters while a third, blocking our way, was offering the girls a string of striking scarlet coral. The bathing and snorkelling were excellent and there was a good hotel on Isla Bosquita south of the anchorage. There are maybe 30 rocky cays in the archipelago and some were so small as to have only just enough space for a house. From a distance the houses looked as if they were floating on the sea. The archipelago is a holiday resort for rich Colombians, charming, picturesque and as yet quite unspoilt.

30 December. A stiff beat back to Cartagena; the first for two years and a sobering reminder of some of the sailing that lay ahead. The four English yachts there saw in the new century, British time, with champagne before tackling the Colombian one with rum at an open air restaurant in one of the city's many sixteenth century squares.

New Year's day 2000. We saw the chance of getting some work done on the boat so we moved into the marina of the Club de Pesca, which is built in a most attractive setting in an old fort. We found people to do high quality stainless steel work, woodwork and varnishing, the latter for $11 a day. There are yards for hauling out further from town and a friend of ours had his boat in one in a travel hoist waiting to be lifted out the next morning, when he was told to move out. He somewhat naturally remonstrated but had to get out when the yard manager threatened to move him by force. After dark and when the yard workers had left, two big trailers arrived with mat black 45ft cigarette boats and manned by black chaps in black overalls. The boats were launched and disappeared into the night. They hauled him out the next morning as if nothing had happened.

Cartagena is said to be the most beautiful city in the Americas and it certainly lived up to its reputation for us. There is as much sightseeing as you want, with early Spanish colonial buildings, good shops, the chance to buy the best of emeralds at a reasonable price and fabulous restaurants which compare most favourably with anywhere we have ever been, particularly if you like shell fish. Above all, the people were charming and friendly. Unfortunately, it is unsafe to travel inland unless by air, and we found it frustrating not to be able to explore the countryside. The harbour is at the northern end of the bay right in the city and the anchorage, though conveniently close in, is very disturbed by the wash of the ferry boats that ply the bay.

There was a light breeze as we sailed down the harbour a month later, bound for Albuquerque Cays, an atoll some 400 miles northwest. I felt quite sheepish when I reefed the mainsail right down, but once we got outside we ran into 35 kts of wind and a nasty steep sea, a horrid shock after a month of high living. Worse was to come; after we had set the Monitor and streamed the water generator line, Sue went down below only to be driven back on deck by dense fumes of ammonia and the gas alarm shrieking. We turned on the extractor fans and when the atmosphere had cleared a bit, started to search for the cause. We checked everything, cleaning materials, batteries (we have sealed ones), engine compartment and fuel but could find nothing. After about ten minutes the alarm stopped and we turned the fans off, only for it to start up again. The cabin was untenable and I was worried about an explosion, but the gas gradually dispersed and we continued on our way. We never found the cause. That night we ate the next day's sandwiches, the first time we had not eaten a cooked dinner at sea for many years.

Three days later we picked up Albuquerque Cays on the radar at 12 miles, and at 0715 anchored in a gap in the leeward reef to wait for better light. Later, we found anchorage between North and South Island, about 300 yards apart, on a patch of sand in 9 feet. Both islands have steep little sandy beaches and are thickly wooded with palm and tropical fig trees and lots of frigate birds. The log says 'wind mostly NNE 20–25 kts, some lop coming across the lagoonal terrace from reef half a mile away. Coral patches to N, W & S but just swing clear. Sandy bottom and Fortress well dug in. Crystal clear water – just what we've come for'. This was the beginning of the snorkelling and reef exploring we really enjoy. Our wind generators and solar panel make enough electricity in these conditions without running the engine, a definite bonus.

We went ashore to check in with the naval post on North Island. They were very friendly and showed us round their camp. There is a small marine detachment on most of the atolls that have solid land and you have to have permission to anchor near them. We got this from the Admiral Commandant in Cartagena before we left. Albuquerque is an atoll in the archipelago of San Andreas and Providencia, which includes several other atolls and coral reefs 100 miles or more off the Nicaraguan coast and separated from the Central American continental shelf by the San Andreas trough. They have belonged to Colombia since 1822, but like other territory in this part of the world, they are disputed, hence the military presence on most of the cays. We were advised not to anchor off any of the uninhabited cays because of Nicaraguan pirates and drug runners.

There were several fishermen from San Andreas camping on South Island and one of them, jet black, wearing a white handkerchief round his head, and looking like an old fashioned pirate came alongside to ask if we had any cigarettes. He spoke fluent English and said he was Lester Hooker and would bring us some fish the next day, which he duly did.

A week later we went out through the northern entrance of the reef and motor sailed in a light head wind and a foul current to San Andreas 25 miles away to anchor by Cotton Cay. This is a safe and convenient anchorage for the town, sheltered from the east by the reef. A ridge of hills run down the centre of the island ending in four bluffs which are visible for many miles off, but it was the sight of high rise buildings when we rounded the south tip that made us wonder what we were coming to. San Andreas is a major tourist resort for Colombians and, with 60,000 resident population, is said to be the most densely populated island in

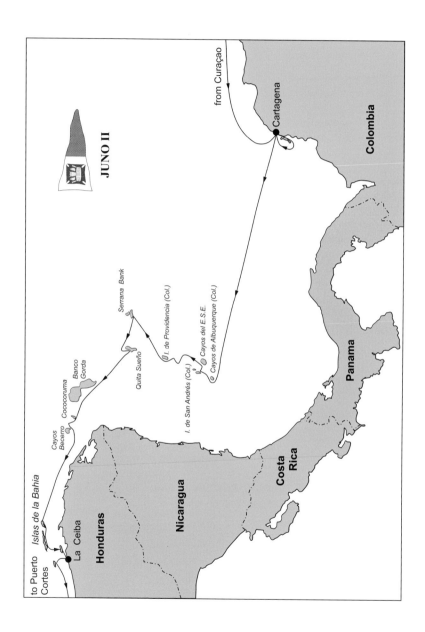

the Caribbean. In the season the population expands to 400,000. The town is not very attractive, but it has good air communications and provisioning. Fred Kemp joined us here from the UK.

The villages outside the town are in a different world and charming. The countryside is lush. The bus took us to Southwest Bay and the Cove, a small inlet with a very narrow entrance, used by the fishermen we saw in Albuquerque. It was also used by British war ships as early as 1808 for shelter during the summer southwesterlies and also for careening and victualling. Robert Felix Esq., commander of the sloop *Beaver* in 1818, says '. . . on the appearance of bad weather we examined the Cove. . . and warped the ship in, placed the best anchor in 12 ft ahead, veered half a cable and secured her by cables and hawsers made fast to rocks and trees on both sides of the Cove. Here we lay perfectly secure.'

5 February. Wind northeasterly F.5/6, bound for Catalina harbour in Old Providence, now Providencia, 70 miles to windward. The leading line for the entrance through the reefs is Morgan's Head, a rocky protuberance on Catalina island, in line with a small peak on the hills on Providencia to the southwest. Morgan's Head is said to resemble the head of the British pirate who used the island as a base in the seventeenth century to pounce on Spanish galleons. It must have served his purpose well as it is well sheltered and hidden from the sea by high hills. It is a very pretty harbour in a beautiful mountainous tropical island setting. It has a population under five thousand.

In the afternoon, the agent Fernandez Bush, the Port Captain (navy), and two Immigration officials came out to clear us in, in a fishing boat with a square glass cabin looking for all the world like a floating hearse. It was run by Jessie, a black gangly native, whom the agent was pleased to call his secretary. Bush charged $40 for his services and was the local Mr Fixit; everybody and everything seemed to work through him. Later, we got talking to Jessie who regaled us with island life. 'There is work for everybody here and everybody has some money; they do not die of heart attacks, they die of old age'. When Fred asked him about ganja, Jessie divulged 'it's best to grow your own cannabis', other drugs just 'float ashore on the beach'.

Like San Andreas, the island was never settled by Carib Indians. Though discovered by Spaniards early in the sixteenth century, Dutch smugglers and English Puritans were the first settlers and from mid seventeenth century to 1822 the islands changed hands between the English and Spanish with occasional settlement by Jamaican pirates. Half the population of San Andreas and everybody in Providencia speaks English, which, while it is not taught in school, is jealously kept up in every family. The officials are mostly Spanish and one occasionally sees notices on trees saying 'Go home Colombians. English is our language'.

We were anchored off Isabel the main village where there were a few shops stocking basic commodities, a few bars, restaurants and small hotels. The town jetty was busy most days with supply ships, smart pensioned off 100ft US trawlers. Everything seemed to be manhandled as neither ship nor pier had a crane. We hired motor scooters to tour the island on a ring road, which was never far from the sea, getting breath taking glimpses through the trees of the brilliant colours of the sea inside the reef. There were a few simple resort hotels under palm trees along sandy beaches and we asked the proprietor at one where we had a drink, 'how do you know when coconuts are going to fall?'. 'In the afternoon,' he said with great confidence, and as he walked away one fell just behind him. He looked back faintly surprised; it was 1030 am. Bush seemed to be one of the most common names on the island and it was also the name of the rum 'factory' at Mountain a half mile out of town. The proprietor, Ben Bush, a sprightly 84-year-old in a bright blue string vest too short to cover his midriff, said he had been distilling for 65 years and had never 'touched a drop'. The 'distillery' was out through the back of the house. There was a 40 gallon oil drum which was rusty but hopefully glazed over with years of sugar. The drum held *panela* (the local bricks of solid brown sugar) fermenting in water. There was also a pile of burnt wood left from the last distillation. We bought a gallon for $12. It was only 18° but had a distinctive tang and was pleasant to drink neat.

3 February. With sadness we checked out and beat up to Low Cay, 12 miles away at the north end of Providencia reef, where we anchored in 15 feet. The next day we started out, fully reefed main, storm jib and staysail, for either Roncador, 80 miles due east or Serrana 100 miles northeast. We made the south end of Quito Sueno Bank, a 40 mile long shallow reef, on the first tack, were only 15 miles north of Providence Reef on the second, and were heading back to the south end of Quito Sueno Bank again on the third. There was a strong west going current, the centre board would not go down, the Monitor was not engaging, the staysail sheet was working loose, the VHF aerial base was swinging upside down at the mast head, and when we had some horrendous squalls, we decided enough was enough and retired to lick our wounds. We had been at it for 20 hours to make 25 miles to windward! It was lovely to be in still water. The hydraulic ram on the centreboard was leaking through the bottom seal but I was able luckily to buy enough hydraulic fluid to work it for the rest of the season.

18 February. We started off again but still had to sail 249 miles to make 99 miles to Serrana Bank. This large atoll is about 22 miles north to south and 12 miles across; it has 5 cays, four along the southern fringe and one in the north. Southwest Cay is the largest and the only one with bushes; it has a marine detachment and a lighthouse which was not working. None of the other cays had any bushes. The southwest reef entrance is easy to identify as there are cays on each side and, just as shown on Richard Owen's chart of 1835, the only one available. There was no tenable anchorage at Little Cay, just inside the reef, where we

Oak Ridge, Roatan, Bay Islands.

had hoped to spend the night, so we had to pick our way across the lagoon to East Cay, two and a half miles away, where we found a reasonable though rather bleak anchorage in its lee, to our profound relief.

We had come to Serrana because of an account we had read of a Spanish seaman who was shipwrecked there in 1528 and had survived for eight years until he was rescued in 1536. We were fascinated to see how this sort of terrain could possibly support any human being for more than eight days let alone eight years. East Cay, where we deduced he must have been, was about 120 yds long and 50 yds wide and covered with coral and mollusc and some tornefortia; nothing else.

The man, Macse Joan, survived there without shelter from the tropical sun, and with nothing from the wreck. There were several sailors at the beginning but some made a raft to try to escape, some died, and he was eventually left with one companion from a later shipwreck from which they managed to salvage some iron and wood. At first he ate raw seal meat, drank the blood and used the skins for shelter. He dug pits and lined them with seal skins to catch water. He made a boat of sorts to visit the other islands for turtle eggs and seals. He eventually built a seal skin shelter, a pit to trap fish and 'two towers, sixteen fathoms around and four high, with their stairways, and we climbed up there to watch the sea'. One tower had 'wood and other things to make smoke so that we might be seen by some vessel if by chance one passed'. When they were eventually rescued the captain of the ship 'took testimony by a notary of everything he saw'. This was the story he presented first to Don Pedro de

Alvarado in Havana and then to King Philip II in Spain. The original account is in the Archivo des Indias in Seville.

During this cruise we explored dozens of reefs and were very sad to find vast tracts of dead coral covered with algae. We saw very few of those especially beautiful blue and purple fans that sway backwards and forwards in the reefs. A field study carried out in the archipelago only 4 years ago has revealed an overall decline of 50 per cent in live coral cover in San Andreas and up to 80 per cent in its lagoonal reefs. Providencia and the outer reefs seem to have fared only marginally better. Although the reasons for the decline are not fully understood and human factors must play a part, it seems that hurricanes, the unexplained and sudden disappearance of the spiny sea urchin, algae proliferation and temperature changes are more probable causes.

24 February. We were under way and past Southwest Cay by 1100 hoping to anchor on Quito Sueno Bank before dark. We thought that we would be helped on our way, at last, by a favourable current. But none was forthcoming and when we got into the lee of the reef near the lighthouse at dusk, there was too much swell and not enough light to dare go closer in through the coral heads to find a tenable anchorage. Reluctantly we set sail again for Arecife Media Luna. Perhaps fortunately we carried on to Cayos Cococoruma in Honduras 155 miles further east. We later heard that a Dutch yacht was attacked a few days before in the anchorage at Media Luna by five Nicaraguan pirates armed with AK47s. And a couple of weeks later we helped a leaking American yacht into a harbour in Roatan, where Fred left us. The yacht had been rammed at night by a fishing boat in the same place. Media Luna is probably too near the Nicaraguan coast for comfort.

It was now all down wind sailing and only the second time we had a full mainsail this season. *Juno II* has only two reefs: the first is a deep second and the second most people's third.

We anchored off the south side of the largest Cococoruma Cay in 18 feet of water with a light swell. The bottom was hard and we dragged at first but eventually stopped when the Fortress dug in. I am a great believer in letting the anchor go on dragging if there is enough room; it usually seems to bite sooner or later. We were surprised to see smoke rising from the trees and an open boat with five men approaching us. The skipper told us they come out from La Ceiba every February to catch shark which was considered a great delicacy at Easter in San Pedro Sula. They said they hoped to catch five hundred in the month they were out. They were very friendly and took Sue and Fred ashore to see their camp where there were masses of frigate birds circling and brown boobies and their chicks in nests right at their feet, they were so tame. They showed them the dried shark meat which they were stacking to cover up for the night. Next morning they came alongside to give us a lobster and snappers they had caught in their shark nets in exchange for cigarettes and beer. They had had a bad night only two small tiger and white sharks, the two most dangerous species! They had no winch nor derrick and must have manhandled them.

Cayos Vivorillo, 20 miles further east, is an unbroken reef a mile long north to south interspersed by cays. The biggest cays which have luxuriant palm trees were at each end and a string of smaller sandy islets between them. The anchorage is easy of access at night with radar, but there was no sign of the lighthouse at the southern tip; it was presumably blown down by Hurricane Mitch on its way to the Bay Islands in 1997.

Cayos Becerro was 5 miles away to the northeast, and has three substantial and four tiny cays all with gorgeous sandy beaches and overhanging palms. They make beautiful fine weather anchorages and, like Vivorillo, its lighthouse had simply disappeared. This was the first cay where we had seen a fishing boat with about 15 young boys in *cayucos*. They were diving for conch, helmet shells and giant whelks.

We then spent the next month in the Bay Islands where, unlike the inhospitable mainland coast 25 miles away, there are masses of protected anchorages, particularly on the leeward shore. Roatan and Guanaja are high while Utila, the third main island, is flat and swampy. A reef runs almost continuously along the north shores of Roatan and Guanaja but there are several narrow down wind openings which can be hair raising and you do not want to make a mistake! In northerlies the whole area is quite dangerous. We think the Cayos Cochinos, between the Bay Islands and the mainland, are the loveliest of all. The two main islands are high

Lower Monitor, Cayos Cochinos.

and densely covered with luxuriant vegetation, magnificent headlands and enticing sandy beaches. The other cays are pretty sandy islets with picturesque native villages nestling under palm trees. There are a few anchorages in trade winds but the wind whistles down the hills in all directions and spun *Juno* round in circles. On clear days you can see the mainland and the Sierra Cangrejal with peaks over 8000ft which forms a magnificent backcloth to the view. The locals go fishing in small wooden *cayucos*, usually in bad shape and leaking but with tiny little gunter sails made of brightly coloured plastic sheeting.

The Bay Islands were discovered by Columbus in 1502 and later used as bases by English, Dutch and French pirates to prey on Spanish galleons. Henry Morgan established a base in Port Royal on Roatan in the mid seventeenth century when there were as many as five thousand pirates on the island. Around 1795 English settlers introduced black Caribs and African slaves to the islands and a large part of the adjacent mainland. These remained under British control until 1860, and consequently some of the population are white and most of them are English speaking. The island settlements are built on piles on the shore or on shallow reefs, apparently to avoid vicious sand flies; the houses are mostly of wood and brightly painted. Seventh Day Adventists seem to be the dominant religious sect. The Caribs tend to live in isolated fishing villages apart from the rest of the community.

17 March. No wind, so we motored most of the way to Puerto Cabotage de la Ceiba on the mainland, where we hoped to leave *Juno* for the hurricane season. This is a little port constructed from a tributary of the Rio Cangrejal with a sea entrance partially protected by two stone piers. Lagoon Marina was hidden up a narrow backwater right in the jungle and we had to ask the locals which turning to take to find it. As the creek got narrower and narrower and still there was no sign of anything, I wondered whether we would be able to turn round. Suddenly, a well built dock and a workshop with an elegant apartment built over it appeared through the trees.

Having established that we could leave *Juno* there for 6 months, we then sailed to Utila and on to the navy yard at Puerto Cortes to haul *Juno* out. However, one look at the place and I realised it would be extremely risky to start work of any sort using the navy personnel if we wished to get out in under a month, perhaps many months. So we just settled for antifouling. We were there for six days, a record not likely to be broken again in a hurry. There were a frightening collection of old wrecks posing as foreign yachts and Honduran naval craft, most of which were unlikely to be fit enough to go to sea again. Also, because the authorities seemed to change the rules and rates quite frequently, some owners were obviously never going to be able to afford to claim back their craft which just sat there rusting away. Breathing a deep sigh of relief as we were relaunched without damage, we sailed back to Lagoon Marina to lay up.

EARNING AN EARRING:
TO CAPE HORN IN *GLORIANA*

by Arthur Beiser

As we flew down the valley of the Río Baker early in January last year the village of Tortel appeared and at anchor before it the blue ketch *Gloriana*. For nearly half a century Germaine and I had dreamt of sailing through the Chilean channels to Cape Horn, and for just as long we could see no realistic prospect of doing so. But here we were, at the invitation of our old friend and her owner Agustín Edwards (RCC), about to join *Gloriana* for a 1300 mile cruise that lasted nearly a month in the extraordinary fjords and archipelagos of southern Chile.

Gloriana is a Swan 76 with a new stern that increases her length to 82 feet. Agustín bases *Gloriana* in Chile and has sailed her down to Antarctica a few years ago; he also owns the magnificent 132ft Hood/Huisman ketch *Anakena* in which he is cruising around the world in stages. Agustín was to meet us in two weeks at Punta Arenas in the Magellan Strait.

The morning after our arrival we left Tortel and headed west for the main shipping channel whose southerly course we followed for much of the way to Punta Arenas. The landscape is rugged here, with mountains plunging steeply into a labyrinth of islands and waterways. It is cool the year round, the snow line only 600 to 700 metres high with glaciers at the heads of many inlets. It is also spectacularly beautiful, especially when the sun shines, which it did regularly if only briefly.

Fresh fruit and vegetables had been unobtainable in Tortel, so we stopped briefly at Puérto Edén, a ramshackle fishing hamlet, to search for some. We had to settle for an armful of greens from the kitchen garden of a friendly resident; the two *supermercados* had only sacks of flour and sugar and a few cans. After Puérto Edén we saw no houses, no roads, no power lines, no signs whatever of humanity on land – except for a very few navigational aids – until we rounded Cape Froward over a week later. What we did see must have been just about what the first European explorers saw nearly five centuries ago.

The day after our visit to Puerto Edén we went up the Seno Eyre to the Pio XI Glacier, a giant tentacle of the South Patagonian Icecap. The approach was littered with car-sized chunks of ice, some a delicate blue, that had tumbled off the glacier's snout. We fended them off from the bow with long boathooks. While *Gloriana* jilled around, several of us took the dinghy in for a closer look at the glacier, which is three miles across at the water's edge. We were to see plenty of other such rivers of ice but none so vast.

Day after sublime day we made our way south past snowy peaks and sparkling glaciers as the weather grew harsher. Temperatures near freezing became more common and it rained, with hail now and then and once with sleet. To keep warm and dry on deck took two fleece layers top and bottom encased in Musto's heaviest oilies plus boots, gloves, and a serious hat. Really bad days called for face coverings and goggles. The rotten weather and clumsy garb should have bothered us but did not: the grandeur of the scene and the exhilaration of sailing such a big fast yacht made up for everything.

In the channels to Punta Arenas we met in all three fishing boats, a ferry, and a Chilean patrol vessel. Wildlife was less sparse, though hardly abundant: birds flew overhead daily, notably albatross and twice, wonderfully, a condor; flightless steamer ducks splashed comically in

Cockburn Channel south of Punta Arenas.

many anchorages, where we might also spy otter and shy deer; occasionally dolphins leapt in greeting; and sometimes we could make out shiny black sea lions basking indolently on shiny black rocks. Here and there knee-high Magellanic penguins stared at us, charming creatures though less impressive than the inflatable Emperor penguin I had brought from home just in case.

We were eight on board, an easy fit in an 82 footer. The capable skipper, John Kenyon, is from Yorkshire and his three hardworking deckhands are young Chileans he trained from scratch. Superb meals whatever the weather were provided by Anita, the full-time cook. Agustín had suggested that Germaine and I bring a friend along, and we invited Alan Oppenheim, who first sailed with us 38 years ago. We three did much of the steering and I helped with the navigation. I had taken along a copy of the Pilotage Foundation's cruising guide to Chile, which was often helpful in choosing anchorages. Here are two additions to its otherwise comprehensive bibliography: *Patagonia*, by Paul van Gaalen, ISBN 9567402051, which is full of fantastic photographs, many taken from a yacht, with an interesting text in English; and the two volumes of *Diccionario de la Toponimia Austral de Chile*, by Carlos Alberto Mantellero Ognio, ISBN 9562350117 and 9562350133, which gives the origins of the names of geographic features and waterways of the Chilean coast. The latter is in Spanish but easy to understand, a fascinating and enjoyable companion for a voyage in this part of the world.

Gloriana sports two jibs set one behind the other on hydraulic furlers. With the wind almost always aft the jibs, singly or wing-and-wing with one poled out, gave us all the push we wanted when it blew hard (F.6–10), which was often. One fine day I was at the helm when we rolled up both jibs as the wind touched F.11; *Gloriana* continued to roar along at 8 knots. Fortunately the seas remained modest in the maze of waterways. To be sure, there were also long periods when the wind relented and we needed the engine to keep up the average that would get us to Punta Arenas by the day planned.

Attractive coves by the score lay beside our path, most of them sheltered by white-capped hills with slopes streaked by silver cataracts. All that rain, 3m per year, has to go somewhere. Alas, these *caletas* usually came with two catches. First, few potential anchorages had reasonable (less than 20m) depths and a number of times we had to drop the hook in such tight spots that lines to shore were needed to keep *Gloriana* from swinging into trouble. The second problem was the *rachas*, violent williwaws that might hurtle down one valley or another at any time. Whammo! Blasted by a *racha*, *Gloriana* would lurch over and jerk at her anchor. In a bad place – hard to predict but soon obvious – we stood watches all night in case we dragged.

We would have loved to ramble ashore but the terrain was uncooperative. Possible landing places were few, and even the best obliged us to stumble over round, smooth, slimy rocks on the way to an uphill slog over spongy turf through dense shrubbery. Twice we had surreal picnics at the water's edge in which we wore oilies as we sat in the drizzle devouring succulent lamb that had been barbecued over driftwood fires. Before us *Gloriana* heeled and swerved as *rachas* swooped down on her, the odd duck paddled by, and the wine bottles grew empty. Bliss.

Ten days out of Tortel we reached Cape Froward, the southern tip of the South American mainland. The cape was so named in 1587 by the English circumnavigator Sir Thomas Cavendish. Froward, a nearly forgotten word that means 'perverse, hostile, odious', is fitting even today to a mariner coming from the Atlantic, since this is where the Magellan Strait turns northwest, right into the usually vigorous prevailing winds. Tilman, in *Mischief*, had a terrible time here in 1956: 'Rain, bitter squalls of hail and snow, strong winds funnelling their way down the channel from dead ahead, were our daily and nightly portion'. Happily we had more clement conditions and were going the other way.

From Cape Froward we went north to Punta Arenas, the only real city in this part of the world. Punta Arenas is an interesting place full of relics of a thriving past when it was a major wool exporter and, before the Panama Canal opened in 1914, serviced shipping between the Atlantic and the Pacific. Facilities for yachts here are nil, and after Agustín's arrival we happily left the miserable open anchorage.

The least exposed route to Cape Horn follows the Beagle Channel eastward and then turns south through the Murray Narrows. Passage

Gloriana at anchor in Caleta Playa, Pauda.

through the latter is normally restricted to Chilean naval vessels, but
Agustín is a reserve naval officer and *Gloriana* was allowed through. We
anchored at Button Island, named after Jeremy Button, one of the four
young Fuegians kidnapped there in 1830 by FitzRoy in the *Beagle*.
FitzRoy brought them to England, where one died of smallpox, to
educate them in 'English and the plainer truths of Christianity'. Three
years later, now with Darwin on board, the *Beagle* returned the remaining Feugians to Wulaia Cove, also in the Murray Narrows and where we

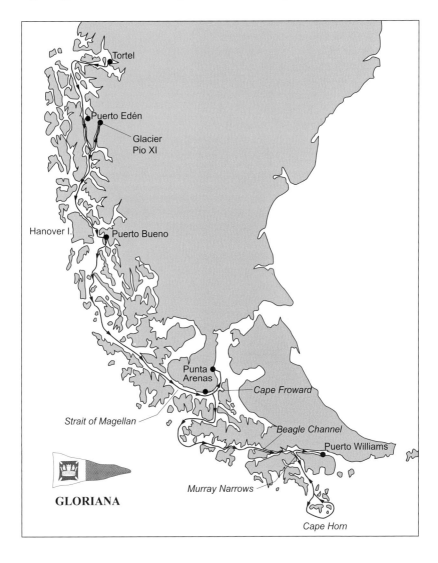

were to anchor on the way back. The Patagonia Missionary Society later established itself in this region and, in a familiar pattern, tried to impose its beliefs on the lesser mortals there, who were exploited and mistreated. In 1859 the Fuegians had had enough and slaughtered eight of the crew of the mission ship at Wulaia Cove. Jemmy Button was on the scene: did he participate? The record is ambiguous. A few decades later European diseases and bounty hunters hired by settlers had wiped out nearly all the indigenous Fuegians.

On 22 January we rounded Cape Horn. The cape itself, only 405m high, is not very impressive to look at, but few landmarks are such potent symbols. We all got a charge as we went past, even Agustín and John for whom it was not the first time. By the way, sailing past Cape Horn provides more than just a thrill, it also gives permission to wear a ring in the left earlobe (I now have one) and to spit to windward (I await a suitable occasion).

A lighthouse stands on a cliff a short distance east of Cape Horn. Below is a cove with a rocky beach from which crude steps lead up to the lighthouse. Holding is poor in the cove and normally yachts stand off while their crews go ashore by dinghy in relays. The young sailor of the Chilean Navy who tends the light lives in a small building near the light with his wife, small son, three dogs and two cats. We were made welcome, signed the guest book (20 to 30 yachts come by each year), and were issued certificates attesting to our visit. Nearby is a generator shack, a tiny chapel, and several monuments that honour Cape Horners of the past. It is impossible to look out to sea from this desolate, windswept place without being deeply moved.

After a few days exploring the islands near Cape Horn we went back up through the Murray Narrows and then east to Puerto Williams. The world's southernmost permanent settlement, its life centres on a small naval base. In the local museum, which features stuffed animals and photos taken long ago of the local Indians, a little boy who might have stepped from one of the pictures asked me if I were a gringo. Yes, I replied, whereupon he beamed – a real gringo! Actually there were plenty of gringos in the nearby Micalvi Yacht Club where seven visiting European yachts were made fast to an ancient naval vessel, its cabin converted to a cosy bar and lounge. (No dress code; excellent pisco sours; kittens available for adoption).

From Puerto Williams we flew to Santiago and then home. In the summer Germaine and I sailed *Ardent Spirit* for the eighth time from our place in southern France to Venice and back, a 3,000 mile cruise that took four months. We half expected to be bored after our robust adventures in Chile, but in fact the contrast seemed to enhance our enjoyment of the tamer but no less real pleasures of the Adriatic. What good fortune to have had both kinds of experience in the same year.

QUIVER'S 'GRAND TOUR'

by Anthony and Monique Browne

Plans for a Grand Tour

In the eighteenth century the Grand Tour to Italy became established as a highly desirable part of the education of the aristocracy and gentry of Europe. Italy was a special destination, with its attractive climate and the lure of antiquity and culture. The tourists would travel from the Riviera down the coast to Rome and as far south as Naples and the Amalfi coast, visiting the amazing discoveries of Pompeii and the great Doric temples of Magna Grecia at Paestum. From there the Grand Tour would continue north, as far as Venice. Our sailing ambitions were curtailed somewhat by work and weddings and the last part of the tour, up the Adriatic, must wait until another year. We managed to get a month off, which we split between Easter, when we sailed from Antibes to Rome, and July, when we cruised around the fascinating and beautiful west coast of Italy.

Easter – the Italian Riviera

The snow shone brightly from the higher slopes of the Alpes Maritimes as we slipped out of Antibes at the end of April. A fair breeze sped us along the mountainous shore into Italy and into new, unexplored waters for us. The breeze wafted us on to Imperia where we tried to anchor in the outside harbour. The anchor could not dig through the thick weed and eventually, in the weak evening sun, we made our way into the inner harbour. We secured between two boats which were wintering here and found an attractive, bustling little town. We left early the next morning in a flat calm. We motored past the lovely Ligurian coast, dotted with perfect cubist villages against a backdrop of thick snow on the hills. Pine covered cliffs sheltered the entrance to Portofino so protectively that it was difficult to spot the entrance. We picked up a buoy then made the stern fast to the small stone quay. We were the only visitor here, in one of

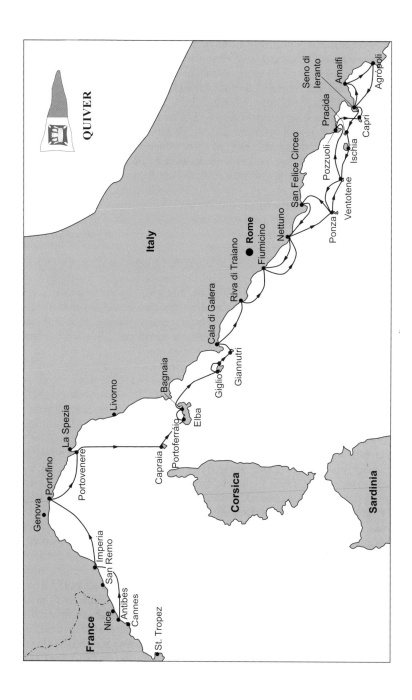

the most famous and picturesque of all Italian resorts. We dined in a pretty trattoria and watched a huge bonfire being built in the main square next to the harbour for the celebration of Easter. Portofino proved to be an excellent place to buy provisions. Another day with very little wind, but today we also suffered from a complete lack of view. We were in thick fog next to the Cinque Terre. We had to follow our progress past the spectacular villages, headlands and cliffs on the radar. At last the fog cleared as we approached Portovenere. A look inside the crowded, tripperish harbour, much loved by Byron and Shelley, decided us to anchor nearby off Isola Palmaria, where we enjoyed a peaceful night in beautiful surroundings.

Quiver's burgee flies off over Tuscany

We had a long hard sail against the wind to Capraia. The 60 miles took nearly 15 hours and it was dark as we anchored amongst several other boats in the bay outside the harbour.

During the night the wind and driving rain funnelled down the hills, blasting the anchorage with vicious bullets which sent yachts dragging their anchors into deep water. We hauled up our anchor in an attempt to avoid the mayhem, and kept watch through a cold and squally night. In the morning we searched for better shelter along the coast, and found a bay a mile to the north. As Monique looked aloft to hold Quiver head to wind while I dropped anchor, she saw that the burgee had blown away. The top half of the burgee stick had broken in one of the violent gusts.

Cala Bagnaia, Elba.

The wind had abated but left a large swell as we sailed towards Elba, the snow covered mountains of Corsica over to starboard. We found an excellent berth in Portoferraio. We wandered round this charming town, clustered around one of the finest natural harbours in the Mediterranean, marvelling at the good fortune of Napoleon. What a great place to be in exile. Across the bay we found a lovely anchorage at Cala Bagnaia, and we enjoyed a good walk through the pine woods, admiring the profuse clusters of wild flowers. Monique identified two dozen different varieties, many of which would only grow in a greenhouse at home.

We had a pleasant sail across a calm sea to Giglio, another of the delightful Tuscan islands. We anchored in Seno di Campese off a fine sandy beach. I spent much of the night on a business conference call, with participants from Australia and the US. Sitting in the cockpit under a full moon and a starlit sky, sipping a glass of malt whisky, I hardly resented the intrusion of work into our cruise. The next day we took a bus up into the centre of the island to the walled hilltop village of Castello. After an excellent lunch we headed to Porto, the small harbour on the other side of the island.

'You should stay in Rome, like we do'

Our next Tuscan island was Giannutri. We set off at the same time as three other boats. We were all different sizes, we all followed different courses, but we all arrived at the same time. The wind was getting up and everyone seemed to be anxious to race us into the anchorage under sail. We anchored in the large bay on the east coast, uncomfortably close to the shore yet still in 18 metres. This was not a place to stay.

In a rising westerly wind we sped northeast under full sail to Cala di Galera. As we made fast Roberto, a handsome bearded Italian, came to admire *Quiver*. We told him that we had to return home in three days and that we were thinking of leaving *Quiver* here.

'You do not want to leave her here', he said. 'It's much too expensive and it's much too far from Rome. You should stay in Fiumicino, like we do. It's really nice up the River Tiber, fresh water, lovely countryside and a very friendly yard. Go on, give Pino a call. He owns the yard.'

We walked along the flower-covered cliffs to Porto Ercole. There is a plaque on the gate commemorating Caravaggio, who keeled over with sunstroke on the beach here in 1610 and is buried in the parish church nearby. I telephoned Pino from a bar. I felt that I was undergoing an interview. 'What sort of boat do you have? Where have you sailed? Do you know so-and-so from the Hamble? I lived there', he said, 'I had a Victoria 34 which I sailed across the Atlantic.' Eventually I had to ask if we could stay for a few weeks. 'Of course you can; we are like a small English club', he replied.

We enjoyed a very slow sail down the coast to another large modern marina at Riva di Traiano. There are no anchorages along this stretch of

Fishing huts at the entrance to the Tiber.

coast, but the marinas are well spaced for day sailing. The coast is shallow some way offshore and a wrecked yacht near the entrance here was a warning of the dangers of this coast.

It was flat calm as we motored south to Fiumicino, guided by the aircraft taking off and landing at Rome's busy airport. The entrance to the River Tiber is extraordinary. On either side of the broad shallow river are rickety wooden huts on stilts. Long curving booms supporting enormous circular nets sweep out across the river from the huts. The effect is exotic, reminiscent of a fishing village in southeast Asia.

We passed a couple of small boat yards as we headed up river, and hundreds of yachts secured alongside the banks. Eventually we came to a little lawn with deck chairs, a bar and a restaurant and as we slowed down a man called to us, 'You must be Signor Anthony. I am Pino. Pass me your lines.'

We were given a very warm welcome at the Nautilus Marina, and we felt confident to leave *Quiver* here until we could return at the beginning of July for a continuation of our tour which took us down to the Bay of Naples and back again to the Tiber.

Quiver is now out of the water and plans are being made for more Italian sailing next year. We found the west coast of Italy to be an excellent cruising ground, with fascinating excursions ashore, good sailing and, in July, generally uncrowded anchorages and harbours.

Quiver is a Bowman 40, built for us in 1987. She is the first of the class and was designed as a good looking and seaworthy passage maker. With her fully-battened mainsail, furling yankee and hanked staysail, she is easily handled by the two of us.

BROWN BEAR HEADS WEST

by John Clothier

Brown Bear's first extended season was planned so that she would arrive in Alaska on 23 June 2000. She left Lymington in August 1999 and reached the West Indies in early December via northwest Spain, Madeira and the Canaries. She then cruised the eastern Caribbean islands and Venezuela and arrived in Curacao in mid-March under the command of the Vice Commodore. She had had twenty-seven different crew members ranging in age from nineteen to eighty. For her toughest leg to date (across the Bay of Biscay), the oldest member was twenty-one.

The boat was set up to be sailed comfortably with two to four people, but as it is always difficult to say no to prospective crew, we would be six on the leg from Curacao through the Canal to the Galapagos and five on to Hawaii. The *Bear* was very pleased to welcome back Meg Clothier and Kath Joy, her two blonde girl friends who had seen her safely from Lymington to Martinique. Joining for their first taste of sailing were two of their university friends, Jack Dancy and Sam Spedding, who had signed up for treatment for post graduation stress disorder! Margaret Kimber (aunt and sister-in-law), who would leave us in the Galapagos, was trading in the responsibilities of late motherhood for some well-earned lazy sea miles and a merchandise-buying trip to Ecuador.

The challenges of the passage, in no particular order, were to maintain cool in Colon, to deny tedium in the doldrums, to reach Honolulu by the end of May and to carry sufficient food and water for the 4500-mile leg from Galapagos to Hawaii. Perhaps a more confident engineer would use different assumptions, but I thought it wise to plan that both watermaker and freezer would fail terminally a day out from Galapagos and that we could share Noel Marshall's experience and spend sixty days at sea.

I chose Curacao as the handover/storing place because of tax-haven standard supermarkets and good communications via Amsterdam. Sera Boca Marina was in Spanish Harbour, on the southeast corner of the island, within the security ring of a private resort estate. A hire car is essential. If you had to leave your boat for a while this would be a good choice, but repair facilities are limited.

Arrivals were as planned except that Meg's bag containing the larger proportion of the ship's library went AWOL in Amsterdam, but amazingly was brought to the *Bear* later the same day by the only man on the island strong enough to carry it. Storing and repairs were largely completed in time for us to take the weekend off and to celebrate my birthday a day early so that we could make a hangover free start. We were in the open sea by 0830 on 20 March wondering how the western Caribbean would live up to its billing as offering some of the roughest seas and strongest winds that are normally encountered on a Round-the-World passage. (Eric Hiscock gave line honours in this respect to the Needles channel!). We were expecting a tough initiation for the 'boys'. With our regular down-wind rig of main and poled-out jib set up, Jack and Sam quickly accustomed themselves to the feel of wind and seas at the helm and had soon mastered the application of Mike Pocock's beautifully thought out rig.

As it turned out, the top wind speed was 28 knots and the log refers to such things as 'full moon, constant wind, regular seas', '*Lord of the Rings* aloud in the cockpit' or 'at 1600 the Ship's band assembled on deck with Sam, director of music, on squeezie, Jack and Kath pipes, Meg cymbals and harmonica.' The wind gradually fell away to comfortable spinnaker flying levels and with the bonus of a strong current (keeping well off the Colombian coast seemed to pay) we were anchoring in Portobelo, Panama on 24 March in 'a beautiful deep-green peaceful bay' in time for a sunset dip. We had covered 714 miles per GPS in four and a half days.

Fishing for visual effect in Portobelo Roads, Panama.

The canal treated us well. We arrived and left as planned, 18 months before! We have a few suggestions, which might help make the transit as good an experience for others as it was for us. A copy of *The Path between the Seas* by David McCullough on board made compulsive reading with a wonderful insight into the French national character through the early years of their endeavour to dig a sea level canal. If you are of an impatient disposition avoid March and early April. The process of getting the paperwork done looks daunting. An agent costs about $500 and takes away the hassle. Alternatively, ask around at the yacht club amongst those already processed for a good taxi driver to sort out what you need and escort you to the different offices for about $40. Either way, the essential first step is admeasurement which you can arrange by radio or telephone. Once you have the completed form you can pay at the bank. Only then do you earn your place in the queue (we paid $450 for transit and $800 for the refundable bond). A strong recommendation is to arrive with enough United States dollars in cash, as ATM machines do not always cough up enough even if they cough at all. We saw several distraught skippers pleading with bank officials to produce the necessary cash. The rule seems to be to get the canal paperwork first then deal with customs, immigration and port authority for the cruising permit. You need four good warps of at least 40m length, lots of fenders (plastic covered tyres were available from local entrepreneurs for $5 each) and, if you do not have closed fairleads, you need to improvise. We used heavy spinnaker snatch blocks on the slotted toerail with the warps led to the primary winches, which gave good control at the stern. We were happy on the much maligned Flats with lots of air, having anchored as close as possible to the yacht club end. Finally, we sat back and enjoyed cheap beer and very adequate food at the yacht club whose services seemed to include the oldest profession of all! Incidentally, one of our crew left her bag including credit cards passport and the like on a table late at night to find next day that it had been handed in to the office by the security guard. Full marks!

Our passage to the Galapagos was pretty windless after a flying start from the coast. We wondered if a more southerly route than the one we took just south of the rhumb line would have paid, but heard others who had tried it reporting no wind as well. This was the first leg on which fishing was taken really seriously. We were completely amazed by the amount of marine life there seemed to be as compared with the Atlantic. Our gear had been significantly improved since my attendance at the annual dinner of a sea-angling club of which I am the woefully ill-informed president. We were now equipped with appropriate rod, reel, line and lures, instead of the home-welded double hooks festooned with strips of old oilskins with which we had tried to tempt the Pacific tuna's Atlantic cousins. Within seconds of deploying our first lure, the rod bent double and a glittering dorado was soon alongside. But, how to land him? The line was grabbed and in one swift movement he was on the side deck, off the hook and back in the sea. This pattern was repeated a couple of times, so we deployed a more savage hook and agreed that hoisting fish direct into the cockpit was the safest fish-landing technology available. The next fish to bite was a really large tuna, which took 45 minutes to bring alongside before shaking free. Finally, we got our act together and successfully landed, slew with a winch handle, filleted and froze two fine fish. Apart from fishing, the band practised regularly with *Spanish Ladies* setting the dolphins dancing, *The Lord of the Rings* was completed, whilst Kath's astro-navigation rendered the GPS redundant and guided us to an evening landfall at the Galapagos.

The Galapagos exceeded all our expectations. I suppose we all had an image of dryish rocks draped with some ugly amphibians cocooned in a blanket whose weft was world Eco-concern and whose warp was Latin-American bureaucracy. Most of the information we had was out-of-date. Yachts are welcome to stay for 21 days and can visit three anchorages without obtaining the hugely expensive cruising permit. This allows exploration of the islands with national-park guide aboard at an all up cost of a couple of thousand dollars. Good food and especially excellent frozen meat are available, as is fuel (filter it carefully), gas and water. In Puerto Ayora, we found Ricardo Arenas and his wife, Yvonne, very helpful in getting the best of what is available at reasonable cost.

We headed straight for Academy Bay and found that we could do most of what we wanted to do without leaving the island of Santa Cruz and paying the national-park fee for so doing. Plans for going off on local charter boats for a few days were abandoned in favour of day trips organised by local entrepreneurs who appeared to have the necessary guide's licences! So we did snorkelling with sea lions, scuba diving with hammerhead sharks and visiting giant turtles on horseback in our own time and at moderate cost. Other low cost delights were surfing the waves and the ether, the latter being an essential therapy to get the news and gossip before the longest haul by far. The other bonus of this arrangement was that we could enjoy the totally unexpected pleasures of the finest nightspot on the equator! Needless to say, the temptation to have a real night out was irresistible and the night before the day desig-nated for victualling and boat servicing finished two hours before work began at 0800! Amazingly all the tasks were achieved by early afternoon. Jack spent two hours in the water beating off the barnacles, whilst Sam and I conducted oil changes in complete silence. Meanwhile, the Meg-and-Kath catering machine ashore was limping to a halt when it was rescued and resuscitated by Yvonne.

As the season seemed to be particularly windless, we invested in cans to give us an extra sixty hours of diesel, to motor clear of the calm at the Galapagos and through the worst of the ITCZ. Shedding Margaret and her belongings on to a scheduled flight to Quito left us still floating

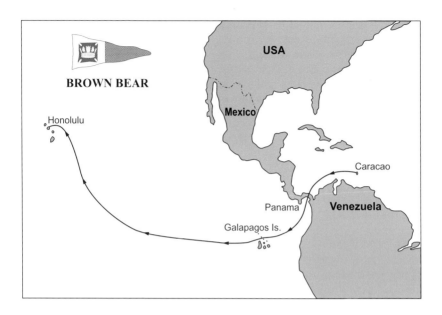

sluggishly below our marks. Departure was as planned at 0900 on 21 April and when the anchor was stowed and the sails set, the arrival sweepstake was posted. The most optimistic male reached for the calculator and divided 4500 miles by six knots (The boat's average speed to date per GPS), yielding thirty-one days. At the other end, I opted for a pessimistic forty, which would still just about keep us on schedule!

Choosing the best route was the challenge for this leg. We would, of course, never *know* whether we had succeeded, but long spells of calm and/or adverse currents would be an indicator of shortcomings. Cornell advises a route for February to May that stays just south of the Equator until crossing at 110°W and rejoining the great circle from Panama to Hawaii. Those who had made the passage recently favoured holding south of the equator until 130°W. We thought we should keep our options open and see what evidence we could collect from weather faxes. We duly motored clear of the Galapagos in a flat calm for about forty hours and then picked up breezes, which were west, rather than east of south. This meant that we were bumping along just south of the equator and probably too close to the ITCZ.

The second day out, we joined an SSB net (Coconut Run 2000) of about ten boats all on their way to the Marquesas, bar one boat bound also for Hawaii. They were all further south and ahead of us. There was no doubt that they had better winds and that once conditions allowed we should try and work south again. With hindsight, we should probably have used our engine hours out of the Galapagos to make for 3°S. On the third day of net chat, the Hawaii bound boat (who was also the group's weather forecaster) announced that, as they were encountering two knots of foul current and headwinds at $3°S\ 110°W$ they had given up on Hawaii and had altered course for the Marquesas. This was rather gloomy news. We looked again at the options and checked that we had a chart of the Marquesas as a fall back! Available weather information showed less wind north of the equator east of $130°W$ than to the south. Apart from the boats ahead, we had no other up-to-date current information, so heading north could also give us a longer spell in the equatorial counter current. Keeping south kept our options open. Meg and I chewed this bit of cud a few times more but we could not convince ourselves that it would pay to do anything other than cross the equator at $130°W$ and head from there on a great circle to Hawaii.

Looking back, we had no regrets. It was a long hard slog. The wind shifted constantly and we realised that we really could get several extra miles a day by hand steering and careful sail trimming, a positive advantage of the larger crew. We too recorded foul current of up to two knots where we expected it to be fair. Perhaps the counter current does indeed operate further south than predicted on the pilot charts, but we would be unable to prove this, as our log became increasingly inaccurate due to the encroachment of goose barnacles. Another phenomenon, reported by other boats too, was short bursts of east going current usually associated with the arrival of squid all over the deck. This suggested an occasional up-welling of the deeper east flowing currents of the Pacific.

After crossing the equator we had a couple of days of perfect spinnaker sailing which hastened us towards our meeting with the ITCZ. Its position was reported moving as much as 100 miles north or south in a day. We had seen just one ship in three weeks, so were completely gobsmacked to hear the roar of a helicopter which came close enough for us to see the glint in the moustachioed pilot's eye as he took in the bronzed blondes sunbathing beneath him. A scan of the horizon identified his base as one of several tuna boats operating in the area.

Deep blue-black clouds heralded the approach of the ITCZ, followed by torrential rain and spiralling winds, but no electrical storms. We got through in the course of a night with the northeast trades filling in just as they should and blowing us quickly on our way. The optimists looked to have gained the upper hand, but a slight rearrangement of the isobars had us slowing from a spate of 180-mile days and gave the prize to the second lowest figure. Sam pledged he would blow his winnings on the finest cocktails in town as our nostrils filled with the scent of fast food wafting off Honolulu's Waikiki beach. We made fast after thirty-four days at sea.

Personally, I could not have dreamt of a better crew or better company. So much so that, when the US immigration official welcomed us to Hawaii with the news that we had each to pay $160 emergency visa waiver or face deportation, I paid out the $800 like a lamb!

The Bear left Hawaii in early June with Peter Lewin-Harris, Sam and Alex Edenborough and Meg and Kath aboard. She arrived in Seward, Alaska on time after a fast sixteen day passage. She is now over-wintering in Nanaimo, Vancouver Island.

Brown Bear was designed by Michael Pocock and built by Stephen Etheridge. She is a close sister of Troubadour. Her vital statistics are: Length overall 13.69m, Length waterline 11.04m, Beam 4.02 m, Draft 2.15 m, Displacement 13,400 Kgs, Sail Area 85.00 sq. m.

Her construction is an epoxy glass sandwich using a Speedstrip Western Red Cedar Core. A layer of Kevlar has been used both internally and externally in the most vulnerable sections of the bows. The rig is heavily specified. The double roller headsail arrangement is designed to provide good windward performance in heavier weather through the high aspect ratio jib set on the inner forestay. The mainsail is fully battened, with batten cars allowing reefing off the wind. The engine is a Sabre-Perkins M65, 4cyl, 3 litre normally aspirated diesel. Fuel capacity is 500 litres and water 400 backed up by a DC watermaker capable of producing 25 litres per hour. She is equipped with most modern aids to navigation and communication, but still uses paper charts!

THE ARC? NO THANKS!

by Trevor Coleman

For my 1999 sabbatical *Takaroa* was joined in Tenerife by Bob Green (alias 'Chunky Monkey' or 'Bits and Bobs') ex CPS Chief, and Sam Berthoud (alias 'Cordon Bleu Sambo' and/or 'Iridium Sam') bringing a little Swiss cuisine and the wonder of modern telecommunications.

After loading enough food for six men for three months, the three of us set out for the Cape Verde Isles on 6 November 1999 at 1105 (5 minutes later than planned three years ago), and were waved goodbye by some of our wives.

The first day was spent diving down into the deep freeze for ice in our Pimms due primarily to an unaccustomed lack of wind in the acceleration zone between Tenerife and Gran Canaria. This eventually turned into a light NW breeze and after 26 hours of frost the tranquil peace of the night was re-established with a brisk northerly breeze almost until we arrived in Puerto Grande Cabo Verde (Sao Vicente) almost exactly six days later when the wind died again. We had to force our way through a motley collection of some fifty Euro-yachts (despite L'Arc) who were on yet another race organised by the French.

This first part of the trip was punctuated by a 26 hour spinnaker run – Roast Lamb with Roast Potatoes, Redcurrant Jelly and Mint Sauce (twice) – Roast Duck À L'Orange – Onion Tart – Vegetables À La Trancha. The wildlife included 20 porpoises, one shark, one tuna and Bananas au Cointreau. Oh and by the way, the trade winds blew for five days! Quelle Joie! 830 nautical miles of uneventful breezes from 6 to 12 November.

Navigation so far caused no problems thanks to no less than four GPS (every good crewman has one!). However, some minor hiccups were caused by the battery charger blowing up with a loud bang whilst we were still (in theory) on 24 volts in Marina Atlantico. This was resolved by some long distance phone calls to Portugal and, after some judicious snipping of wires, there was a ceremonial ditching of the Solent charger followed just south of the Cape Verde Islands after five years use (clearly exceeding its sell by date). Surges of up to 480 volts reported in Marina Atlantico in the yachting press this summer explained the cause of the problem. The boat is now floating much higher in the water.

A special mention must be made of Sam's agricultural expertise, which is only exceeded by his culinary exploits. He waters his mint, chives and parsley daily and can be seen talking to them exhorting them to greater efforts to keep up with the consumption of Pimms and other delicacies.

The Cape Verde interlude cannot be concluded without mentioning Bob's 'drawing' power, whilst away for two minutes phoning my electrical engineer, I returned to find a very large and 'loving' Maria perched on my chair at the bar looking 'ravishingly' at Bob – who only just escaped 'unhurt' (we believe!). We dragged him away eventually – reluctantly.

Puerto Grande is a safe harbour with good holding, fair provisioning and diesel from Shell on the main quay. Having seen the colour of the fresh water on the quay from the hose we kept our Tenerife supply intact. Nelson our boat boy kept everything running smoothly including our laundry and, once he had stripped Bob's tee shirt off his back and his baseball cap, he was only disappointed by the lack of shoes. My own fashionable towelling shirts were not in demand!

We failed to contact emigration, despite many efforts, and left without clearance but we were more successful with the Port Captain's documents.

By 15 November we were more than ready to leave and put both foresails on the roller gear, set the trysail and had a good gently rolling sail downhill. 1970 nautical miles to go on 282° if the four GPSs were to be believed.

Notable events over the next few days included half an hour of 100 porpoises playing around the boat – Bob's birthday – Champagne cocktails and a six course meal lasting from noon till 1800 including salad, smoked salmon, fresh fish caught by the fishing officer himself and lemon pie and birthday cake with candles. Five pilot whales spotted and a bloated puffer fish identified. Wednesday and Thursday were noted for unseasonably heavy rain and squalls from SE. We had to lower the trysail our steadying sail and do a long tack down to the south in heavy swell from NE. We passed 60 miles south from our position on 21 November 1972 (27 years on) in our Seacracker *Buttercup*.

Iridium Sam gave us encouraging news of Hurricane Lenny sitting stationary over Antigua with 135 knots of wind as we approached the halfway mark.

Sam's agricultural efforts also excelled by turning owner's bed into a mud bath thanks to an exceptional wave. Sam's reputation saved by roast lamb for dinner.

Full sail on Friday, which kept up our average speed of 137 nautical miles per day.

No sign of any trade wind yet but rain and squalls continue apace terminating in a 27 knot squall and teaming rain for three hours in the skipper's watch (no less), after which both rain and wind gave up and we had 24 hours of nil wind under the Iron Genoa – good for the iced Pimms and batteries but little else.

Swims, spinnakers and heat became the order of the days as flat calm set in for 3 whole days. Sam's wife 'Mim' predicts two more days flat calm before our 'white' spot on the Internet chart turns to green (10 knots or more!).

The morning of Tuesday 23 November is devoted to poetic musings for the benefit of Lucy's (my sister in law's) impending nuptials on Saturday 27 November at Powderham Castle in Devon. A suitable email was prepared as a joint effort causing a few hours of hilarity on the suitability for inclusion of certain events in Lucy's life. There are only 1,000 miles to Barbados now and we are over the halfway mark.

Spinnaker up for nearly 6 days on and off, but found a mysterious tear in it one morning. We could only conclude that the pin in the end of the snap shackle caused the problem and tape it up – instantly repaired and then up again.

Various dorados caught en route which proved excellent eating. Light winds continue for further three days but squalls resulted in lowering of spinnaker by night and back up by day. Our Health & Safety Officer burnt his hands on spinnaker halyard and Sam tried to go down fore hatch bottom first, however spinnaker eventually raised.

Sighted *Moonstar* (RCC) a 42′ Halberg Rassy which took nearly 24 hours to pass us.

Sam maintained his culinary skill by cooking flambéed peach and spilling most of contents on his feet and the galley floor – shortly after he had a rare shower on deck – from one of the Solar showers.

Bob landed a 4lb dorado on 1 December which we duly ate with roasted almonds – very good it was too.

On 2 December, we sighted Barbados and had a good run in round Island in 20 knots – another crossing successfully concluded – 23 days – same as 27 years ago almost to the day. Bob won the arrival time bet and a free meal at the Brown Sugar restaurant.

The 'high' lights which made the trip most memorable were:-
> Ice in Pimms and mint.
> Autohelm worked all the way.
> Beautiful starry nights.
> Six days spinnaker run.
> Dorados on demand.
> Bob's 'take it easy' approach.
> Sam's roast lambs and ducks.

The 'low' lights were:-
> Lack of wind/slatting of sails
> Too many other yachts in the Atlantic.

MARY HELEN GOES SOUTH

by Donald Tew

This log records the family cruise for which the Grace Cup was awarded to Helen Tew.

There was a fateful moment in 1999 when my mother said to me, 'Find out what is happening to *Mary Helen*, I want to buy her back'. In the following eighteen months, well over 1000 miles have slid under her keel. She is further south than she has ever been before and has spent more nights at sea at one time than ever before. At 63 years old, the ship has started a second childhood. Normally we do our cruises when younger and our vessels newer; indeed *Mary Helen* did exactly that, winning the challenge cup in 1938, a year after being launched.

You may be wondering where this is leading. It is a preamble to a remark I made to Mama in March this year, when I suggested heading south, saying, 'Let's see how far we get.' I thought, perhaps, that she would say that doing three millennium meets would suffice for this year. In fact, she went for it and asked when and where were we going! 'Oh, and by the way', she added, 'let's do the meets anyway'.

I persuaded her to drop two of the meets, because, going south, we might turn right: things would need doing to the boat for such a trip.

My brother James (RCC) spent a week cruising in the Channel Islands with mother, before leaving *Mary Helen* in Guernsey where I worked. At the end of June, Mama and I left Guernsey, on the day I retired, to go to the first of the millennium meets in Jersey, Minquiers, and Iles Chausey. How kind everyone was to Mother – especially Michael Allo and his son, who ferried her (and me) about. Anchoring in the Minquiers was a first for *Mary Helen*, and particularly exciting, our thoughts having been moulded by the late Hammond Innes.

From Iles Chausey we returned to Beaulieu on 4 July to fit out for the trip south. I had set a departure date for 1 August, which was not going to be missed. There was much to be done, including fitting a

219

windpilot, radar, weatherfax, autohelm and a thousand and one other things.

1 August was looming. I had been out with Datayacht to check radar, autopilot and weather fax; all were working! Mother made up the shopping list for a voyage of 'some duration' and my kind wife Lucy spent a small fortune and filled many supermarket trolleys following the list! Where would it all go? I had used up some of the space to stow water: forty-eight one and a half litre bottles behind the settees, eight two gallon cans elsewhere about the boat. The main tank holds about ten gallons, so overall enough water at half a gallon a head per day for two people to last at least thirty days with a fifty percent margin.

Everything was stowed and the only real sign was that *Mary Helen* was just a little lower in the water. These main stores were for later, when crossing the Atlantic. In the meantime, the ready use locker would hold enough for the shorter passages.

The evening of 1 August finally arrived and the family came down to see us off. A drink or two was had and at last when the tide was high enough (*Mary Helen* has an inside berth at the Bucklers Hard Marina) we left under power. My nephew Michael joined us for the first part of the trip and it was useful having a third hand.

It was late; how quiet and peaceful the river was, no wind and the stars shining. Dark shapes of boats on their moorings could easily be mistaken for the wooden warships being towed down the river by oarsmen in small boats. Wherever one goes, there is nothing, so far in my experience, to beat the Beaulieu River. We made fast to the Beaulieu River Sailing Club's pontoon at Needs Oar, had supper and turned in.

We had intended to be away early to catch the tide down the Solent, but, as I suppose I could have expected, the wind had sprung up from the southwest and was beginning to blow. So much for the easterlies that had been around for some ten days prior to our leaving! Nevertheless, despite F.7 at times and showers, there were odd jobs to be done that should have been done before and, with Michael's help, they were all completed.

At 1230 on 3 August, we left the pontoon under sail; the wind was westerley, F. 3–4, but more in the squalls accompanying the rain. Cowes Week was in full swing and there were many boats about. None of them was flying a racing flag, so *Mary Helen* sailed through the various fleets close hauled on starboard tack and believe it or not, was given due courtesy for age and rig! I took a reef in halfway down the Solent as we were being hard pressed in the squalls. *Mary Helen* made good time with a fair tide out to the Fairway buoy off the Needles. There was a confused steep sea and we could not lay our course for Ushant. *Mary Helen* did not like this, nor did the crew, so with a little help from the engine, we made for Studland Bay. As we closed Old Harry rock, the sea calmed down and Michael, who had succumbed to seasickness, perked up. We made our way into the bay and picked up a mooring. It was clear that the wind had shifted to the northwest; maybe we would make real progress tomorrow.

We got away from Studland at 0345. There was a fresh northwesterly wind and *Mary Helen* was tramping along at over six knots in the right direction. It did not last, as the wind slowly died, but we did just save our tide at Portland, although the Bill remained in sight for a long time!

It was a clear sunny start, but later clouded over and the wind headed, although we were able to lay our course. I put the yankee up and this increased our speed quite considerably. By dusk, we were being pressed, so the big sail was handed and replaced with the much smaller jib. A moderate head sea made the motion a little uncomfortable, but *Mary Helen* ploughed on at four and a half knots seeming eager to head on south. Michael was feeling a lot better after yesterday's dusting.

A cool night followed with lots of ships about. At least with modern electrics, we no longer had to light the paraffin side lights and then take them forward for fitting! By dawn the wind had died, so the engine was used, but not for long as a light west-northwesterly breeze had sprung up, allowing us to hold our course at three and a half knots. I again put up the yankee and this increased our speed. The motion of yesterday had eased and as the morning wore on the sky cleared. There were many gannets about, but as Michael does not like fish, I did not put the line overboard. By the evening there was no wind, so wanting to get round Ushant as soon as possible we made use of the engine.

On Sunday 6 August, Ushant was abeam at 0320. When I came on watch at 0400 the visibility was down to less than a quarter of a mile. At least we had radar. Wet drizzle set in and for a short while conditions were somewhat unpleasant and we went through two oil slicks, which smelt horribly. Dawn did break, but with some reluctance. The skies were heavily overcast and the cloud was very low. The wind picked up from northwest by west, so on the watch change we stopped the engine. The sun tried hard all day and it was as dusk fell that it made an appearance with a spectacular sunset.

During this day we were making five knots, but as the wind veered to the north and died, progress became slow. The yankee was up again and boomed out. Just at sunset, there were some very odd cloud formations at sea level, just as one remembers seeing in horror films. In the end, the moon shone through with its twinkling light rippling on the calm sea. This did not last and those strange clouds lost their phantom image and took on a real form as the fog rolled in. Not much fun in the dark!

By dawn the heavy mist had left us and the sky was clear. There were ships on both sides of us and it would seem that we were in the clear zone in the middle of the shipping lanes. The sea had changed to that cobalt blue colour, now that we were off the continental shelf. *Mary Helen* was making some three knots with the fair wind. There was a slight swell. As the day progressed, the wind veered to the east and increased. We gybed and the speed improved to over five knots. This was more like it! *Mary Helen* was now half way across the Bay of Biscay and as the hours went by, further south than she has ever been before. With the increase in the wind, the sea built up with the odd crest breaking nearby.

We went into the night carrying the yankee and full main. The moon again shone, with its silvery path for us to follow. Through the night a slow increase in the wind pushed our speed higher. By the afternoon it was F.5–6 from the north east and our speed was touching seven knots at times. It was time to reduce sail and I put one reef in the mainsail as well as handing the yankee. Things calmed down a little and the motion became easier.

By dawn on 9 August, the breeze of yesterday had departed. There was a heavy mist in the air and our speed had fallen to two and a half knots. The sea was confused and sharp and we had to motor. Ships were appearing when not expected. Either I was overtired or there was fog about. Indeed the fog closed in as we approached the northwest coast of Spain. The radar and GPS really do work and, without such aids, I would have gone out to the west, away from the shipping lanes and waited until it cleared. As the afternoon wore on, my nerves were well tested with visibility almost zero and what I hoped was Cape Villano very close. I had decided to go into Camarinas just to the south of the Cape. After continuous plotting and radar watching, I announced that we should see something on the starboard bow as I altered course eastwards in the swirling fog. At 1745 a glint of sun shone on land to starboard: the instruments were right after all! The relief was tangible as we left the fog and entered the Ria.

From 10 August *Mary Helen* sailed down the west coast of Spain and arrived at Lagos, her first objective achieved. Those stores purchased for a "voyage of some duration" are perhaps soon to be used.

VOYAGING IN VENEZUELA

by Tom Fenwick

In years gone by I had been up and down the Caribbean islands but had not been to Venezuela. I had heard a lot about it and now was the time to spend the best part of a season there. *First Lady* had been laid up in Trinidad in August 1999 while we were in UK. We returned to the boat in late January 2000. For the following two months we fitted out, prepared for Carnival and then enjoyed this amazing event, all the while enjoying the help and hospitality of our Hon. Foreign Representative, Don Kelshall and his wife, Cathryn. Both Don and Cathryn were a patient source of information and great fun to be with during our time in Trinidad. It was difficult to leave but we set off at the end of March heading for Los Testigos, those magic islands so well described by Trevor Wilkinson in the 1998 Journal. Magic they were for us, especially for the less humid climate and clearer water. We enjoyed snorkelling, swimming and a lobster feast before sailing on to Isla Margarita to meet Gill Lloyd who was going to have her first cruise since reaching eighty; she would be with us for two weeks.

If you look at a chart of Venezuela you will see several distinct regions; the islands south of Isla Margarita (Coche and Cubagua) then south of this the vast Gulf of Cariaco. To the west of the gulf is Mochima Marine National Park with a mass of inlets and Puerto La Cruz at the western end. Then there are the outer islands of Tortuga, La Blanquilla, Los Roques and Los Aves.

Los Roques is a National Park and as such you not only have to pay to go into it but only get 14 days – and this costs £75. You can make your time extend by not checking in too soon (by hanging out in some out of the way anchorage) and by hanging around a bit when you check out – we had three weeks on this system. Many boats just going through on their way to Los Aves and Bonaire do not check in. I must say it is a glorious cruising ground for although much of it is shallow the deep waters are nearly all protected by outer reefs. Every little island has

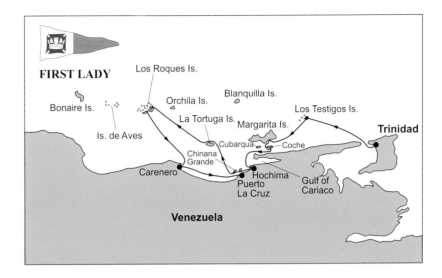

magical fine coral sand beaches, usually with mangroves in some area, and the fishing is excellent. I even managed to trap an 18 inch ray at low water, driving it into the real shallows until I could stun it with my plastic shod heel. Raie à la crème was for supper that night. Francisqui, where many Venezuelan boats were left at anchor, is a lagoon with a mini lagoon inside it and then the most superb snorkelling lagoon on the weather side. The variety of fish was stunning, as was the coral. The only problem with Francisqui was that the big day charter catamarans came in (the punters having flown to Gran Roque from the mainland) but by 1700 or earlier they had all gone. From here we moved back to Gran Roque to store up as best we could. It is very hit and miss as to whether the stores have come in the day you shop, otherwise as each day goes by there is less and less. It is also expensive, but there is nothing else for 80 miles. Gran Roque has a permanent population of about 800 and is the only island in the group that is more than 30 foot above sea level (and those are only dunes). The Rock itself is some 800 feet high with a lighthouse on top.

From Gran Roque we ran down to the lagoon at Noronsqui, a mere four miles and then worked our way round coral heads and into a comfortable spot. From here we ran on down wind the 15 miles to Caya de Agua, at the western end, passing Sarqui, Crasqui and Carenero on the theory of 'let's have a good run down wind and then short hops to get back uphill'. We were the only boat in Caya de Agua and we found it a little open, but the sand dunes were spectacular and the cay does have some fresh water (if you dig for it) and a few palm trees. Two days there were enough before heading back to Carenero. This turned out to be the

Sardines on the BBQ – Gulf of Cariaco.

gem of Los Roques. There was a lagoon with mangrove trees to windward, protected through 330 degrees, and you looked out to the west
over multi hued shallows to where the finger of Carenero stretched some
8 miles. The bone-fishing here was excellent. Los Roques is the bone
fishing capital of the world – you fly-fish for them. The dinghy sailing
was divine – we could have all stayed for weeks – but for foreigners that
was not allowed. So we gave ourselves six days in this spot of paradise
before moving back upwind towards Gran Roque, visiting Sarqui and
Crasqui on the way. It was as we were coming round the south end of
Crasqui where we were motoring up the channel, directly into the wind,
and then having to round a coral bank before hoisting sail that we had an
interesting problem; I had just began to alter course to port round the
coral bank (with coral to starboard as well) when I felt the steering go
very stiff and I wondered if by some malfunction the Autohelm had been
turned on. I yelled down to Trish. 'No,' came the answer. 'Well look into
the pot cupboard under the cockpit where the Autohelm gearing is
installed.' Back came the reply, 'No that looks alright – wait a minute –
oh hell, there is a plastic spatula jammed in the gearing and I can't get it
out.' At this point we had not quite rounded the end of the coral so were
able to put the engine out of gear and drift back down the channel until
we were clear of the coral and then with limited steering head in behind
it and drop the anchor. By this time the spatula had forced the chain
linkage so that it was sitting on top of a sprocket tooth, but also jammed

up against the bearing housing and so the steering was well and truly locked. With anchor down and the socket set out it was only a matter of minutes to slacken off the bearing housing retaining nuts to free the spatula and the chain, then tighten up again. We were off again in less than half an hour but if the whole shenanigan had happened five minutes later there could have been a different tale – no steering and coral reef just to leeward of us. How the spatula got up there I do not know for there is 18 inches clearance; anyway spatula stowage will be high on the check list in future. We had a glorious close reach to Gran Roque, cleared out and went off to Francisqui with its lovely snorkelling pool to spend a few days 'waiting for the weather'.

Before laying up at Puerto La Cruz we decided to take a trip inland; in the sixties I had been to a talk by Eric Hiscock and he had shown a slide of the Angel falls, deep in the interior; he and Susan had flown over it. We decided we would go by dug-out canoe from Canaima, some 50 miles short of the Falls. To get there we first took a bus to Ciudad Bolivar on the Orinoco, then flew in a small plane the 140 miles to Canaima before setting off up river with a side trip or two in a 40 foot dugout with a 40hp outboard on the stern. I reckon we were going at near 20 knots a good deal of the time. We spent one night in a campsite sleeping in hammocks before the final run up the river which took us over many shallows. We then walked mostly uphill the last 2 miles through the jungle to near the base of these 3300 foot falls. Wow, that was something, for when we arrived the upper two thirds of the falls were obscured by cloud, and then the clouds started to clear – it was magic. The whole area is dotted with *tepuys*, very ancient flat topped mountain areas with vertical sides. Since we were in the rainy season much of the time they were obscured – then the rain would stop, the sun come out and all around you there were waterfalls pouring down. Watching these from our camp on the second evening was enchanting. The trip down from Angel Falls was more exciting than going up as you had the extra speed of the water going with you over the shallows – the Amerindian helmsman lifting his engine in many places. The flight back to Ciudad Bolivar was also interesting – a somewhat battered 4 seater, pilot very macho with much gold on and my safety harness would not do up. 'No problema,' said the pilot, but I noticed that there was nothing wrong with his belt. Trish, sitting behind me, swore that the starboard wing strut had come away from the wing. Anyway we made it back to ground without mishap.

First Lady is a Midshipman 41' ketch designed by William Garden and built in Taiwan in 1978 by Transworld Yachts. We bought her in Holland in 1997.

LA SNOOK, THE GRANNIES AND BEYOND

by Gill Lloyd

The tubby 25ft *La Snook* and 'The Grannies' have become somewhat outdated in the modern world of large, fast and sophisticated yachts full of electronic gadgets, but perhaps our humble potterings can encourage others that it is still possible for ancient mariners to keep going and have fun at moderate expense.

Nevertheless change there has to be. After ten years of the three of us happily sailing together, Liz Bate and I have lost our most venerable companion, Helen Tew, back to her lovingly rescued and restored *Mary Helen*, and off with son Donald across the ocean. Fortunately we have been joined by another highly experienced RCC granny, Carol Ridout, David's mum, three generation family friend, and like-minded scrabble and whisky enthusiast. We have also modernized *La Snook* by installing a rolling jib and home-designed lazy-jacks for the main. This has made deck work for the ageing grannies a good deal easier and means we can carry sail longer.

We set off from Lymington on 13 June into the usual southwesterly weather, but finding the Needles Channel too unattractive settled for a wet, roughish beat to Studland Bay, followed by a sheltered layday getting shipshape. Our reward was a pleasant twelve hour channel crossing and after a sunny day in Cherbourg, with fog at sea, we set off downwind with a nice E.4 forecast. Alas, it died on us after an hour, and under main and motor we whistled spookily round Cap de la Hague on a swirling, glassy sea, to creep into Diélette with 1.5m. under us. The echo-sounder battery had gone flat and was irreplaceable in France. So back to ancient lead-line marked in fathoms. Drinks time brought surprise visitors, Geoffrey and Sue Nockolds RCC, just arrived over by car for a week in their nearby delightfully rural cottage. They invited us to a sumptuous and leisurely Sunday lunch the next day in perfect summer weather.

Another foggy day, then on to Carteret through two tremendous thundery downpours. Here strong onshore winds kept us three days in port. We we were consoled by the friendly welcome in the yacht club, a colourful market day and, from a long walk across the marshes, a ride home on the little toy train from Portbail. We hitched a lift by a level-crossing, where the grannies were inelegantly hauled aboard up off the track by the Thomas-the-Tank-Engine crew, via an upturned milk crate provided by the engine driver. We escaped the next day but were rewarded by a roughish but exhilarating sail to the anchorage in St Catherine's Bay on the northeast corner of Jersey. Thence an early start on a beautiful morning to catch the tide to Granville.

Arrival in Granville was a near disaster. Carol missed her footing getting onto the narrow, wobbly finger pontoon and ended up hanging precariously onto the ship's rail, half in the water. We tied a rope round under her armpits, and with the long boarding-ladder hung close by, got her back aboard wet only to the waist. Liz had managed to secure the bow-line, but on our attempt to moor back alongside, she stepped onto the pontoon with the stern line, only to stand wobblingly rooted to the spot, and I eventually had to crawl on hands and knees to fix it to the end ring. We must in future have the *grabbit* ready in the stern for marina berthing. Luckily there were no spectators about, and Carol was none the worse back in dry clothes. We recovered with strong rum and limes all round.

Excellent very French supper 'chez Pierot', then out the next afternoon on the falling tide for a delightful sail to Isles Chausey, against the stream of returning weekend boats, to pick up an empty buoy in the sound where we ate supper in the cockpit on a perfect evening in the setting sun. We had a great sail with a beam wind to St Malo to visit our dear French friends of over thirty years, Jean Pierre and Florine, at Minihic. We drank champagne in the sunny garden looking out across the Rance to St Suliac.

Then back to Chausey for another perfect evening, where we picked up a buoy in the northeast corner of the sound, among smallish boats: HW at drinks time and our 6 fathom lead-line just touched bottom, with tidal range of 11.4 metres. Our doubts were cured by another whisky, and there were no bumps in the night! We pottered on to Jersey to meet up with the assembling RCC fleet in St Helier marina for a convivial meet whence the Grannies flew home, leaving *La Snook* to be sailed to south Brittany by the next generation, Sarah and Giles Gleadell, on a four week cruise. Back at Lymington, she was off again with the third generation, grand-daughter Katy as skipper for the first time, down to Weymouth and back, gathering friends en route. On one night they had five sleeping aboard!

Between whiles faithful *Snook* has also taken all my three great-grandchildren to sea at various times in the Solent – four generation sailing is fun, if at times slightly fraught! But *La Snook*, twenty six years in the family, happily and safely accommodates all ages.

TO THE DENMARK STRAIT

by David Lomax

For *Cloud Walker's* millennium cruise, Judy and I hoped that the effects of global warming might allow a yacht to explore the world's largest fjord, Scoresbysund on the east coast of Greenland across the Denmark Strait from Iceland.

We sailed by way of two rolling meets to the Faeroes. At the fogbound entrance to Tórshavn a guard boat asked us to stooge around for an hour because the harbour was full of racing skiffs with crowds ashore cheering them on. Out of the mist came hearty crews heaving on their oars as they propelled their brightly painted whalers towards the finishing line somewhere out of sight. In front of us was a cabin cruiser from which a Faeroese radio reporter was giving an excitable and infectious running commentary. It was impossible not to be carried away by the competitive atmosphere in spite of not being able to see much of it.

This was our fifth visit to the Faeroes but we had not realised that this weekend coincided with St Olav's Day, the most important holiday in the national calendar. The entire population seemed to be out in the streets in traditional costume, with mobile phones and open bottles of beer. It took us sometime before we could enter, make fast and join in. Next day with the crowds lining the route of an annual ceremonial procession we watched while the Faeroese church hierarchy in robes and stiff white ruffs led local parliamentarians to a church service and then a reception in an ancient turf-roofed office block. The entire procedure was broadcast live on Faeroese television although it seemed as if most of the audience was already present.

One reason for visiting the Faeroes was to allow Jim to explore his roots. During the war his father was the medical officer in charge of a hospital for the 8000 British troops building the airport at Vagar. Jim wanted to find out more. Some post-war snap shots of Faeroese women had been found in his late father's effects. After a night disturbed by nearby revellers who sang and danced on the quay until dawn, we

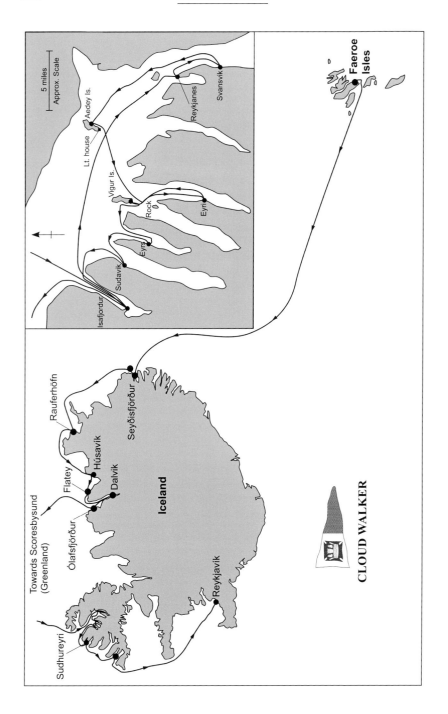

slipped away and were soon on a spirited broad reach in a W4 with huge swirlies. In a brisk westerly we beat to windward down Skopunarfjørður, with an ebb tide of 4 knots carrying us past the glowering shapes of Hestur and Koltur (Horse and Colt islands), and finally motored into Miðvágur, where we tied up alongside the fish factory and next to an abandoned trawler.

According to Jim's father all the islanders were friendly when the troops first arrived but did not seem to know whether the newcomers were British or German. Jim's photographs intrigued some of the older locals, who recognised one of the girls and pointed us in the direction of an old people's home. Sadly, the matron reported that Elli (84) was too ill to see us. We took a taxi past the airport to the awesome cliffs over-looking Mykenes, inspected a plaque in the church at Sørvágur which recorded the gratitude of the British occupiers, and next day, set off under the precipitous Witch's Finger down Vestmannasund. On either side sheep with apparently magnetic hooves grazed the almost vertical slopes, their brown and dirty cream fleeces the exact colour of the local sweaters. The spring tide sluiced us through to the open sea.

After resting and refuelling in Seyðisfjörður we set course for Langenes and the north coast. This was again a long motor, much of it through thick fog and a sloppy swell, with millions of cavorting seabirds. In Rauferhöfn, Iceland's most northerly port, we moored alongside the same wooden fish dock we had visited five years before and found the same family running the local hotel. They provided showers and intro-duced us to a new delicacy, lake trout smoked in sheep manure.

There are times when the summer climate along this coast lets you sail in a T-shirt, in scorching sunlight with a visibility of 50 miles. Judy gut-ted cod, and as we crossed the Arctic Circle we celebrated with a dram – with an offering over the side to appease the deities. Húsavik, which had grown since our last visit, has a superb local museum and an excellent fish restaurant on the quay where one no longer has to consult the IMF before ordering. An overnight gale started to clear the following after-noon, so in a northwest F.5–6 we beat across the bay to the island of Flatey, stopping briefly for a walk ashore then running along the coast and 30 miles up the next fjord, dodging outbound cruise liners.

In Akureyri the manager of the local tourist office, could not have been more helpful. Knudur advised us about where we might get parts for some minor repairs and showed off his home-built steel sloop. *Go Go* had taken him 14 years and was, he told us, ready for a Greenlandic adventure. She looked considerably more substantial than our craft. It was here that we collected our borrowed polar bear weapon, enjoyed a swim and hot pot in what must surely be the finest swimming pool in the country, swapped crew, and indulged in guillemot in blue cheese and chocolate sauces (on separate evenings). Over the next two days of provisioning and repairs, James Nixon RCC, who had replaced Jim, demonstrated that he is as good at mending bilge pumps as hips and kneecaps.

Icelandic weather forecasts are excellent for the immediate period but do not take into account local effects. In spite of the northern coast's promised south F.4, the fjord treated James to an initiation of north F.5 gusting 6 and heavy rain. Our beat to Hrísey was wild. Next day the island, which lies near the mouth of the Eyjafjörður, rewarded us with a rugged walk around a vast rocky bird sanctuary with ptarmigan, whimbrel, rock pippets and golden plover. We were towed back there after having fouled the prop with a vast floating trawl the following windless morning. A frantic session with boat hooks from the dinghy eventually freed the offending object. The tow cost us a bottle of Scotch, but we were then able to beat vigorously northwards to Ólafsfjörður and then 30 miles offshore to the island of Grimsey, which lies on the Arctic Circle.

When we left for Scoresbysund it would have been good to have more long range weather intelligence than our Navtex could give us. We had plugged into the internet café in Akureyri, but had not been able to find any decent up to date ice information. As the weather appeared reasonably settled, we decided to push northwards anyway. As Grimsey retreated the weather was reasonable, the boat in good order and our morale high. We bucketed along at first in ESE F.4–5 then took in reefs as the wind and sea increased.

Twelve hours later serious waves were tramping past and often breaking over us. One bent a stanchion. By midday on Sunday 13 August when we were about 100 miles off Scoresbysund we decided to heave to on the starboard tack. The breaking seas on all sides seemed to be getting bigger. That evening the wind was over 40 knots. I saw 44 on the dial but there were obviously heavier gusts. One sea then stove in the spray hood, drenching the mate who was not amused. Another dollop managed to woosh over the cooker. None of this was exactly life threatening, but it did make one wonder how long it might continue and whether it was wise to proceed.

I imagined we were somehow being squashed between another low brewing off Cape Farewell and an increasing high in Greenland. We were now under bare poles making about 3 knots to the west where we knew that somewhere in the fog, perhaps at 50 miles, there was a vast raft of pack ice being ground into the coast. Perhaps in retrospect we should have continued, but at this point both Judy and I had the same idea simultaneously, 'How far is it to northwest Iceland?'

Although in no real danger, we were wet, cold and hungry and not in a position to hold our own against ice. As we turned down wind and let out a scrap of jib *Cloud Walker* rushed down the long seas which were trying to overwhelm our quarter. She managed to maintain her heading on autohelm, and gradually we were able to tidy up. James managed to light the cooker and noted that the inventor of *cuppasoup* deserved a

Cloud Walker in Isafjordur.

Nobel prize. For 30 hours we forged our way towards Isafjörður with the wind and sea gradually dropping until it was necessary to start the motor abeam the stark headlands of Hornstrandir.

Ísarfjörður could not have been more welcoming. The manager of a prawn processing machine shop took us under his wing, and within two days all damage had been repaired; we had bathed and feasted and been taken on guided tours. Sigurdur and his father own the only two yachts in this part of Iceland and know the shrimp boat skippers who fish in the rarely visited fjords to the east. We decided to leave East Greenland for another year and spend the rest of our cruise exploring these. There are still white areas even on Icelandic charts, but a shrimpboat skipper advised where there were good places to shelter.

A brisk westerly carried us up Ísarfjörðardjúp past a procession of snow-capped crags, waterfalls and valleys with isolated summer farms. We tried to follow the beacons and land at Reykjanes, on the point between Reykjarður and Ísarfjörður, but there did not seem to be enough water or shelter. As the Admiralty pilot confirmed, Svansvík a few miles further up provided a safer anchorage. We crept past a long low rock covered in slumbering seals and felt our way into a gravel bay under a farm with gently sloping fields of sheep and cattle. Next morning, once ashore by dinghy we started walking towards Reykanes along a single track road graded from the lava. A farm jeep stopped and gave us a lift for the rest of the way. Its occupants were on their way back to Reykjavik after a farm holiday. A notice at the hotel spa where they dropped us warned that the crumbling geothermally heated pool might be danger-ously hot. We could just about bear its scalding waters at the end nearest the sea. When we had finished our swim the farmer at Svansvík, who was having coffee at the hotel, was persuaded by the manageress to offer us a lift back. He was the only Icelandic we met who spoke no English.

In the next few days we explored three more fjords (Skotufjörður, Seyðhisjördur and Álftafjörður), saw a rare white tailed eagle and visited two inhabited islands. The first, Æðey, had a small inner pool over-looked by a farmhouse. We were offered the owner's vacant mooring and greeted by an escort of inquisitive greylag geese destined for Christmas. Later the farmer's two teenage boys showed us over the island and its lighthouse. We sat on the cliff edge watching a huge whale breaching and heard how the family collects eider down from nests in the season. Reefs marked by tiny buoys flank the landing on the neighbouring island of Vigur, which seems to have many more visitors and is inhabited by two related families all year round. 'It's a pity that the birds have all gone now,' one of the residents told us, but we could hardly hear him for the sound of the millions of sea birds still present. Perhaps he meant the puffins which burrow into the cliffs and which he harvests every year. His wife is an opera singer who also makes excellent pancakes, and his mother runs a minute post office.

Each port along this coast seems to have a surprise. The open-air vol-canic heated swimming pool at Suðureyri, for example, was being super-vised by Debbie from New Zealand, who had come to the village to work for a spell in the fish factory 19 years ago and was now married with 4 children. A few years ago, she had seen another RCC yacht in those parts, *Sai See,* and helped her crew with their laundry. Another surprise was to find a lagoon flushed by the tide through a pipe under a newly constructed road and holding a thousand huge cod. These were being fed on the waste from one of the baiting sheds. Jens Holm who had set up this experiment took us to watch him feeding his pets. As they thrashed around him he lifted a couple out of the sea and cradled them in his arms. Later he took us berry picking in the neighbouring valley and caught a trout in the stream that gushed from the lava field.

In Patreksfjörður we sheltered for a day from a sudden storm. A hire car let us explore further via a pass over the rain swept mountains that looked like the other side of the moon. The rain and overcast somehow added to the power of a monstrous waterfall in wedding cake cascades foaming down a mountain. Then it was time to push on to our promised winter berth in Hafnarfjörðdur next to Reykjavik.

Cloud Walker has been left afloat at rates somewhat less than those of the Solent and looked after by friends who live nearby and who have been good enough to store all our gear. There are, we are assured, no ice problems. We plan to return next season for another attempt to reach East Greenland, this time with better equipment for predicting weather and keeping in touch with the outside world.

ROLLING ROUND THE HEBRIDES

by Jim Pitts

Our last four summer cruises have been something of a bash with definite objectives in mind.

This year we had a better idea; to sail where the wind would take us. There was just the merest hint that should it be in the general direction of St. Kilda then we would be very happy. In fact we had a Roving Commission.

I had attempted to go to St. Kilda on two previous occasions. Our first was abandoned due to awful weather; on the second, in perfect weather, I fell down a cattle grid at Rodel in Harris. Yes, I know, farmers are supposed to know about cattle grids! This reminds me of the remark made by a friend to Catherine whilst I was in Stornoway Hospital. He knew I had a reasonable sized yacht however he thought it must be a big one if it has a cattle grid on it!

This year the weather and the cattle grids were less obstructive. We reached St. Kilda where we had to pick the dinner up off the cabin sole and then rolled on round the Butt of Lewis and down the Minch to Dunvegan where we found a really old fashioned baker's shop. The smell of fresh bread takes some beating (along with new cut grass in spring) and we returned with hot rolls and wonderful bread.

We sailed off our anchor and fetched out to Dunvegan Head before running with little wind past Neist Point. A yacht coming towards us was flying the red and white burgee. Field glasses were brought to bear; we discovered she was *Adrigole*, but in spite of frantic waving we failed to excite the crew! All very strange. About half an hour later Jeffery O'Riordan called us on the radio saying his new crew dared not wake him from his siesta and he apologised for the lack of a joyous greeting!

Sailing slowly into Loch Bracadale close to the spectacular MacLeod's Maidens rock formations we came to in Gusto Bay on the east shore at the entrance to Loch Harport. A very pleasant spot with a distant view of the Cuillins showing over the green fields close by.

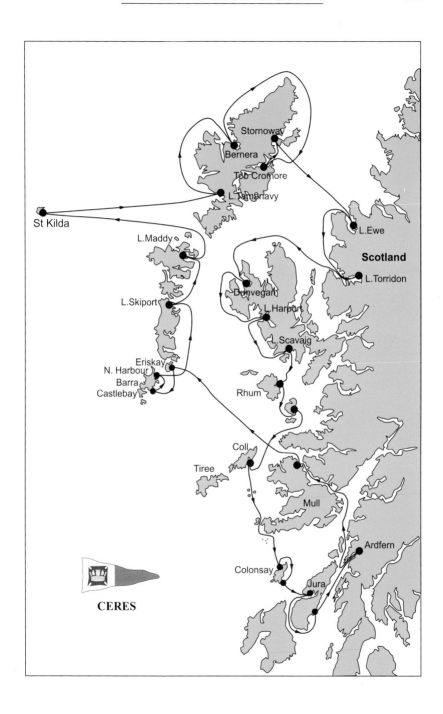

CERES

We received news of a remarkable phenomenon: England had won a Test match!

Next morning we took advantage of the quiet conditions by sailing to Loch Scavaig, surely the most dramatic place to take a yacht in Britain. My descriptive powers will fail to do justice to the place and it has been well described in the past. In this part of Skye Gavin Maxwell's ghost is never far away; over on Soay are the remains of his shark fishing works whilst in the Sound of Sleat at Sandaig he wrote *Ring of Bright Water.*

After lunch and a pleasant meeting with *Janjo of Arisaig* belonging to a neighbour at home, we sailed off for Rum. Great civil engineering works were in progress, we discovered that a new roll on/roll off ferry pier was being built. Later we found the same was happening on the tiny island of Muck. Someone has surely got their sums wrong. There is hardly a road on Rum and the Scottish National Heritage do not want you to go anywhere; Muck is even smaller! Of course its all EEC money so its not coming from you and I. Oh! Is not it!?

In very light winds we made Eigg the following morning. I wanted to find the grave of an old friend of C.C.Lynam RCC who was buried here in about 1924. In the tiny harbour the water was so clear that we could see the chain all down to the anchor. We went ashore but found the cattle had got at the headstones in the cemetery. The view from the graveyard was spectacular, overlooking the harbour, away to Arisaig and Loch Moidart, and all of the Ardnamurchan peninsular. The lighthouse on the point stood out bold and clear like an umpire's finger when giving out! Approaching Muck we saw huge construction barges and cranes working on the new pier. We tarried not at Port Mor and sailed on to Coll where, with all the visitors buoys occupied, we anchored in fine sand. We were beginning to look at the date (I see there is no reference to any so far in this log) We discovered it was 4th July and and we had to be back at Ardfern tomorrow!

ESCAPE TO WASHINGTON

by Mike and Pat Pocock

It had long been our ambition to take *Blackjack* to Washington. In the past we have sailed in her to a number of the world's big cities, New York, San Francisco, Vancouver, Auckland, Sydney, Perth and Capetown. It seemed right to add Washington to the list. We were in Elizabeth City, North Carolina, when the die was cast. Our next commitment was two weeks away in the Piankatank River and given a fast run to Norfolk, Virginia, we should just have time.

From Elizabeth City there are two ways to go north to Norfolk, through the Dismal Swamp or back down the Pasquotank River into Albemarle Sound and through the Virginia Cut which is the better alternative, with deeper controlled depth. *Blackjack* draws 7ft and there was no way we could attempt the Dismal Swamp, which is apparently a good deal more attractive than the name suggests.

We motored out of the berth in Elizabeth City at 0630 and almost immediately were able to set full sail and lay down river on one board. As we reached eastward in the Albemarle Sound the wind freshened and, rather than risk a down wind grounding under full sail, we dropped the main as we bore away into the North River. There followed the most amazing day as we reeled off the miles, through the Carolina Cut, up the Currituck Sound, a quick pit stop for cheap fuel at Coinjock and into the North Landing River. Late in the evening we swung westwards for the final leg in the Albemarle and Chesapeake Canal. After hours of high speed running, we were faced with a head wind. We rolled up the genoa and fired up the motor to take us to Great Bridge, just above the lock that drops one down into Norfolk. Here we made fast to a free pontoon, exactly 12 hours and 70 miles logged from our starting point and nearly all of it under sail. Others may like to know that our 7ft draft never caused any problem in the ICW, except when, off the route, looking for an anchorage and twice between Beaufort SC and Charleston, where I misread the best water on two bends. On each occasion the contact was extremely gentle, the bottom as soft as it comes and backing off was easy. Beaufort SC was our starting point and by all accounts further south the depth, or lack of it, is said to be a greater problem. It is also said that those with greater draft go aground the least because they are inclined to concentrate on the plot that much more. Every time we passed a marker, everyone of them with sitting ospreys in residence, I jotted down its number in the margin of the chart. This is an aid to concentration and an instant reference if one has lost one's place.

The bridges that have to be passed going down into Norfolk are all closed at rush hour so that there is no way one can pass the first one before 0900. By 1045 we were at the Tidewater Agency by Mile Zero and quickly ashore to buy the chart book of the Chesapeake and swiftly away again. With a little, but not much, help from the motor we reached Mobjack Bay and anchored above 'G13' close to the east shore. We spent the next day, which was windless, in this peaceful river cleaning the stains of the ICW from the topsides. The run-off from the peat makes all the water into strong tea with no milk and the effects, particularly on our less than perfect topsides, were horrendous. We subsequently learnt that the quite expensive preparations sold in the chandleries are hardly any different to 'Bar Keepers Friend' sold very cheaply in the bigger supermarkets.

The following day was still pretty windless and, despite 5 hours of motoring, we only reached Dymer Creek, one of the branches of Fleets Bay. During the day we had crossed the mouth of the Piankatank our destination for when we eventually emerged from the Potomac.

We motored out of the creek at 0600 next morning to find 25 knots of wind. With two slabs and a reduced genoa we had a very fast and very wet ride before we were able to ease sheets in heavy rain, as we bore away into the Potomac. We were back to full sail and the wind easing by 1100. We were beginning to enjoy this mighty river, at this stage five or six miles across. It is not easy to identify good anchorages for the night because the scale of the river is so large that what may look, on the chart, like an attractive creek turns out to be quite a wide river in its own right. For our first night having logged 57 miles we chose to beat into the Wicomico River on the Maryland shore and anchor just north of the White Point Bar. It was a peaceful enough spot and we enjoyed a quiet night but, nonetheless, we were way out in the river with half a mile of shallows between us and the bank.

Once again we ate our breakfast underway, having weighed at 0630, and motored back into the Potomac. There we were able to set sail once again and make good progress up river towards Cedar Point, a significant landmark on the north shore, where for a while the river narrows, relatively, and the ebb and flow runs faster. Our early start had ensured a fair push through this section as we passed under the Route 301 bridge. Shortly before Cedar Point we were hailed on VHF and politely advised to stay close to the yellow buoys on the north side, as the proving range would become active at 1000. Sure enough, with due punctuality a minor war appeared to break out and firing commenced from the Naval Proving Grounds straight, we hoped, down the middle of the river.

Beyond this point the Potomac begins to wind somewhat and our fair wind came steadily ahead as we approached the bend round the Tayloe Neck. We made slow progress as we took one tack to get clear past markers 'G23' and 'R24' until we could ease sheets again up the next reach. Close hauled, close to the trees on the Maryland shore we saw two bald eagles, not it would appear a pair as they were clearly disputing the rights to the territory.

We knew that on weekdays the Woodrow Wilson Memorial Bridge (vertical clearance 51ft), which carries the Washington Beltway, would only open for yachts between midnight and 0500. As daylight was fading and we were approaching this bridge we attempted to raise the bridge tender on VHF to obtain confirmation but without success. All we could do was anchor clear of the channel outside of marker 'R90' and set the alarm for just before midnight. It was a glorious evening that had provided some delightful sailing and the return of the flood tide had helped us to make the final miles under sail.

The alarm woke us and we duly presented ourselves to await the opening of the bridge. Only after repeated calls did we get an answer, only to be told that 24 hours notice was required for an opening even within these permitted hours. Imagine our horror, after all our efforts, to be faced with a full day to be spent anchored in a position entirely without facilities or opportunities for landing. We had not been ashore since Norfolk and without a mobile phone we could not have given such notice had we known it was required. As the traffic thundered over the bridge, even at this late hour, he kept us on edge for a while, until he admitted that there was a Naval vessel due to pass through at 1130 next morning. If we were on hand, we could go through immediately astern of her. So, back to our previous anchorage and turn in, and there was not even any point in rising early!

In fact it is infinitely preferable to be able to go through in daylight with a ship, if there is one, but the traffic of large vessels is very small. The short distance from the bridge to the centre of Washington would be an anxious business if doing it for the first time in the dark. On the other hand, in daylight, it is a fun way to arrive with lots to gaze at on the way. Any members heading that way armed with a mobile can call the bridge tender on 202-727-5522. For ourselves we made a strong point of booking our bridge time for our downstream opening as we went through, close behind the USS Mohawk.

Visiting yachts anchor in the Washington Channel, a quiet backwater, flanked on the one side by the East Potomac Park and on the other by the Gangplank Marina which stretches almost endlessly along the shore

The USS Mohawk leads Blackjack through the Woodrow Wilson Memorial Bridge.

on the city side. The marina staff are most helpful to anchored yachts and for $5.00 a day we were given the benefit of secure dinghy mooring and use of the toilets, showers and laundry facilities. From the marina gate it is a short walk to the main attractions of the city, including the White House.

For two and a half days we behaved, very happily, just like any other tourists and did the sights of Washington. We both agreed that the greatest thrill was the Smithsonian Air and Space Museum, a superbly presented collection of aircraft and space paraphernalia. To us, the most striking item was the World Voyager, the Dick Rutan designed aircraft in which he and a female companion flew non-stop around the world, without in flight refuelling, remaining airborne for 9½ days. It was an epic story at the time and to see this remarkable flying machine, suspended from the ceiling, almost within touching distance, was a memorable experience.

Everything one needs is within easy distance of the dock including, wonder of wonders, a Safeway supermarket. Throughout the USA, the chances of being able to buy any food items, without the use of wheels to the nearest mall, are very slim indeed. In Beaufort SC the marina in which we lay allowed berth holders the use of a courtesy car for just that purpose. No shop within the town sold foodstuffs and the nearest supermarket was well beyond walking distance.

We left Washington on a Saturday morning when the permitted opening hours are extended to 0700. We had booked our opening for 0645
and when it came to the time there were three other yachts in the convoy
as we set off down river. Our efforts at sailing were not so successful this
time and we were obliged to motor until 0830, when a following wind
gave us some gentle sailing until around 1330, when we were back close
to 'R24'. We motored in the rain until the river bent back to the south
and we could see the Highway 301 bridge once again. The motor was
stopped and the log records good sailing for the rest of the way. This
time we chose to anchor a mile or two short of the Wicomico off the
mouth of Piccowaxen Creek between Cedar Point and Swan Point on
the Maryland shore.

Sunday saw us under way at 0530 determined to be close to the mouth
of the Potomac by evening and hopefully to avoid too much motoring.
Sadly, the wind failed us by 0930 and we needed to motor until 1215
after which we were able to beat the last ten miles in fluky conditions,
anchoring in a delightful quiet spot in Smith Creek off Calvert Bay.

Monday was Memorial Day and with a forecast of NNW 25kts we
elected to use the day to sail across to the east shore of the Chesapeake
to visit Crisfield, where we were lead to believe there was a seafood
restaurant of some repute. Once under sail and heading east under the
north shore of the Potomac the conditions deteriorated markedly, with
winds that were coming across the deck at 35kts to 40kts. Believing that
we were in relatively sheltered waters, we were sailing without our third
reef pennant rove which left us over-canvassed with two reefs and only
our staysail. We made the prudent decision not to cross the Chesapeake
after all and we bore away south to the Great Wicomico River, this one in
Virginia. Very wet and slightly chastened we anchored in Cockrell Creek,
the first branch of the river on the starboard hand, just above Reedville.
After a miserable passage it was a haven of peace. The sun came out and
so did the rum and we unwound very thankfully.

Two days later we were in the Piankatank in good time for our commitments there.

DARWIN TO SOUTH AFRICA

by Mike Thoyts

The distance across the Indian Ocean from Darwin to South Africa is roughly 6000 miles and there are not many stopping places on the way. Christmas Island and Cocos Keeling Island are obvious possibilities, and I had charts for both. But while each are Australian territory, Christmas Island is regarded as being ecologically part of Indonesia so, if you call in there, and then go on to Cocos Keeling you may have all your honey, tinned ham, fresh fruit and vegetables confiscated – even if you had originally bought them in the land of Oz! So it has to be either one island or the other. As Cocos Keeling is almost exactly half way to Mauritius, the decision was easy.

I locked out of the marina in Darwin at 1000 on 28 August in a light northeasterly wind which veered to the east as predicted and remained very light until 1330 the next day when I could turn the engine off and set the main and genny wing-and-wing. By the following morning I was clear of the continental shelf and the cluster of oil rigs west of Darwin so at noon I set my two genoas and put the cover on the mainsail. I was hoping to carry this running rig for the 2000 miles to Cocos Keeling but a day later the wind veered to the southeast and freshened, so it was another major sail change and back to reaching with a reefed main and genoa.

This part of the Indian Ocean is still full of fish, and there were plenty of birds about as a result. In one day I saw Albatross, Petrels, Boobies, Shearwaters, White-Tailed Tropic Birds, Frigate Birds and Terns. The Boobies were a nuisance as they would roost aboard, even on the turning wind generator, and each morning I had to clean up after them. But it was pleasant sailing. The big difference between the North Atlantic and the Southern oceans is that south of the equator there is usually a long swell coming up from the Roaring Forties; as a result in easterly trade-winds there is normally a crossed swell which induces an irregular motion. In light winds this can be marked and it makes it difficult for the wind pilot to cope. So in anything less than 10 knots I usually needed to rig the *Autohelm* 'Tinley' fashion so that it operated the wind vane. This arrangement works so well that I too now always use it when motoring.

However the trade-wind gradually increased to its, by now familiar, 'reinforced' strength of around 30-plus knots, and so I changed down, yet again to storm-jib and trysail. This rig is ideal in heavy weather, and the boom-gallows which I had had made in New Zealand made the sail changing easy. I finally made landfall on Cocos Keeling Islands at 0645 on 11 September, and was securely at anchor in Direction Island by 1030. This is a fascinating small archipelago, a thousand miles from anywhere, which was until recently the personal domain of the Clunies Ross family who traded in copra, and ran it as a feudal fiefdom. It is now a separate Australian state. With the decline of the Copra trade the people there have had a difficult time earning a living, but they are now developing fishing and horticulture for export.

Direction Island was for many years the site of the cable and wireless station linking Australia, South Africa and Ceylon. During the First World War the German cruiser *Emden* put a landing party ashore there to demolish the installation, however whilst they were busy doing this, *Emden* was caught and sunk by the Navy, leaving them marooned. The demolition party later commandeered the Clunies Ross' schooner and used her to make their escape back to Germany. There are photographs of the raiders destroying the telegraph office in the little museum there, but not much to tell how they got home. It sounds like a good escape story which deserves to be better known. Today there are only scattered traces of the telegraph station to be found as it was abandoned with the advent of satellite communications, and it has recently been bulldozed into the ocean. The five large submarine cables however are still visible as you snorkel along the shore.

Facilities are basic, but the Australian government has built a large barbecue shelter for the use of yachtsmen, with a roof which is also a water catchment, and so some freshwater is available. There is also a solar powered telephone, which works well for international calls when the sun is shining. They have also built a 'long-drop' earth closet there, but as one cannot dig deep pits on coral reef, it has been built upwards and is quite a tall building! Formalities are relaxed, and performed after a long, wet dinghy ride to one or other of the adjacent islands where a few, very limited, supplies are available. Coconuts however are plentiful and free for the taking. The Clunies Ross mansion can be visited, but was locked when I went there, however the gardens alone are worth the trip. The house is a substantial building clad in dazzling, white-glazed bricks and one can see through the windows some impressive teak joinery inside.

Because it is almost the perfect desert island, and there was congenial company there, I stayed until 1 October and then left for Rodrigues. The

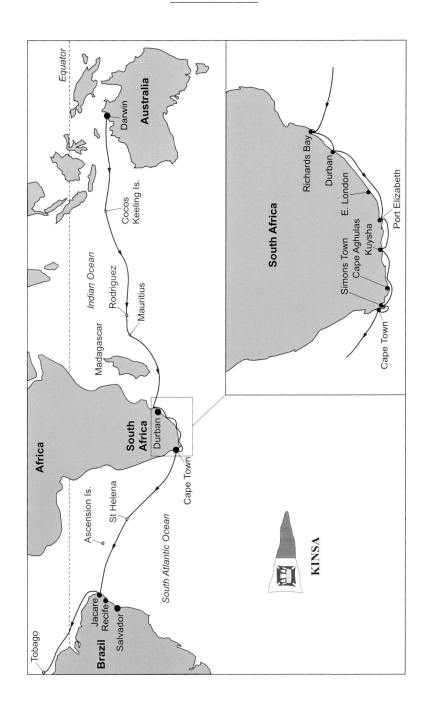

weather had been wet and windy for a few days, so after motoring clear of the anchorage, and finding the wind easterly at 25 to 30 knots I again set the trysail and storm jib wing-and-wing with the clew of the trysail lashed to the boom. This again proved a very comfortable and easily handled rig in the conditions which continued to blow at F.6/7 for the next ten days. The lower centre of effort reduces the rolling considerably, and when the wind went lighter I could unfurl some genny, which because of the low cut of the trysail set well without being blanketed.

I wrote on 13 October, 'Wind and sea on the port quarter. Wind 25–35 knots, swell from the northeast, about 4 metres with a rough sea on top which hits the boat occasionally covering everything with spray. Sky cloudy with bright patches. Very few birds, no other sign of life. This is a big ocean! When the sun is out it is vigorous heady sailing. Cockpit gets a good dollop aboard about every two hours.' And on 6 October: 'Still a big lumpy sea (which climbs into the cockpit occasionally and splashes the galley from time to time). Still about a four metre swell with a F.6 sea on top.' The next day, 'Wind freshened to 35+ knots, furled Genoa completely leaving *Kinsa* again running under storm jib and trysail. Took in starboard dodger which has been torn by a sea, for repair'.

The weather was in fact considerably more boisterous than I had expected, and on 9 October I got a weatherfax from Darwin showing that a tropical storm had been upgraded to Cyclone *Celia* 900 miles to the northeast. This explained much and I altered course away from its predicted track. Within 48 hours the wind was much lighter and we were slopping about in the aftermath of the strong winds. Two days later *Celia* had disappeared from the synoptic charts and I was sailing under full main and genny in bright sunshine, drying out the boat as best I could. The biggest problem was that spray had dried all over everything and with the strong sunshine there was thick salt-rime everywhere as high as the crosstrees. I prayed for rain, and that evening a heavy rain-squall obliged by washing the boat down most efficiently!

This stretch of the Indian Ocean was remarkable for being almost totally devoid of any sign of life. I saw the occasional shearwater but, apart from these few birds, there was nothing. I can only suppose that it has been fished out by massive, indiscriminate over-fishing. One morning, towards the end of this leg I was working on the foredeck, tidying up after a night-time sail change. I had been there for about an hour when, glancing up, I saw an enormous car-transporter about 300 yards to leeward. I had heard nothing, nothing at all of its approach. I had not seen her, and she certainly had not seen me, nor did she answer my VHF call on Ch. 16. She crossed my bows close enough for me to smell cooking and cigarette smoke. It was only a near-miss, but I shall never feel the same again about the name *Toyota*! This was the only other vessel I saw in over 4000 sea-miles. I finally made landfall on Rodrigues at 0500 on 16 October, and dropped anchor in Port Maturin Harbour at 0915. All told the whole 4125 miles from Darwin had taken 31 days 23 hours sea-time, an average of 129 miles per day or 5.3 knots.

Rodrigues is an island I have wanted to visit ever since I was in the Suez Canal Zone as a National Serviceman with Mauritians. Our Regimental Police were all Rodriguees, and very good they were. I said this to the Immigration Officer who cleared me in, and he replied that his father had served there at the same time, but sadly he had died two years previously. The island today is still unspoiled; they have two small hotels, and live by fishing from sailing boats and rearing cattle which are exported on the weekly mail boat. Together with two other yachts I was anchored in the turning basin for the mail-boat. There were only the three of us there at the time, all British, wearing masthead burgees, showing anchor balls by day and a light by night and all hoisting and lowering our ensigns at 0800 and sunset. An unusual experience and quite unrehearsed. The other two boats were *Moonlight of Down* (John and Pat Driscoll, OCC) who had left Falmouth at about the same time as *Kinsa* in 1994 and *Wylo II*, a lovely little steel gaffer designed and built by her owner Nick Skeates in New Zealand. Nick is now on his second circumnavigation in her.

On 24 October I left Rodrigues towards Mauritius with a fair wind of 15 to 20 knots and covered the 366 miles in 67 hours, an average speed of 5.2 knots. This was remarkably good sailing for a boat only 27ft on the waterline, which had been in tropical waters for over six months without a scrub. It was due, I felt, to those excellent new sails and an increased surface drift due to the stronger winds. Port Louis is a large, modern city, the capital of Mauritius, which is a beautiful island but is heavily into the holiday industry, mainly aimed at the wealthy end of the South African market. I went north to Grande Baye for a few days and saw the various sights until 10 November, when I left for South Africa.

The crossing to Richards Bay was a further 1559 miles which *Kinsa* managed at the even more remarkable average speed of 5.5 knots, thanks to fair winds and a favourable current. The Pilot recommends keeping 100 miles off the southern tip of Madagascar, but this still meant crossing the continental shelf and I found it extremely rough going. I was able to suggest on the radio to John and Pat in *Moonlight* that they avoid it altogether by keeping south of the 100 metre contour, which they did and had a much easier ride. Richards Bay claims to be the largest coal terminal in the world, and one should seek permission to enter from Port Control. This was given readily with the warning to mind the Grey Whale and her calf just outside the entrance. I passed them on the way in. They were swimming gently along on the surface as I came up to the harbour entrance.

There is a small marina at Tuzi Gazi which is much used by long-distance small boats in varying stages of rest, recuperation or preparation. Formalities and shopping are all done in the 'Commercial District' some ten miles away. Transport was by a friendly local taxi driver who has appointed himself as 'Mister Fixit' for yachtsmen, and who has thus made himself almost indispensable. He drove me in on my first morning as I needed to go to the bank before anything else. So we parked and walked in through an American type shopping mall to find a full scale armed robbery in progress at the bank with a fair amount of shooting going on. We beat a hasty retreat and read about it in the papers later! It seemed that an armed gang had held up a Securicor van and escaped with two million Rand. The police were rightly praised for swift, effective action as they had quickly arrested the robbers and recovered the money, but what apparently impressed the reporter most was that the police had actually handed all the money back. This unusual event he said, showed what a remarkably fine, honest police force they had in Kwa Zulu Natal!

The local travel agent, through whom I booked a flight home, also offered an amazingly cheap price to visit one of South Africa's most prestigious game parks for two nights, which was a wonderful bargain. The Driscolls joined me, and not only did we see lion, cheetah, hippo, giraffe and rhinoceros at amazingly close range, but we were fed and housed in conditions of absolutely sybaritic luxury. After several months at sea this came as a wonderful treat. I then flew home for Christmas with my family and returned on January 22.

The passage south around the South African coast presents a number of challenges. The main challenge is that if the swiftly flowing, south-going Aghulas current is met by the prevailing strong south-westerly winds, an exceptionally big dangerous sea rapidly builds up. The distance from Durban to East London is over 300 miles, and there is no shelter anywhere on this stretch, so one needs to wait patiently for easterly winds. It is not easy to judge the weather for the necessary three or four days ahead as, although the large lows which bring predictably strong winds regularly coming across from the South Atlantic are well shown on the synoptic charts, the large differences in temperature between the southern oceans and the land mass of South Africa create numerous small, localised, very intense low pressure systems all around the coast which can generate prolonged squalls with dangerously strong winds. These little lows are so small that they often fail to show up on the excellent weather faxes put out by the Pretoria Met. Office. I found however that a telephone call to the local airport and a talk to the duty Met. Officer always got a friendly and very helpful response.

I left Richards Bay on 17 February at 1700 and was securely berthed in Durban Marina one hundred miles to the south by 1000 the following morning. Whilst we were in Richards Bay, John Driscoll and I had met a local tugboat skipper who had taken us out for a day and even allowed us to drive his tug. This was a unique experience as it was equipped with Voight-Schneider drive units which meant that as well as being able to turn in its own length it could be manoeuvred backwards or sideways with equal facility, great fun! Whilst we were in Durban, the captain came down and took us for a three day tour of the Drakensberg Mountains which must be among the most beautiful places on earth. It was a wonderful experience.

I left Durban at 1500 on 1 March and made fast in Port Elizabeth at 1100 on 4 March after an easy 423 miles passage, missing out East London on the way. 'P.E.' is a busy commercial port and the boat was rapidly covered with fine black abrasive dust which got into everything so I left as soon as I could manage after a necessary engine service. My next stop was at Knysna, a wonderful small harbour at the eastern end of the famous Garden Route from Cape Town. The entrance between massive cliffs, is extremely narrow with a rock in the middle of the channel. The strong tides and big swell in the area make it imperative only to enter and leave at slack water. This tricky entrance is made much easier thanks to help from 'Knysna Base', a local volunteer coastguard who will talk one in through heads on VHF – in my case he actually drove up to the eastern cliff top to do so. Once inside there is a small town, a friendly yacht club and a luxuriant wealth of the gorgeous flowers, fruit and vegetables for which this area is famous.

Whilst in Knysna I flew up to stay with cousins in Pretoria who made me most welcome and took me into the Kruger National Park for two days. On my return I was delighted to find *Wylo II* alongside and a few days later we prepared to leave together. The day before we left however the community was shocked by the loss of a fishing boat which had tried to leave through the heads against the flood, contrary to advice, and had been backward pitch-poled in the entrance with the loss of two clients. Nick and I left exactly as instructed, and then on the way we had a photo session before setting off on the final leg, he to Cape Town and I to Simonstown.

I spent the next night at anchor in the lee of a headland to let a front go through before passing three miles south of Cape Aghulas, the most southerly point of Africa at 2100 on 26 March. Having marked the occasion appropriately with a small libation as we passed into the southern Atlantic Ocean, I finally reached Simon's Town at 1330 the following afternoon. There I left *Kinsa* in the little marina whilst I again flew home, this time for the marriage of my younger son Robert.

This is part of a circumnavigation which began with a passage from England to New Zealand between September 1995 and November 1996. The circumnavigation was completed with a further leg of 6830 miles to Trinidad in November 1999. Most of this voyage has been single handed. Kinsa is a Rustler 36 built in 1991.

BEADS AND BEARS

by Kitty Van Hagen

Spring was late this year but April is known to be a cruel month. In Sidney, Vancouver Island, the daffodils nodding beneath the flowering cherries, a riot of wallflowers and tulips in the municipal flower-beds all gave a false promise that the sun held warmth. Snow-capped mountains in the distance ranged postcard pretty against a cobalt sky but the bitter wind kicked up a short chop on the open water. We had left *Duet* ashore on Vancouver Island for the winter months and now, after a week of preparation, we were ready to set off again to continue cruising at a leisurely pace.

Last year's cruise had been a marathon. We departed Trinidad in September 1998 to cruise a bit in Venezuela before heading back to Trinidad to pick up more anchor chain before heading out to Tobago. We cruised up through the Leeward islands to St Martin and St Kitts where we spent Christmas and New Year. We then sailed on to the British Virgins before turning around and dashing back down to Venezuela and the offshore islands. We enjoyed a couple of weeks in Curacao as well as a bit more of mainland Venezuela before heading through the Panama Canal in February 1999. From Panama we went to the Galapagos where we spent a couple of weeks before leaving for Hawaii. That leg was the longest, nearly 5000 miles that took us 32 days, 16 hours and 42½ minutes. We spent a month in Honolulu before heading up to Kodiak, Alaska and Prince William Sound. Then we had to dash across the Gulf of Alaska and down the inside passage. We had schedules to keep and we kept them at the cost of not lingering longer in areas where we would have liked to have stayed. Reflecting on last year's speed and endurance sailathon, a total distance of 12,500 miles, we promised ourselves that this year there would be no schedules, no long distances but maximum cruising and pottering time.

Our shake-down sail took us across the Strait of Georgia to Vancouver City. We enjoyed a couple of weeks there as well as a land-based trip before stocking up *Duet* and setting off. We sailed northwards with a cold but fair wind up the Strait of Georgia to Desolation Sound, a beautiful area for cruising at this time of the year when you have the place to yourself. It was still cold and the mountains wore a fresh dusting of snow every morning. Dark, sombre pine trees clothed the slopes down to the shore-line interspersed with the tender green leaves of the alder trees. Ashore the salmon berries were flowering, providing a feast of nectar for the humming birds that come each year from Mexico and central America to breed. We spent a week in Desolation Sound enjoying the peace and the areas of untouched forest. The gashes of clear cut logging run in swaths across so much of the area leaving a litter of trunks and stumps in their wake. The mountain sides look battle torn and raw. On the water snub-nosed tugs hauled the tons of logs, their tow at least 500 metres long, sometimes appearing even longer. This is an area were it is unwise to sail at night as the enormous amount of logging debris in the water can be dangerous. This includes everything from smallish branches to huge logs and worst of all, deadheads. Deadheads are logs or stumps that are so waterlogged that only the top eight to ten inches or less show above water. Like icebergs there is more to them than meets the eye. It is easy enough to miss them in broad daylight. We removed the log impeller on about day six by hitting one such horror without having seen it. We are also happy to have an aluminium yacht! Kelp is also another hazard: it's long, it's tough and loves to wrap itself around the propeller. Several times we had to get into the water to cut it off, wet suits really come into their own here when the water is a chilly 8°.

Instead of heading at speed up through Discovery Passage, we elected to take the scenic route north. This involved going through all the narrow passes where the water squirts like a high-pressure water hydrant hose. The maximum rates at the biggest spring tides can reach dizzy-making speeds of 15 or more knots. The first passage was through a delightfully named 'Hole in the Wall'. We were half an hour late for slack water and already the water was streaming through but we did not think that it looked too bad. The chart showed that there was plenty of water and that there were tide rips but no whirlpools. By now we were in the grip of the stream and there was nothing for it but have the engine at full power so that the propeller had something to grip. It was an exciting ride with the SOG reaching a dizzy 14 knots at one point! We were fortunate. In 1792 when the Spanish explorers, Galiano and Valdes aboard the *Sutil* and *Mexicana* were exploring this coast at the same time as Vancouver they did not have such a good time of it. The *Mexicana* managed to get through one of these passes but the *Sutil* got swept into the jaws of currents, 'They (the currents) were violent and the whirlpools frequent, and so strong that one, which the *Sutil* could not avoid, turned her around completely three times, at such a lively rate as to be surprising......' No

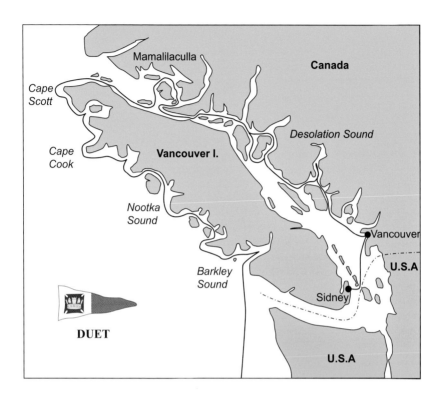

wonder the early Indians believed that they were protected from marauding northern tribes by the resident sea monster who pulled invaders' canoes under the water in this pass.

During the 1920s and 1930s, the commercial fishing industry created thousands of jobs for the native Indians when canneries were built all over this part of the west coast. When the industry floundered it left whole villages to rot alongside the abandoned canneries. We visited one such village that had been abandoned, Mamalilaculla. The name rolls round the mouth in such a satisfying sound. We had read in our cruising guide that there was a native guardian who camped there during the summer months but the place was so overgrown that it would soon disappear. We had a pleasant sail short tacking up between the scattered islands. With a flat sea and a gentle 15 knots of wind, it was one of the best sails we had had for some time. Four hours later we were dismayed to see that the anchorage marked on the chart was almost filled by a float house and a couple of rickety pontoons. We dropped the main sail as we motored towards it gingerly ascertaining the possibility of dropping the anchor close by. A figure hailed us, beckoning us to come alongside one of the pontoons.

'Hi – I'm Tom, how are you folks doing?' He greeted us as he took our lines. 'Welcome to Village Island.' His flattened Indian features creased in a wide grin and his puppy made as if to jump on board.

'He's called Land Rights – watch him carefully – if he pisses on your boat it's mine!' Tom laughed.

'We've read about you,' I said showing him the book that devoted a whole page to him. He was pleased as well as surprised. This was the first time he had seen the *Waggoners Guide*. He told us he had done a lot of clearing and now most of the village could be seen. He promised us he would take us over to the village the next day.

The following day it was raining with that persistence that means it is going to last all day. A long legged bear was roaming the beach flicking over boulders with a casual toss of his paw. He looked as miserable as the sky. Land Rights sat shivering in front of the cabin door with his gaze riveted on the bear. Tom came by a little later on and invited us over to his house. We spent a fascinating afternoon drinking endless cups of tea sitting by a roaring log fire listening to ancient Indian history, legends and lore. Tom is one of those born raconteurs and the hours flicked by.

The following morning Tom came over for a coffee and invited us to return the following week when he was hosting a special party to which he had invited representatives from local tourist bureaux and press. The idea was to publicise the village and to encourage the tourists to come out from Campbell River and Alert Bay. Before he left he pointed out to us on the chart where we might find pictographs on rocks as well as beaches where it was still possible to find trade beads. Blue, red, brown and black beads as well as tools, weapons, kettles and nails were used extensively by the Europeans to trade with the Indians for furs in the eighteenth century. I knew it was still possible to find beads on the beaches and had had no luck so far. On Tom's advice we scoured the beaches around Alert Bay and other anchorages and were rewarded by finding two blue glass beads. We never found the pictographs but instead the remains of a Bhuddist temple that had been built on an island by a Chinese settlement sometime in the early 1900s.

We returned to Mamalilaculla the following week. The day of the party dawned bright and clear and from early morning people began to arrive by boat as well as no less than three float planes and a genuine war canoe. Tom, dressed in full regalia, welcomed his guests and invited them to walk around the island to the village. He had been hard at work slashing down brambles and clearing the path. There stood the remains of six houses and posts of the old Long House which had been in the past the ancestral home. When the crowd was assembled Tom entertained us for an hour and a half of legends and the history of his people and the village. Afterwards was a fantastic feast of crab and salmon which we ate with our fingers whilst sitting in the grass in front of the ruins. Then came the highlight of the day – traditional dancers.

There was a banging of drums, some blood-curdling yells and the
troupe of dancers leaped out from behind a tarpaulin screen. I do not
pretend to be an expert on Indian dancing. To the uninitiated, once you
have seen one lot of men wearing masks smeared in mud and wearing
nothing but a few strategically placed branches of fir tree stamping their
feet, jumping up and down accompanied by a great deal of grunting and
yelling, you really have seen the lot. After a bit my attention began to
wander and I could not help thinking that the blankets that the band
were wearing looked suspiciously like rugs I've seen recently in IKEA.
The music, which Vancouver had described as being not too unpleasant
to the ear, consisted of various drums and some rather unmusical sound-
ing chanting. It was time for us to leave.

We were looking forward to rounding Cape Scott, the northwestern
corner of Vancouver Island as it marked the turning point for heading
south. From the charts, it looked quite dramatic. Needless to say it was
flat calm and foggy so we did not see a thing.

Our first anchorage on the west coast was Sea Otter cove. There were
shown on the chart two mooring buoys, but we had no idea what to
expect and, if they were there, what kind of condition they would be in.
They are huge iron can shaped buoys with tractor tires on the sides. On
top there is a high standing V shaped bar on to which you moor. These
looked in reasonable condition and we could see the chains either side of
the bay onto which they were anchored. The chain looked large enough
to hold several trawlers. The pilot book mentioned the buoys saying that
they were laid by the fishery department and that anyone could use

them, it was just a case of first come. They were far too heavy to lift up out of the water so the problem was how to stop the boat riding up on the buoy as the edges were rough and anyway we did not want our sleep disturbed. It was simple enough to attach one line to the bow and another to a cleat half way down the toe rail, thus holding the buoy half way along the bow. A fender between the hull and the buoy kept it off and all was peace and quiet.

The anchorages on the northwest coast of the island are all deep inside the sounds. Dark green pools of water surrounded by sitka spruce, cedar and hemlock trees that crowd down to the water's edge, branches sweeping the water. The steady drip, drip of moisture adds to the impression of being inside a rain forest. Cosy for a day but, for five when we were storm bound, claustrophobic. The small communities of Natives and Canadians are scattered and their access is either dirt track or a weekly ferry. There are few facilities but a warm welcome for the occasional visitors. Once south of the notorious Cape Cook the sun came out and the sea sparkled.

We spent a happy couple of days in the Bunsby islands looking in vain for the sea otters that were reputedly in residence. Sea otters had been hunted to near extinction for their fur, the last one having been shot near here in 1931. Many had survived in Alaska and some had been transplanted to the Bunsby Islands where they had re-established themselves successfully. We discovered later that they had moved from here to further south having cleared out the Bunsby islands of clams, abalone and sea urchins that form their staple diet. From the Bunsbys it was a short trip of ten miles to our next destination, Kyuquot Sound. We picked our way through the rocky channels that are clearly marked on our charts and as the visibility was good, there was no problem. When we left Kyuquot sound we had a longer passage to make to Nootka Sound, the scene of Cook's landfall. This passage was one of the more exciting of our trip. The wind was blowing far harder than we anticipated, it picks up quickly here, and we were going far too fast for the tricky passage so called 'Clear Passage'. We reefed right down but it seemed to make no difference so we dropped the mainsail and proceeded still at 8 knots with the smallest jib half rolled. The sea was rough even though we were in the shelter of the reefs, but shoal water makes for lumpy conditions. Our route was safely stowed in waypoints, but this was the moment that the USA obviously decided to de-tune the satellites, or whatever they do, so the GPS kept bleeping 'no fix, no fix' and then went totally blank. So it was back to plotting in the old fashioned way as the rocks spun past at a quite terrifying speed. At one point we had to make a dramatic alteration of course as a huge patch of kelp was too close for comfort and the depth shallowed alarmingly quickly. The sea was breaking just ahead and there was a patch of kelp too, we thought it might be a sneaky rock that had not been marked on the chart, so we altered course to pass it close by. It took a huge amount of concentration to pick which rock was which, steer a steady course, and plot the course as we went. There were several rocks shown on the chart that lurk just beneath the surface, although some were not, but kelp patches were always shown.

By mid June the weather was perfect. We enjoyed plenty of day sailing through the rock-strewn inlets and channels. We anchored off islands. We watched a land otter fishing, and mink and racoons swimming from islet to islet in search of food. We saw grey whales and calves feeding in the plankton rich waters. We watched sea lions on the rocks and bears were daily visitors to the beaches and, if we did not see them, we saw their tracks in the soft sand. We caught crabs, picked oysters and dug for clams. It was an idyllic time. This is the most wonderful cruising area we have met with so far. The only problem is the weather but, as it is the same latitude as the UK, it is not dissimilar. August is locally called fogust with good reason. Fog rolls in every afternoon and only lifts for a couple of hours at midday. The pine trees look depressed and the mournful sound of whistle buoys accentuate the general sense of gloom. It was time to be heading south again. But not before we had photographed eagles catching fish. Earlier when we had been going through the rapids, we had seen a mass of dead fish floating on the surface of the water that was attracting hundreds of bald-headed eagles as well as sea gulls. The air was thick with swooping, feeding birds. We had no idea what had caused this as on closer inspection the fish seemed only half-dead and were definitely still wriggling. A fisherman explained it to us. The larger fish are strong enough to cope with the extreme force of the tides in these rapids, but the juveniles cannot. The effect is they are caught in the whirlpools, forced to the surface at such a speed that their air sacks expand and burst.

We knew that eagles ate floating fish so we bought bait and chucked anchovies into the water underneath a tree where a pair of eagles sat. It is possible that they did not notice in time but at any rate the fish sank very quickly or were gobbled up by sea gulls. Simon suggested that if the fish floated for longer we might have more success. So whilst he was poised in the dinghy with the camera, I got out a syringe and inflated the herring. It worked! Not only did they float but the eagles came, snatched the bait and flew off. We feared that flatulent eagles on the wing might make a huge mess on the deck so we sailed out of Barkley Sound into yet more fog to head south for San Francisco. It is 780 miles from Barkley Sound to San Francisco. *Duet* covered the distance in 4½ days:

> *It's North you may run to the rime-ringed sun,*
> *Or South to the blind Horn's hate;*
> *Or East all the way into Mississippi Bay*
> *Or West to the Golden Gate.*
>
> *(Rudyard Kipling. The Long Trail.)*

CLUB MATTERS

THE 2000 AWARDS

Judge's Commentary by Oz Robinson

There were some 27 log entries this year, plus one elegantly presented account which arrived far too late for inclusion. Some logs reflected major ocean passages and cruises in far distant waters. Others recorded carefully thought out coastal cruises. There was a good batch of qualifying logs of cruises in home waters, partly inspired by the Rolling Meet. Overall, the logs present as wide a geographical distribution of adventure as ever, from pole to pole – well more or less – and from 0°E to 0°W via 180°E or W depending on which way you approach that line. Collectively the Club has occasion to be very well pleased with the range of activity. But there is a downside to this judgement and it is that the quality of the logs themselves varies tremendously. Some are very well presented, well written and with the information sought by the FPI, the Pilotage Foundation and the Judge properly set out. On the other hand, there were logs without even a sketch map, logs which were late (which gums up the administrative machinery) and logs without the name of the skipper or boat. The worst sin was that 18 of the 28 entries had no port or pilotage information as such, not even a comment to the effect that there was nothing new to report. This is a competition. Read the competition rules (which are a mess and need revision) and combine them with Club Rule 2 and you will see why such logs suffer.

The Grace Cup *Helen Tew*

We will start with a properly presented log. The one family cruise reported this year was from Guernsey, via the first of the millennium meets and Bayona, to Lagos in Portugal made in a 65-year-old gaff rigged cutter manned by a crew of Tews. The youngest Tew, who had not been offshore before, had to leave in Bayona, leaving uncle and grandmother to continue. Grandmother of course has come to notice before. On this voyage she, at the age of 88, was a major factor in the success of the voyage and also a great example to anyone or any ship who thinks she may be past it. The Grace Cup, which is for a lady on a family cruise, goes to Helen Tew aboard the *Mary Helen.*

The Sea Laughter Trophy   Mary Thornhill

This is awarded in relation to a well conducted cruise of a month in the Inner Hebrides skippered by a cadet member. What marks the operation out as special is that the skipper had aboard two lots of four crew and a first mate, all of whom she had trained from scratch. I did observe that this skipper, being prudent, had earlier in the year given the first mate a preliminary course aboard a wreckable charter boat in the Aegean before she risked him aboard her father's boat. The Sea Laughter award goes to Mary Thornhill aboard *Sai See.*

The Claymore Cup   Richard Wakeford

Now a cruise made to look straight-forward but which was in a difficult area and which had its problems. Starting from Tierra del Fuego, the cruise went across the Drake Passage to the Antarctic, in and around the islands and the ice on the fringe of that continent and back, minus one crew, to the Falklands. The crew, apart from the RCC skipper, was made up of two RCC cadets, both ladies, and two potential cadets. The only event I will mention is that after one of the crew suffered a very painful accident ashore, the sufferer first had to be manhandled back aboard the boat as painlessly as possible across the rocks and ice and eventually evacuated to Argentina by the Russians. For achievement in terms of political persuasion, of seamanship and of good sense shown in an inhospitable environment, the Claymore Cup is awarded to Richard Wakeford aboard *The Alderman.*

The Cruising Club Bowl   Peter Ingram

A good east-bound Atlantic Crossing from the Caribbean undertaken at very short notice (and that is important). It was skippered by a RCC cadet supported at first by two contemporaries and reinforced after the Azores by another RCC cadet. The passage demonstrated a high degree of ready competence on the part of the skipper. It also happens to reflect the high level of maintenance of the family boat which earlier had been taken to the Caribbean by a gang of ladies skippered by the matriarch. But the real point is that the cadet knew his onions and had no brushing-up to do. Moreover he presented his log properly. The Cruising Club Bowl goes to Peter Ingram aboard *Troubadour.*

The Juno Cup   Stephen & Sue Lennane

Back to the cold: the Club does not seem to be able to keep away from miserable places. The Juno Cup goes for a well conducted cruise, the thought of which caused the Norwegians and others to fall about laughing when they heard of the plan. The cruise was from Stockholm to the

head of the Gulf of Bothnia (where very few yachts have been), then by
lorry to the Barents Sea, round North Cape and southwards to Tromso.
It was the reverse of the track taken by *Blue Dragon* 88 years ago except
that *Blue Dragon* was moved on her side by train, not vertically by lorry.
This log was properly presented. It notes cold, murk, lots of fog and has
serious pilotage notes. The Juno Cup goes to Stephen and Sue Lennane,
aboard *Arcadia of Glaven*.

The Founder's Cup   Michael & Julie Manzoni

Now to some warmer weather. This cruise started in Curaçao and
achieved its objective of visiting Cuba, the Caymans and Belize which
has seldom been visited and which is a fascinating area with the second
longest barrier reef in the world. One of the factors which influenced this
award was that this cruise showed the lowest use of engine – a mere 3.9%
of time under way On all cruises the judge takes in to consideration the
inevitable use of the engine. In the area of this cruise the weather pattern
and open waters favour sailing. Even so, 3.9% is an exceptionally low
figure – 20 to 25% is more usual. I am sure the Founder would be
pleased by this and the Founder's Cup goes to Michael and Julie Man-
zoni aboard *Blue Sonata*.

The Royal Cork Club Glass Vase   Peter & Gill Price

First the Royal Cork Glass Vase. This goes for a more old fashioned
cruise, not an oceanic bash nor a struggle with the elements or with sea
monsters. It was a 2000 mile, 14 week cruise by a crew of 2 in the
Adriatic finishing at Dubrovnik but starting nearer the Pillars of Hercules.
The cruise was very well managed. The narrative is a very readable story.
More than 70 anchorages were visited and in every single place where
there was an item of port or pilotage information to be noted it was
properly entered in an appendix to the log which can be seized upon by
the lucky FPI editor and converted in furtherance of rule 2 of the Club.
Apart from the content, this was the best presented log as was only to be
expected as the skipper in question seems to hold a PhD in communications, computers and common sense and, besides, was our Secretary.
The Cork Vase goes to Peter Price, most ably supported by Gill.

The ICC Ships Decanter   Ann Fraser

The next venture has points in common with the last. It is for a cruise of
about 2600 miles, visiting some 75 anchorages along the way. But in this
case the route lay through inshore passages where the wind is either on
the nose or up the backside, where the tidal arrangements make Corry-
vrekan a mill-pond and where rocks awash submerge at the first hint
of fog – in short, past places where the closest attention to pilotage is
required. Part of the cruise was in the company of the West Coast
Station of the CCA. They tend to think that a suitable boat for the area is

a 12 knot power cruiser with central heating. *Gollywobbler* is not like that. For this cruise, from the border of British Columbia to Glacier Bay which is north of Juneau in Alaska, and then back, the ICC Ships Decanter goes to Ann Fraser, aboard *Gollywobbler II.*

The Romola Cup   John & Sally Melling

A cruise by a crew of two and taking a year, from the UK to Brazil, Uruguay and Argentina and back. Apart from the pleasure of cruising, the aim was to climb in Patagonia. There is a Tilmanesque echo here except that for Tilman, the boat was a vehicle to get him there (which is why he bothered to learn sailing from Bobby Somerset) and anyway women were out. This whole cruise was a considerable achievement and the greatest part of the return voyage was single-handed. A proper log also contained excellent pilotage and port information. For this, the Romola Cup goes to John and Sally Melling aboard *Taraki.*

The RCC Challenge Cup   David Mitchell

A remarkable crossing of the Pacific from Cairns to Vancouver over the course of a year, cruising en route in the Solomons, Papua New Guinea and the Philippines, calling at Hong Kong and Japan and then passing rather too close to the Aleutians for the crew's peace of mind. The log is very well presented. The pilotage and port information is first rate, covers little known areas and was delivered in proper form. You will have to read all about it in the Library but I will mention that the crew devised a method, novel to me, of conning the ship through reefs by leading tiller lines to the lower cross trees and steering from there. Later, in mid-Pacific, this single handed crew had occasion to go no less than four times up the mast in bad weather to make do and mend. For this extended cruise, the RCC Challenge Cup goes, for the second year running, to David Mitchell aboard *Ondarina.*

The Goldsmith Exploration Award   David Mitchell

And that is not the end of it. After consultation with the Hon Sec of the FPI, the Goldsmith Exploration Award also goes to David Mitchell aboard *Ondarina* for his pilotage and port information about places little known to the sailing community.

The Vice Commodore's Prize   Graham Morfey

This prize is awarded for a venture which does not come into the category of any other prize, but is worthy of recognition. It is awarded for a cruise which has, in addition to being well planned and executed, produced a wealth of port and pilotage information to update existing publications for the Pacific. Although not being in little known or uncharted waters it will prove most valuable. In addition to this, *Flight of Time* rescued the crew of a small foreign yacht which was in danger of sinking in mid ocean due to failure of a keel bolt. This was conducted in moderate weather but a heavy swell in the exemplary manner which one would expect of a member of the RCC. For all this, the Vice Commodore's Prize is awarded to Graham Morfey and *Flight of Time.*

The Medal for Seamanship   Nicolai Litau

The Seamanship Medal is awarded to Nicolai Litau, skipper of the Moscow Adventure Club yacht *Apostle Andrew*, for the first yacht voyage around the continents of Europe, Asia and Australia. The yacht left St Petersburg on 14 November 1996 and passed the Baltic, Kattegat, North Sea and English Channel into the Atlantic. She sailed via Dakar (Senegal), her furthest west, to Capetown, the first visit there of any Russian yacht. She then headed east and on 18 May 1997 lost her steering and sustained other damage in a severe storm in the south Indian Ocean. She made Fremantle under sail, steering mainly by sail trim with help from a jury rudder, arriving on 16 June. Following repairs, she went on to Sydney, through the Pacific by way of the Caroline Islands, logging her best day's run of 215 miles, to Petropavlovsk-Kamchatsky where she spent the winter not so far from the Aleutian Islands. The voyage recommenced the following June and continued via the Bering Strait to attempt the North East Passage. They were caught by an ice barrier and forced to turn back at 75° 30′N; 121° 32′E. A second attempt also failed and the yacht was forced to spend another winter, this time in Tiksi, Siberia. They started again when the ice broke up in late July 1999 and this time there was no stopping them. By 11 August they had succeeded in rounding Cape Chelyushkin, the most northerly point of the Eurasian land mass, and they arrived in Murmansk to complete the first transit of the Northern Sea Route by a yacht on 12 September. They continued around North Cape (Norway) and crossed their outward track in the Kattegat on 14 October 1999, having logged 31,000 miles. *Apostle Andrew* finally arrived back in St Petersburg on 11 November 1999.

Apostle Andrew is a 51ft steel ketch with a displacement of 22 tonnes and an auxiliary engine of 74 hp. The voyage encompassed all conditions from tropical to polar, and the ship and her crew were heavily reliant on their own resources. It is for this that the RCC Seamanship Medal in this millennium year is awarded to Nicolai Litau.

The Tilman Medal   Sverre Kraemer

Sverre Kraemer left Oslo in his 23-year-old 37ft yacht *Quest* and sailed single handed to Tromsø where he was joined by two friends. They then sailed from Tromsø for Svalbard on 16 July 2000 to give the best compromise between ideal ice conditions and the ability to return south before the autumn storms began. Despite ice information from a charter vessel that the Hinlopen Strait was blocked, they pressed on and found the ice predictions to be pessimistic. With improving weather they passed to the north of the Svalbard archipelago, making a furthest north of 81°00.6N, 20°40'E, believed to be the most northerly latitude ever reached by a sailing yacht. Heading on, they came to the northeast point of the island of Kvitøya in 80°13.4'N, 33°30.4'E. in rapidly deteriorating weather. Despite this the skipper landed, though only briefly due to the sudden appearance of a large male polar bear less than 60 metres away. They headed south for Kong Karls Land where they sheltered from a storm for 2 days before riding the tail of the gale back to Tromsø where they arrived on 12 August. For a voyage conducted in the best tradition without fuss or outside help the Tilman Medal for the year 2000 is awarded to Sverre Kraemer.

Medal for Services to Cruising   *Scrap Batten*

The number of members who contribute to the RCC Pilotage foundation is considerable, both in providing part of the information needed for keeping the pilot books they publish up to date, and, more onerous by far, running the organisation, writing and publishing the books. Scrap Batten has been closely connected with this operation for a long time, becoming chairman in 1991 and taking on the mantle of Director as well in 1995. By the time he retired in 2000 the number of titles of the pilot books which the foundation publishes increased from 10 to 22. Few cruising yachts are without at least one of these books on board, and it is for this work he is awarded the RCC Medal for Services to Cruising.

The Dulcibella Prize   *Heather Howard*

The Dulcibella Prize is awarded to Heather Howard for an account of a voyage all the way from Clachan Sound to Connel Ferry. It is the most entertaining of logs in that it conveys the simple joys, delights and pleasures of the simplest and gentlest of cruises in a yacht no larger than the *Dulcibella*.

FLEET MOVEMENTS

Yacht	Skipper	Area Cruised
Adrigole	Jeffrey O'Riordan	West coast of Scotland
Aenigma	BarryWoodhouse	Tromso to White Sea, Arkangelsk, Solvetski Islands, Belamorsk, White Sea Canal, Lake Onega, Volga-Balt Canal, Volga River, Volgograd, Volga- Don Canal, Azov, Sea of Azov, Black Sea, Yalta, Istanbul
Artemis of Lleyn	John Hodges	Stockholm to Copenhagen and then through Denmark to lay up on Jutland
Assent	Willy Ker	West coast of Greenland
Aurora	Graham Adam	Portugal, Southern Spain & Balearics
Ayesha of Yealm	John Lawson	Faeroes, Shetlands and NW Scotland
Barada	Ted Hawkins	Channel Islands and N. Brittany
Black Velvet	Ewen Southby-Tailyour	Rockall area (3 weeks: Iceland, failed) West Ireland.
Blackjack	Mike Pocock	Caribbean, East coast USA (S. Carolina to Maine), Nova Scotia (Lunenburg and Chester only), St John's NF, Ireland S. coast and home.
Brilleau	Sam Bayliss	Brittany and Vendée to La Rochelle and back by Ushant and Iles Chausey
Capercaillie	Hugh Wallace	Scottish Islands Three Peaks Race
Carina of Wight	Iain Eaton	Antigua to Cowes via Leeward Islands, British, US and Spanish Virgins, Puerto Rico, Dominican Republic, Cuba, Florida. Bermuda, Azores and home.
Celadus	Paddy Carr	Chesapeake Bay, Azores, England
Ceres	Jim Pitts	West coast of Scotland and St Kilda
Cerulean	Peter Snow	Venice to Dubrovnik
Charlsian	Adrian Biggs	West Indies
Cresting	David Brooke	South and West Turkey
Dodo's Delight	Bob Shepton	West coast of Greenland

Eila Rose	Edward and Thomas Bourne	North Western Spain
Feanor	Jeremy Parkinson	Aegean, S. Turkey, Ionian Islands
Felicia	Robin Faulkner	Channel Islands, N Brittany North Biscay incl the Golfe du Morbihan, Houat and Belle Ile
Felicia	Robin Faulkner	South and West Brittany
Fera	Nicholas Charman	South Brittany
Fillette	Harry Ross Skinner	Southern Turkey and Aegean
Flight of Time	Graham Morfey	Windward Islands, Panama, Marquesas, Tuamotus, Society Islands, Cook Islands, Tonga, New Zealand
Gas Pirate	Mike Pidsley	Around Britain with the Rolling Meet.
Gefion	Max Ekholm	Finland, Copenhagen, Göta Canal, Finland
Gemervescence	Michael Bonham Cozens	Leeward Islands, US and British Virgin Islands
Gemervescence of London	Michael Bonham Cozens	Helsinki, Estonia, Gotland, Gota Canal, Gothenburg
Gollywobbler II	Ann Fraser	Anacortes, Washington State, Pacific Northwest. British Columbia to Juneau, Alaska
Halcyon of Hebe	Jeremy Gurney	SE Aegean and south coast of Turkey as far as Gazipasa.
Holly	Peter Poole	Scotland, Western Isles
Hookey of Hamble	Martin Walker	South Coast Turkey between Bodrum and Mersin, Syria, Lebanon, Israel, Egypt, Cyprus
Hosannah	Bill and Laurel Cooper	North Sea
Houdalinqua II	Julian and Sheena Berney	Lagos (Portugal), Cadiz, Gibraltar, Caletta de Valez, Morocco (Marina Smir – El Jabha, Al Hoceima) – Spain (Almeria – Catagena, Alicante, Ibiza, Barcelona, Ginesta)
Ilex	John Webster	North Brittany, Channel Islands, and West Country
Irish Mist	Charles Nodder	Brittany and Channel Islands
Island Moon	Peter Craig-Wood	Eastern Caribbean
Juno II	Geoffrey Nockolds	Colombia, Nicaraguan Atolls and Reefs, Honduras
Kwai Muli	Kit Power	Channel Islands to Stornoway, Scottish Western Isles
Lectron	Peter Price	Spain, Sardinia, Sicily, Italy and Croatia
Libertà	Sandy Watson	West Country, Channel Islands and N Brittany
Maia of Dart	Robin Leuchars	Balearics, Spain
Mermerus	Christopher Lawrence-Jones	Turkey, Greece
Migrant	John Roome	Ionian Sea and South Adriatic

Morning Sky	Oliver Roome	Channel Islands, North Brittany, West Country
Morning Star	Dick Trafford	Eastern Aegean
Mor-Ula	Guy Morgan	Croatia
Mutineer	Jonathan Trafford	Outer Hebrides
Ocean Grace	John Sharp	Algarve, Azores, North Western Spain, Britanny
Ondarina	David Mitchell	Australia, Solomon Islands, Papua New Guinea, Philippines, Hong Kong, Japan, Canada, US.
Pemandia	Peter Fabricius	W. Coast of Scotland
Penelope's Ark	Tony Vasey	Alsace to Burgundy
Quiver	Anthony Browne	South of France and West Coast of Italy
Rafiki of Lymington	Bill and Hilary Keatinge	Preveza (NW Greece) to Kemer (S.Turkey) via Athens, Istanbul (Sea of Marmara)
Roving Topsy	Conrad Jenkin	Ionian Sea
Sarakiniko	Andrew Phelan	W. Scotland, Galloway, Isle of Man, Pembrokeshire
Shadey Lady	David Beckly	South Brittany
Shadey Lady	John Beckly	South Brittany
Shiant	Christopher Corbet	Loch Melfort meet and west coast of Scotland
Squander	James Beattie	West Country, North & South Brittany
Sundance of Suffolk	Colin Barry	Lagos, Grand Canaria, St Lucia, St Vincent, Grenada, Martinique, Saints, Guadalupe, St Barts, St Martin, Virgin Isles, Algarve, Western Mediterranean
Surgical Spirit	Alan Gardner	Burnham on Crouch, Channel Islands, North Brittany and Round Britain
Tacit	Hugh Marriott	Indonesia and Thailand
Taichi	Henry Hugh Smith	Cuba (north coast), Florida, Maine, Virginia, Bermuda, St Lucia.
Taraki	John Melling	Brazil, Uruguay, Argentina, Azores
Thetis of Tamar	Jeremy Bradshaw-Smith	Normandy, Brittany, Spain and Portugal
Tricula	Terry Gerald	North Brittany, Channel Islands and West Country
Twayblade	Jonathan Virden	Plymouth to Stornoway and back via Rolling meets, CCC Classic Malts and the West of Ireland
Upshot	Foster & Jeremy Swetenham	Round Scotland
Warrior Shamaal	Richard Clifford.	Channel Is, Portugal, Spain, Morocco, Balearics, Corsica, Sardinia, Pontine Islands, Italy.
Wender	Sam Poole	SW England, Channel Islands and N. Brittany
Westernman	Tom Cunliffe	Around Ireland

THE ROUND BRITAIN ROLLING MEET 2000

Edited and Compiled by Jonathan Virden

Kit Power, Commodore during the planning of the Round Britain Rolling Meet

In the middle of 1998 Millennium fever was hotting up and the committee considered how the club would mark the event. Ashtrays, tea-towels and other mementos were briefly discussed, but we felt that by the time the year rolled round to 2000 we would all be awash with such artefacts. What was needed was an event, but it should be different so that we would remember it as being special. And it should be something in which all members, wherever they lived in the British Isles, could participate. And so the idea of the 'Rolling Meet' was born. There would be a sequence of meets moving clockwise from the Channel Islands, up the Irish Sea, round the top of Scotland, down the East Coast and finally reaching Beaulieu in time for the meet there in September. It was hoped that members would attend the meet nearest their home ports, sometimes sailing in company to adjacent meets as well. Some stalwarts might even do the whole circumnavigation but the main objective was simply to involve as many members as possible at one stage or another.

Richard Clifford organised the event with great energy and care. He planned a sequence of ten parties, each organised by a Local Meet Organiser (LMO), so that every one of the local meets had its own character. There were to be barbecues, pub lunches, dinners and receptions in Yacht Clubhouses or hotels, raft parties, and so on with a mixture of formal and informal events as appropriate. The plans seemed to strike a chord and some enterprising members put their names down as potential participants, most of whom eventually took part. By the beginning of July all the pieces were in place and on a beautiful evening in the Elizabeth Castle overlooking St Helier the first party took place and the Rolling Meet was under way.

Ile Chausey
18 : 7 : 00

Richard Clifford, Chief Organiser

The Rolling Meet was Kit's idea. It was discussed during the ski meet in 1998 and I agreed to take it on. Kit's aim was to have a series of meets around the UK to gather in members, in particular, where they do not often have meets. And it had to be sequential so that the intrepid or those with time could get to them all.

With this directive I first had to decide which way round to go and to find members who were prepared to organise a meet in their area. The direction was easily resolved; clockwise like the Round Britain Race seemed the best way. With Peter Price's assistance a trawl through members scattered around the coastline soon gave me a framework plan. The only clash seemed to be with an invitation from the Clyde Cruising Club to their Millennium Cruise event. We ended up with LMOs who meticulously planned the meets in their area and in their style.

With approval of the committee I designed a pennant like that for the centenary for members to fly in 2000. We sold just under 100. The whole event was to be non-profit making; we ended with just over £100 in the kitty. Three months before the event the instructions prepared by the LMOs were put into a single document and dispatched with tickets, 519 in all. Mike Pidsley won the prize for purchasing the most tickets – 52.

Sandy Watson: Le Cricket?

The finale of the Channel Islands Meet was a sort of cricket match played in Iles Chausey. The ground will probably be unfamiliar to most cricketers because, being situated just to the south of L'Enseigne beacon,

The Minquiers Meet: June 2000 (Jonathan Virden).

it is only available for play at certain states of the tide, and arguably could be considered to be *in* French territorial waters.

The players were drawn from the crews of seven RCC yachts which were anchored in the pool to the north of the beacon. The prelude to the match was a most convivial barbecue on the nearby rocks. Although not quite a bacchanalian feast, there was both conspicuous consumption of food and worthy attempts to make inroads into the seemingly endless supply of wine and beer that had been laid on by the organisers. As the tide fell, dinghies had to be periodically waded off ever further into the middle distance and re-anchored to avoid much portage later.

There was some debate as to how the teams should be constituted. Eventually East Jersey v West Jersey and the Rest of the World was decided upon as the best balance achievable. But any distinction was soon lost as only the batsman wasn't fielding, and the important thing seemed to be to get whoever was in out or to make as many runs as you could when in. The ground was, for the most part, distinctly soft and not entirely level sand. With the stumps still being in Jersey, an Avon dinghy seat was pressed into service as the batsman's wicket. Players' reactions were a little dulled by lunch, and most attempts at athleticism were foiled by the ground giving way under their feet in moments of stress. Left-handed batsmen caused minor problems as several fielders had to be deployed into shallow pools. At the end of the day it was thought that East Jersey had lost by one run, but no-one was quite sure, and nobody minded at all after such a fun occasion.

Hugh Davies, LMO Helford.

The biggest RCC meet ever in the Helford river? I am not sure, but big enough to stretch local facilities. Happily not to breaking point, as all 24 yachts found comfortable moorings, a few were rafted up, and the Ferryboat Inn at Helford Passage rose to the occasion and served an excellent buffet lunch to the 83 members (Richard Clifford had calculated 82 on 6 June. How's that for inspired staff work?). The pub had cordoned off half of its dining/sitting space for the Club, having been warned to prepare for up to 90 RCC members and crews, in addition to a normal July Saturday influx. Weather was what worried us. Fine, and we could spill out onto the terrace. Wet and windy: Oh Dear!. But it was fine, or at least fine enough, and although a trifle crowded, the decibel level indicated satisfaction. What a relief!

Yachts attending were *Astros*, *Caressa*, *Gas Pirate*, *Harrier*, *Isis Tres*, *Jessamy*, *Juno*, *Kataree*, *Kwai Muli*, *Merlintu*, *Morning Sky*, *Nansida*, *Salvation Jane*, *Southern Comfort*, *Sumarel*, *Surgical Spirit*, *Tallulah*, *Tatsu*, *Twayblade*, *Wandering Moon*, *Wenda*, *Wish Hound II*, *Yara*.

John Marsh, Harrier. *Helford to Dunlaoghaire*

James Tree (ex clipper crew *Taeping*) joined me for the passage from Helford to Dun Laoghaire. We left Helford on Monday 10 July at 1715 and experienced northwest F.6/7, touching F.8 until well round Lands End. This became northerly for a while on Tuesday afternoon, and it was not until 2100 on that day that we were able to log 'on our way at

The Helford Meet (Hugh Davies).

last'. Then it was a pleasant sail, reaching Dun Laoghaire at 0045 on 13 July. Sheila sensibly flew to Dublin.

Colin McMullen, LMO Dun Laoghaire.

The Dun Laoghaire Lunch was preceded by ten days of strong northerlies, leading to doubts as to how many boats would arrive in time. In the end, most boats arrived in the nick of time. We wondered how Cormac McHenry would make his way from the National YC. Would he bring *Erquy* the necessary half cable or be driven by the boatman, keeping his tootsies dry? Perhaps the answer should remain a mystery so that Cormac might not, in his own words, be exposed as a fraud.

Fifty-five members and friends assembled for the usual magnificent lunch provided by the Royal Irish YC; Irish lamb for most, swordfish for a few. The Nixon brothers had their parties at the same table, as if to prove that brotherly love still exists or perhaps due to a scarcity of volunteers. The Commodore of the RIYC gave a fascinating history of the club and in the double entendre of the millennium referred to that great RCC and RIYC member and Irishman, whose bust (presented by RCC members) adorns the foyer, as 'Conor Cruise O'Brien'! (For the uninitiated Conor Cruise O'Brien is a recent public figure in Ireland and Conor O'Brien cruised south of the three great capes in the 1920s JV)

Talking of history, it is one of the quirks of Irish Independence that both the major gun-running voyages to this area in the 'War of Independence' were carried out under the club burgee.

Main cabin of Nordlys, at anchor in Strangford Lough.

Jonathan Virden, **Twayblade**

Twayblade followed the rolling meet from Jersey to Helford and then up
the Celtic Sea until we were frustrated by contrary weather from getting
to Dun Laoghaire in time for lunch. We retreated to Dale, finding an
unexpectedly good place. From Dale we motored hard to Howth, on to
Bangor where we joined in the reception and dinner, and on to Skye. It
was more effort than had been planned, but the rewards were great. The
sunflower raft, ceilidh and buffet lunch at Talisker were memorable.
Thereafter we motored to Mull for a picnic lunch with the Royal Highland YC and on to Loch Melfort. Then to Kerrera for dinner with the
Clyde Cruising Club and Classic Malts. We reached Stornoway late but
just in time for dinner. From Lewis we sailed south to Oban, for a crew
change, and then home to Plymouth by way of the west of Ireland,
mostly motoring past picture-postcard coasts. Our first venture to Scotland was very successful, much helped by calm sunshine, great gather-
ings and huge quantities of diesel, all stimulated by the Rolling Meet.

James Nixon, LMO Bangor

I was pleased to be asked to help organise the Royal Cruising Club
Rolling Meet around Britain in 2000, and tried to join in as much as
possible. It causes no hardship to get away from Northern Ireland in
July. Patrick Knatchbull and I sailed *Ardnagee* to Dun Laoghaire, stopping at Carlingford and Howth on the way. Entering Dun Laoghaire we

James Nixon and Alexander taking Corryvreckan fairly seriously.

felt that the digging machine building the new port-hand breakwater should have been coloured red. It was green which caused us great confusion. Paddy Doyle, the head boatman at the Royal Irish YC, remembered me from my quiet student days at Trinity and we were given the plum berth at the pontoon in front of the club. Throughout our stay an elderly flatulent grey seal entertained us. He had taken up residence in a chamber under the boat deck.

There were many RCC boats in Dun Laoghaire and an excellent lunch was enjoyed in the Royal Irish, organised by Colin McMullen. Ed Wheeler joined us for the trip north; we stopped at Ardglass, and then motored on to Bangor.

I tried to get back to business for a few days but RCC business is important. I helped *Cloud Walker* with repairs and supplies of duty-free liquid for Iceland and beyond. I had a vested interest as I was to join them there later. The dinner in the Royal Ulster YC was convivial and the fleet then dispersed north.

Ardnagee went north too, with Katherine, and daughter Holly with the husband James Somerville. We stopped at Gigha, visited Achamore gardens, and had to move across the Sound of Gigha to a more comfortable berth. Before we came to Ardfern we spent a night in the 'lagoon'. We motored through Corryvreckan to anchor in Bagh Bleann nam Muck at the north end of Jura. This is a wonderful natural anchorage and the strong tidal stream across the entrance ensures that no swell enters.

Landing for dinner at Loch Melfort (Stuart Ingram).

Shiant, Christopher Corbet, RCC came in that evening and the roar of the Corryvreckan carried over to us on a calm evening. We sailed to Loch Melfort to join in the raft and dinner. We were made very welcome and lots of people came on board. It was reassuring to see the lack of discipline in the sail-in-company behind *Troubadour.*

Heather Howard, Jubilate *takes the High Road*

Having gone to the Helford meet with Christopher Buckley, we trailed *Jubilate* from Hampshire to Loch Melfort, a two-day journey, and joined in the raft-up and the dinner. On the way south, again by road, the jeep was stolen and *Jubilate* came home behind the AA. We then went to the Deben meet in a Wayfarer and found magnificent hospitality from Mike and Margaret Spear. What a beautiful river! Finally we came to Beaulieu.

Mike Pidsley, Gas Pirate

We departed Bangor on 19 July and crossed to Loch Ryan for the night. Next morning, we had a glorious sail up the Firth of Clyde, past Ailsa Craig, Lamlash and Holy Island and dropped anchor off the quay at Millport on the south of Great Cumbrae Island. Here we went ashore for our first taste of Scotland. During the next few days the sun shone down on us. The wind was somewhat fickle. We coasted gently up the Gareloch in the lightest of breezes, and made a flying pick-up of Mark and Fiona Adams RCC off Rhu in the RIB without actually stopping sailing. We spent a beautiful morning sailing through the Kyles of Bute and next day traversed the Crinan Canal. While others paid good money to eat at the famous restaurant in the Crinan Hotel we consumed a double rib of Aberdeen Angus beef sitting on deck. We enjoyed a balmy evening and watched the sun setting over Scarba, Luing and the more distant island of Mull. It was stunning; cruising at its very best. Even the midges were well under control.

Bill McKean, LMO *Loch Melfort*

The Millennium summer proved to be a truly memorable summer on the west coast of Scotland with Caribbean blue skies day after day and the largest fleet of RCC yachts to gather in these waters. The meet was timed to allow members to 'island hop' between Bangor and Stornoway and to take in some of the Malts cruise if their taste desired.

The fleet began to gather on the morning of 26 July in Loch Shuna. Some had anchored off the Loch Melfort Hotel for the previous evening. Others of us who had been sampling distillery products left Tobermory early that morning and burst the last of the flood stream at Cuan Sound to join the fleet shortly after midday.

Rear commodore Stuart Ingram, together with John Clow formed the nucleus of a raft and within the hour twenty-four club yachts rafted together awaiting the arrival of the commodore and vice-commodore who had travelled north to be with us. By the time Christopher, Valentine and Michael arrived the raft had safely survived a swing in wind direction. With anchors holding, the cocktails and many other tales were flowing freely.

The fleet remained rafted together until later in the afternoon before easing apart and moving to the head of the loch where we moored for the evening's activities.

Over 140 members and guests dined ashore in the Melfort village hall, a perfect venue for that number, easily approached by dinghy and only a short walk from the beach. As in previous years the buffet was prepared and presented on stage by Steven and Alison Hyatt of the Shower of Herring Inn. What an act they have to follow!

Later that evening (very much later for some) we made our way back on board feeling very satisfied with life. Good food, good wine and the good company of fellow RCC members had made for a very happy day.

The 24 yachts present in the raft were; *Jubilate, Alakush, Jesta IV, Islay, Quaila, Siolta, Capercaillie, Harrier, Jessamy, Kwai Muli, Troubadour, Nordlys, Oriole, Ceres, Foggy Dew, Venture, Ayesha, Francesca, Gas Pirate, Borialis, Sarakiniko, Twayblade, Ardnagee, Shiant.*

Mike Pidsley, Gas Pirate

On the morning of 26 July yachts were appearing from all directions as we began to assemble in Asknish Bay. After much use of channel 72 it was decided to raft up in south Loch Melfort. We numbered twenty-seven yachts abreast. Midst all this activity I noticed that one of the small craft amongst us had found less water than expected. I dispatched the RIB with my trusty crew to pull him off. There was some discussion as to whose line should be used, the word salvage being mentioned. Later he sailed gently past and handed a bottle, with wired cork, in gratitude; such a gentleman.

Jim Pitts, Ceres

When I first heard of the idea of a Round Britain Rolling Meet about a year ago I thought, 'What a splendid idea, I'll do that'. However milking cows and the harvest limited us to the meets at Loch Melfort and Stornoway. Catherine joined *Ceres* on the morning of the meet after *Ceres* had spent the night with *Troubadour, Harrier* and *Oriole* in the bay below the Loch Melfort hotel. We joined in the raft and the supper party which was a huge success whether judged on numbers, food (quality and quantity of which defied belief) or conversation and friendship; this last point is always so vivid at any RCC gathering and always amazes this relatively new member! Next *Ceres* collected more crew at Oban, visited Loch Aline, Loch Skipport and Loch Scadabay among others. We saw many porpoises, whales and sharks and met T*roubadour* at the Shiant Is. taking photos of puffins which have no fear of humans. We also met the Traffords on *Mutineer*. After much use of diesel breeze so far, we had a quiet sail into Loch Leurbost. On the way into Leurbost we spotted four female forms on the shore who responded to our greetings; this was as near as we got to seeing mermaids as requested by the Editor. The raft at Loch Leurbost and the gathering at Stornoway were organised with great skill and hospitality by Audrey and Bill Speirs. ·

Christopher Corbet, Shiant

Like most guests with the least far to go we arrived late at Loch Melfort, but that was because we were prepared to sail in. To do it with a little panache we anchored under sail. Out went the chain in the right place, the jib furled, the mainsail dropped. We were about to drop back nicely alongside the last yacht in the raft. But the catting pennant was still made fast to the pulpit so the anchor eventually dropped in quite the wrong place. There were a lot of kindly faces pretending not to notice.

Pam and Bill Kellett, Islay

Leaving Loch Melfort we made our way to Loch Leurbost, but saw very few of the other yachts of the fleet. We stopped at Loch na Droma Buidhe, having chosen to leave Skye to port. On the way into Inverie, Loch Nevis, we towed a RIB home. We had reserved a table at the Pier House restaurant, and the Ingrams with Michael Lewin-Harris joined us from *Troubadour*. A great meal, aided by extra wine provided by the owner of the RIB in lieu of salvage. It is not recorded which of Pam or Annabel danced on the table.

Next we called at Rona after a slow day of light wind. We failed to find the church in the cave, but the shower in the crofter's cottage, fed from the pool in the hills was heated and as modern as any in the isles. The crew of *Troubadour* joined us for a jolly unplanned supper. At the Shiant Islands, we found several other RCC yachts north-bound and the Traffords aboard *Mutineer*. A grand reunion luncheon ensued before we moved on to Loch Leurbost and found the missing RCC fleet!

Sally and Jeffrey O'Riordan were Lurking in the Isles in Adrigole

On our way from Arisaig to the meet in Stornoway and going back to Ardfern *Adrigole* perfected a new technique. For this it is important not to decide where you are going until the last possible moment. The night before might be convenient but it is far too early. For example when heading for the Outer Hebrides from Rhum we agreed on a course that was generally westerly but it was not until we were half way across the Minch that it was reasonable to decide that Eriskay was the ideal target, allowing for the prevailing wind. Anything further north would have had us close hauled. Once safely anchored there we could agree that it was the perfect place to go. On the jetty if you're lucky there will be a fishing boat waiting to give you some scallops and we mean give. Ashore you can marvel at the machair, that remarkable mixture of sand, shell and earth that allows even wild orchids to flourish. The more energetic can wonder where they could find the Eriskay ponies which are said to be living fossils. Back aboard you could read Whisky Galore with greater insight and wonder if you are on Little Toddy especially as we had been given a lift to the shops by the parish priest and regaled with an account of life on the island.

To get the best out of the 'Loitering in the Isles' principle you need to be in no hurry. If going north up the coast to Stornoway is not appropriate, why not cross the Minch again, say to Gairloch? In doing so, remember that in Scotland the same name is used for places that are quite far apart, so be sure to be looking at the right chart. We made one serious mistake in deciding that *Adrigole* needed to go to the Summer Isles on a particular day. The wind, and there was plenty of it, was coming directly from there. This was bad for the digestion and we were glad to find a hurricane hole in a recess of Loch Ewe, favoured by seals. Once you do get to the Summer Isles be sure to divert to the nearby mainland, to land in a dinghy and locate the Smoke House. They supply smoked fish to a couple of London grocers, one in Knightsbridge, run by an Egyptian, and the other in Piccadilly, run by a man in a frock coat. The Smoke House also sell locally.

RCC displaying some discipline entering Stornaway (Stuart Ingram).

Stuart Ingram, **Troubadour**

The following day, Tuesday 1 August, we moved on to Stornoway, which was in the midst of its Maritime Festival. The co-ordinated entry of the RCC fleet into the harbour made such an impression that it was covered on local television and a photograph graced the front page of the weekly *Stornoway Gazette*. Bill and Audrey Speirs, supported by their son Richard, had worked to make this something special and we were particularly grateful when next day they took us together with David and Annette Ridout for a tour of the island and its ancient sites. This was to be a parting of the ways for the RCC fleet. As the majority turned south, the Ingrams on *Troubadour* and Ridouts on *Nordlys* set out on the 200-mile passage to Shetland. To begin with there was little wind and we motored towards Cape Wrath but then the breeze filled in from the southwest and with the genoa boomed out we ran on south of Sule Skerry with deteriorating visibility and increasing wind. We took in a reef during the night but when it eased the following morning we were too slow in shaking it out and *Nordlys* pulled ahead. We blessed the GPS and radar as we ran towards the windward side of the Shetlands. Twenty miles off I was able to contact the Commodore thanks to Vodafone and get details of where to go in Scalloway. We followed *Nordlys* in and moored in the harbour at 1700. We had taken just over 30 hours to cover the 209 miles.

Scalloway on 4 August 2000.

David Ridout, Nordlys

By now the fleet was thinning out and there were only two of us who set out for the Shetlands. We rounded Cape Wrath with little wind and a lumpy sea. *Troubadour* was six miles ahead of us. With the afternoon turning to twilight the wind filled in from the southwest giving us a fast sail. The genoa boomed out to port, our working headsail set in the gap between forestay and mast and the mainsail bowsed town tight to the starboard rail *Nordlys* ploughed on through the low cloud and rain squalls averaging a shade under eight knots. Annette having crossed the Atlantic last year on *Troubadour* has split loyalties and was quite sure we would not loose out but would not catch up. By 0200, the wind was up to a gusting seven and as we hit thirteen knots I put a reef in the main. The dot on the radar screen was out to starboard but only three miles ahead. Later in the morning the reef came out and as we came up to Fuglaness light off Scalloway we were two hundred meters ahead of our rival. For those who are used to sailing in such northern climbs such a passage is easy but for us it was a step into the unknown and having chats on the radio with *Troubadour* every few hours was very reassuring. We eventually made fast alongside each other in the commercial part of Scalloway harbour at 1700. There were 201 miles on the log and a polite harbour master saying we could remain for three days for £6.50. The post passage whisky tasted very good.

Christopher Thornhill, Commodore and LMO Shetland.

The fine weather on the west coast of Scotland did not continue beyond Cape Wrath. *Sai See* was faced with northeasterly F.7 at the Cape. Shetland in early August was exceptionally cold.

The unsatisfactory weather and a disappointing turn-out led to a last minute abandonment of the whole plan. We substituted ad hoc mini-meets and an early departure southwards. We had started with fairly firm commitment by 11 yachts and 37 people. By the time of the Jersey meet the count was down to 8 yachts and 24 people and about 10 Shetlanders with a yacht or two. Finally only *Troubadour* with two Ingrams and *Nordlys* with two Ridouts joined *Sai See* at Scalloway. There we found John Armitage in *Kyrah,* quite unaware of the meet, but he was a welcome addition.

Saturday 5 August, the key day for making our way northwards was so foul, windy, wet, foggy and cold, that the nine people voted to abandon sailing, hire a minibus and do the antiquities of the Mainland. The day was a great success. We inspected Jarlshof and the Iron Age excavations and reconstructions at Scatness, and had lunch in the Sumburgh Hotel and ended with a good dinner in Lerwick. It was a great relief when Alistair Pratt telephoned while we were sheltering in a Lerwick pub and we were able to divert him southwards. *Copihue II* eventually joined *Sai*

See and *Troubadour* in Fair Isle (North Haven) on a beautiful evening for a very jolly dinner on *Sai See*.

Unscrambling the dinner arrangements and local invitations was a little embarrassing. However, although disappointing in many ways, with the weather quite unsuitable for the planned assault on the Outstack, 5 RCC yachts and 11 people met in Shetland and had a good and interesting time. The yachts returning southwards were glad to get away ahead of schedule. I hope they will all return to sail the islands properly.

Stuart Ingram, Troubadour *at Hartlepool*

We were now under pressure of time to reach Hartlepool. We left next morning, Tuesday, to find the northwesterly wind dying away leaving a lumpy sea. After a few hours with the motor the wind returned from the southeast and we started a slow beat towards the Moray coast. It was not enjoyable. We finally rounded Rattray Head in poor visibility amidst fishing boats and tugs towing oilrig equipment. We battled on down towards Aberdeen before the wind relented and went round to the west. On the second night it picked up and we had to reef in the small hours but as we did so the main halyard suddenly gave way, not parting but stretching considerably. In the dark it was difficult to see what had happened but eventually we managed to get the mainsail set up double reefed. If we tried to pull it up further the halyard jammed. In daylight it was apparent that the outer covering of the Spectra line had parted although the core was intact. Later a visit to the top of the mast in Hartlepool to sort out the wind instruments, which had also gone on the blink during this passage, revealed the whole story. The Tufnol spacer between the two sheaves for the main halyard and topping lift in the mastbox had at some stage shattered; the jagged edges left had cut the Spectra line. We switched to using the topping lift to raise the mainsail. After all this we were glad to reach the excellent marina at Hartlepool where we met with *Gas Pirate* and *Surgical Spirit*.

Gas Pirate *drops in on the Whitby Folk Festival*

For our entertainment Whitby had laid on their annual Folk Week. Everywhere you looked there were violins, guitars or accordions strapped to peoples backs. Music and beer flowed out of every pub. The atmosphere was very pleasurable. In the evening, as we waited for the tide to lift *Gas Pirate*, I visited the rowing club bar on the quay alongside us. There where ten violins, three accordions, two melodeons, two concertinas and one guitar. As one musician started a jig or round, so the others gradually joined in, until the room was full of genuine country sound. Then as if by magic, but I'm quite sure they had all carefully been counting the bars, it would cease and someone would play on into another tune only for the others to pick it up again. We were very sorry to leave Whitby but the Deben was calling

Mike Spear, LMO Deben

The venue picked for the East Coast Meet was the Rocks Anchorage in the river Deben – a very pretty spot – privately owned and no road access! We then went ahead and notified those interested and sent charts of the entrance to the Deben which could be tricky to those from away. As it happened the entrance, metes and buoys were all changed after the charts were sent – so they were re-drawn and sent to Alan Gardner to distribute as some were already on their way.

People were very interested and we soon had several acceptances. As this year's climate was dodgy, it was decided to barbecue on the foredeck of *Zeeuwleeuw*. We cajoled our Haven Ports Club Steward, Des, to come and do the cooking. This worked very well and about 50 people enjoyed the evening. We rafted with *Gas Pirate* on one side and *Surgical Spirit* on the other. They set up chairs and tables on their decks and it all looked terribly civilised! At 1800 we assembled and drinks flowed; others kept arriving. A Wayfarer even came loaded with several children who clambered over all the boats and climbed various masts and had a good time on ginger beer!

The Rear Commodore was here with 'Dear All' of e-mail fame, with their wives. The barbecue menu was steaks, chops, sausages, baked potatoes and salads followed by strawberries and cream, all washed down by various wines in vast quantities. The whole organisation worked well; cancellations balanced last minute requests for tickets!

The Gas Pirates at Beaulieu on 9 September 2000.

Alan Gardner, LMO Burnham

The RCC event in Burnham took place on Monday 28 August. Commodore Cathy Herring and the Flag Officers of the Royal Burnham Yacht Club attended a drinks party in the new River Room followed by an excellent dinner with dancing afterwards for those still on their feet. Boats present were *Surgical Spirit, Moonbeam, Troubadour, Hermione of Burnham, Gas Pirate* and *Zeeuwleeuw*. Around 25 RCC members mingled noisily with local friends at the Burnham Week Cruiser dinner. Incidentally *Surgical Spirit* won class 6 at Burnham Week. (Is this cricket? JV) After all, racing is fast cruising is not it? (No! JV)

Kit Power at the Beaulieu Meet

An unpromising long-range weather forecast for the week-end of 9/10 September became less and less threatening as the date approached and in the event we enjoyed two days of sunshine and moderate winds. This was the final meet of the Round Britain Rolling Meet. On the central raft were *Troubadour* and *Gas Pirate*, both veterans of the RBRM circumnavigation, together with *Wombat*, and Leslie and Margaret Jones' beautiful and brand new *Namaqua*. Both Lord Montagu and his son Ralph attended the Commodore's drinks party at noon on Saturday. A better than average number of new members attended the lunch which followed. The 'Gas Pirates' turned themselves into stewards for the occasion. The big boats on the central raft provided plenty of space for a well-attended sing-song that evening.

MEETS

Christmas meet

After weeks of rain it was very nice to be onboard in the sun for the visit to the Folly pontoons where Francis Hicks had arranged berths. For those coming from Lymington there was a fair tide both ways and a light NW wind assisted. *Kataree* took the opportunity to air her sails before proceeding up river. A variety of vacuum flasks were in constant use along the pontoon dispensing mulled wine. The following vessels attended: *Brilleau, Kataree, Meandro, Squander, The Otter, Tricula, Wandering Moon.*

JB

Eastern Mediterranean Cruise in Company

It says much for Harry Ross Skinner's charm and gentle persuasion that six yachts were safely anchored at Gumusslik, near Bodrum, on Saturday 27 May. The last to arrive was 28ft *Feanor*, the smallest yacht having travelled the greatest distance. With three young grass widows aboard she quickly became a most popular ship. Prior to the start of festivities two former Commodores and the Club Secretary with their entourage visited Bodrum Castle and the new and fascinating Underwater Archaeology Museum by minibus. It was a hot and rewarding trip.

Whilst no yachts were rafted up we were all in close company and enjoyed visiting before twenty-four of us sat down for an entertaining Turkish dinner at the Bati restaurant. It was a lively happy party where tentative plans for the week were made. The following morning all yachts left in hot sun and gentle breezes bound for Cökertme some 30 miles to the southeast. The Kos Channel between the high hills of Turkey and the mountains of Kos and Kalymnos made a fine sight as the cruise started. Everyone arrived at Cökertme in good time for a noisy drinks party aboard *Fillette*. Laughter and anxiety were mixed when it became known that a rat had joined a club yacht which also had a split stainless water tank. No evidence appeared that the two events were connected and both problems were resolved by the end of the week. There was another full complement for dinner ashore at the Mary Rose. The fleet dispersed on Monday morning in light conditions planning to meet near Göcek for the final party on Friday. During the day it became clear that the high mountain ranges on the nearby peninsulas made VHF communications unreliable. Not to be outdone Richard Clifford on *Morning Star* determined to keep in touch with club headquarters and with the aid of a temporary dipole raised Peter Price at sea between Minorca and Sardinia. Rendezvous for the next few days were haphazard but most yachts met up at one or more of the many fascinating anchorages where visits were exchanged. The most popular of the anchorages were ancient Knidos at Cape Krio, Port Losta Keci Buku and Dirsek in the Gulf of Doris, and Bozuk Nuku Serve and Ekencik, all on the way towards Göcek. Newcomers and old hands were spoilt for choice as anchorages were found in one historic place after another. Many were surveyed by Captain Beaufort from 1810 to 1812 and the charts are still accurate. By Thursday the weather forecasts became mildly worrying with severe gales expected in the southeast Aegean due to arrive for our final parties in Skopea Liman. Many yachts had exciting sailing and we became involved in the Turkish Fleet manoeuvres in the Rhodes Channel; the leading squadron of frigates gave way to a yacht under sail as salutes were exchanged. Our own fleet had by now arrived in Tomb Bay and with great thunderclouds gathering over the distant 7000ft mountains and squalls in evidence anchoring became interesting. We all anchored Mediterranean style with lines ashore. The forecast did not prevent a thoroughly enjoyable farewell drinks party aboard *Fillette* after which five noisy full dinghies crossed the darkening bay for the final dinner at the shoreside restaurant. After a surprisingly peaceful night the fleet dispersed but not before the lively arrival of the Gleadells with Sam and Sue Poole aboard their charter yacht. Everyone who made the effort to join this cruise in company thoroughly enjoyed exploring the beautiful coast. Here hot sun and good breezes combine with warm swimming and safe anchorages to make an ideal cruising ground. The late Henry Denham would have been delighted to think that more than fifty years after he first explored and then wrote his Sea-Guides the Club was following in his illustrious wake.

Twenty two members attended. The six yachts were *Cresting*, *Feanor*, *Fillette*, *Halcyon of Hebe*, *Morning Star* and *Eros*.

RHT

Cadet Meet.

The RCC cadet meet was one of the most successful in recent years. Stuart Ingram and Trevor Wilkinson kindly lent *Troubadour* and *Wombat*. Richard Wakeman, fresh from the south Pacific, in *The Alderman* and John Trinder with *Saga* completed the sailing fleet. We did a couple of circuits of the Western Solent in F.3–4 northwest with massive offsets of 45 deg for the spring tide when crossing the Solent.

A traditional raft-up on the harbourmaster's buoys off Needs Oar Point followed. *Troubadour* had a push-pit BBQ from which Jamie Lewin-Harris managed to feed 30 cadets and others. This allowed time for much consumption of wine and beer. Then Giles Gleadell, the foremost guitarist of the RCC, with his family, joined from *Fidget*. An uninhibited serenade of the gulls and geese occupied the next three or four hours of a beautiful evening as the sun went down and the air cooled near midnight.

AG

OBITUARIES

Reverend Canon Roslyn Aish

Roslyn died in September 2000, aged 80, after a long illness. He was a man of many parts.

After obtaining a first class honours degree in electrical engineering, he joined the RNVR and soon found himself swept into WWII where he served with distinction for four years as a naval officer. It was during this period, given just one day's leave from his ship in Weymouth, that he married Jean.

War service over, Roslyn entered the prosperous and respected business of Aish & Co, electrical engineers, Poole, which had been founded by his grandfather. After some years, however, Roslyn decided that his true calling in life was with the Church.

He started as a curate in Coventry and Bournemouth. Then, from 1963 to 1973 he had ten very enjoyable years as vicar of Hyde, a small country parish on the edge of the New Forest. His later appointments and voluntary work focused more and more on the rehabilitation into society of the mentally ill. He worked directly with several mental hospitals and became director of the Bournemouth branch of the Samaritans. These were services to the community for which not many of us, the writer included, would have had the patience or stomach. In 1983, in recognition of his Christian work, Roslyn was created an Honorary Canon of Winchester Cathedral.

Little of the above was known to the many friends who knew Roslyn only as a quiet, but intrepid, yachtsman. A member of Parkstone Yacht Club for over sixty years, he was very much a cruising man. Not for him, though, weekends and day trips throughout the season. Rather his sailing was usually compressed into one hectic three or four week holiday each summer during which he cruised to France, Spain and as far as North Africa. It was, however, for his Norwegian exploits that Roslyn will be chiefly remembered.

The writer first met Roslyn in the early 1980s after a talk I gave on my

287

own cruises in west and north Norway. He confessed to me later that this was what gave him the idea to go to Norway, with the thought that, 'if H can do it, I am sure I can!', I am still not quite sure how to take this.

No less than ten annual cruises to Norway followed, each one reaching further and further north. During this time we were all getting rather worried as he suffered several mishaps, including a medical emergency and a dismasting, chiefly on the long return journey from north Norway to Poole. I tried to persuade Roslyn to leave his yacht in Norway for the winter, as I and others had done, but to no avail.

Finally in 1996, on *Ondine's* third visit to Svalbard, Roslyn achieved his ambition of being only the second yacht after Tilman to circumnavigate West Spitzbergen. For this cruise he was rightly awarded the Challenge Cup.

For such a kindly man, Roslyn was not the easiest of skippers to sail with. Impervious to seasickness even in a full gale, he would set the A*utopilot* and go below to organised chaos, with hatches battened down. With the possible exception of the ocean yacht master crew who jumped ship in the Shetlands after a particularly rough passage from north Norway, he attracted great crew loyalty. This even included the distinguished medic and regular crew who wrote an amusing article in a leading yachting magazine entitled, *'To Hell and Back with Roslyn Aish'*.

It gave me great pleasure to propose Roslyn Aish for membership of the RCC in 1994. He truly represented the best Corinthian spirit of this Club.

HS

John Bush

John Bush, who died in January 2000 aged 92, was an inspiration to all those who were lucky enough to sail with him. He was a truly exceptional seaman and navigator and a tough sailor but with a well developed sense of the ridiculous and an infectious enthusiasm for the moment, regardless of the prevailing weather conditions. This combination of talents had a profound influence upon the many young people who he introduced to offshore sailing.

At Sherborne, he met Howson Devitt who was to become a lifelong friend. John spent the pre-war years cruising and racing on Howson's yachts *Spray* and *Lady Maud*, and after the war (during which he served with distinction in the Royal Artillery, mainly in the Middle East), he became Secretary of the RORC yacht *Griffin* for eight years.

Those were days when the distinction between the cruising and ocean racing disciplines was far less marked than it is today. It is hard to believe, in this modern high tech era, that *Griffin* (a heavy engineless gaff rigged cutter) competed in every RORC race during John's eight year term, usually with a crew of novices and frequently with great success

John Bush.

thanks to John's canny navigational skills. He went on to become Vice
Commodore of the RORC in 1952 and was a Trustee of the Admiral's
Cup from its inception in 1957 until 1986. He was a regular crew on
Bloodhound when she was owned by Miles Wyatt, and was honoured to
skipper her in her first ocean race under royal ownership (a rough race in
which she leaked appallingly but was driven on to take line honours and
a telegram of congratulations from the Duke of Edinburgh).

John then bought *Jouster* one of the first Nicholson 32s, in partnership
with Hugo Walford. *Jouster* competed in almost all the RORC races in
the late 1960's and early 1970's with her happy crew of family and friends.
As always, she was driven hard and was often in the money, but the
laughs were the same regardless of the outcome. *Jouster* did not linger on
her moorings for long and became something of an institution.

John took *Jouster* on some notable cruises and was elected to the
RCC in 1972. In that year (following his retirement from the shipping
agents Benjamin Ackerley) he and Isobel cruised 2624 miles to Scotland,
Norway, Denmark and Holland. His log in Roving Commissions refers
to atrocious weather from Gosport to Inverness, including eight gales,
but is brimming with fun and enjoyment. He had the true cruising
yachtsman's interest in the history and culture of the places he visited,
and he loved meeting the locals and joining in with them, (including, on
one memorable Spanish cruise, demonstrating how the British could
also dance on the tables). His description in the 1975 Roving Com-

missions of a *Peaceful Sunday in Houat* is an object lesson in how humour and tenacity can overcome the frustrations of a crowded harbour.

He was always modest about his achievements, but took a close and enthusiastic interest in the sailing exploits of his family, friends and protégés. At his funeral, his son Graham recalled one wet early morning off St Catherines when John appeared on deck – damp, salty, unshaven – but with whisky glass in hand – and supremely happy. He would wish for no better epitaph.

NJW

Paul Caswell

The strength of the RCC is the variety of activity embraced under that 'furtherance of the best aspects of cruising under sail' which is an object of the Club. Some members cross oceans; others work their little ships among estuaries and shoals. Both groups call on skills and qualities of character which one can call seamanship.

Paul was a little ship man. I remember him enthusing about single-handed and self-sufficient cruising in an open boat with a tent arrangement for use at night in some snug anchorage. Then for several years he owned *Alghero*, a Johnson and Jago five tonner in which, with two others, he did a fine cruise in the Baltic written up in the 1965 journal. He later owned *Pepper*, a Van de Stadt six tonner.

Taking up school-mastering (at Oundle and Brighton) after some experience in the world of business, Paul was the sort of school-master who did the marking of his pupils' work thoroughly. His cruising style with its attention to detail, to getting things technically right, had similar quality: nothing flashy, it was all quite modest stuff. One man and his boat.

Paul retired to Fowey. Fowey would have understood him and he Fowey. As was written about the late Sir Arthur Quiller-Couch ("Q") perhaps Fowey's most famous citizen, 'boats, oars and sails provided his chief relaxation throughout his life'.

M van H

Philip Stewart Francis

Philip joined the Royal Navy at the age of 13 in 1921 when he went to the Naval College at Dartmouth. There he learnt to sail but he excelled at games, particularly squash, despite his modest stature. His interest in sailing however really came to the fore when in 1932 in Hong Kong he and four other young naval officers decided that they would jointly buy a boat and sail her home to the UK.

Unable to find a suitable craft they commissioned the Hong Kong and Whampoa Dock Company to design and build a 54ft Bermudian Ketch at the massive cost to them of £800. She was built of teak with pine decks and Junk type masts of China Fir. Money was a major problem so economies were made. The boat had neither engine nor heads. The latter deficiency was considered relatively unimportant at sea when a skilfully designed bosun's chair could be used to leeward but was more of an issue in harbour in an age before marina facilities in every port.

She was named *Tai-Mo-Shan* the name of the highest mountain in the then New Territories. Sailing "east about" they were obliged to follow a northerly route across the Pacific to avoid headwinds and went north of the Aleutian Islands into the Bering Sea. Southwards down the coast of Canada winds were fair but south from San Francisco was very slow averaging only 50 miles a day. Passage through the Panama canal was achieved by bartering a coil of rope for a tow by a banana boat.

The lack of an engine became a serious problem in the Bahamas where a sudden and unusual shift of wind to the southwest found them on a lee shore and they were driven ashore at the top of spring tides. It took a fortnight of hard work to get her afloat again and they finally got into Dartmouth 364 days after they set sail. Soon after this he joined the RCC.

By this time Philip was an experienced submariner and in 1937 he was given command of his first 'boat', *HMS Spearfish*. Two years later he married Ruth Schreiber.

In 1941 in command of *HMS Proteus* in the Mediterranean he headed the list of enemy tonnage sunk. In one incident when an Italian destroyer tried to ram him whilst on the surface he turned towards and nearly sank the destroyer as the boat's hydroplane sliced a massive gash in her ship's side. For this and other incidents he was awarded two DSOs. Incidentally the five who sailed in *Tai-Mo-Shan* shared a VC and four DSOs between them.

When he retired after the war he owned a 30ft sloop called *Peter Rabbit*, cruising extensively in the Channel and North Sea. His other great interest in life was horses and in one race meeting in the Far East he managed to ride the winner of every race in one meeting.

A quiet and modest man, he nevertheless held strong beliefs. Sadly both his wife and daughter pre-deceased him.

Cocky Landon

Lieutenant Colonel Lionel Landon, universally known as 'Cocky' from a very early age, died in February aged 92. A colourful, genial person with a sparkling sense of humour he lived life to the full. Born in India, after Marlborough he spent a year at Lausanne University before winning a modern languages scholarship to Clare in 1926. Unusually, he then joined the Army and was commissioned into the Royal Artillery and served initially in India. Already at home in the saddle, he became a superb

Cocky Landon.

horseman. He spent most of the war commanding Indian mountain artillery units. In his working life Cocky enjoyed four Defence appointments in France, where he made many friends.

Cruising under sail was Cocky's other lifelong passion, along with riding. And under sail meant under sail – the engine was seldom used. What if it did mean another night at sea? He had owned small boats from an early age, having been thoroughly taught by his uncle, Noël Baxendale RCC, in his 60ft *Halloween*. In 1947 he bought the first of four beautiful wooden boats that he was to own and sail for the next twenty-five years. He joined the RCC in 1952. The first of these boats was *Falcon*, a 1903 53ft Fifer that 'could not have been better bred'. There followed over the years *Singora*, a 45ft gaff yawl built in 1896, *Seajack*, a 59ft 1934 bermudan cutter from Phillips of Dartmouth and finally the lovely *Morva*, a 1938 56ft Mylne-designed sloop for the last ten years. In these boats he cruised with his family and friends to Brittany, Spain, the Baltic and round Ireland. At other times the boat was cruised adventurously by his wife Bess or by one of his children, or generously lent to friends or the Sea Cadets. On selling *Morva* he and Bess cruised under power and Cocky sailed a Finn at home in Yarmouth, Isle of Wight. In addition to the RCC he was a member of the Royal Yacht Squadron, the Royal Ocean Racing Club and the Royal Solent Yacht Club.

A companionable, larger than life person to the end, he leaves Bess, the wife of his second marriage, herself the daughter of a 1920 RCC member; and his surviving son and daughter who, together with one of his grandchildren, all became members of the RCC.

OMR

Commander Graham Mann

Graham Mann died at his home in Lymington on 1 April 2000 aged 76 after a full and distinguished lifetime which revolved round the sea and seafaring.

The son of a submariner, he learnt to sail in dinghies in Portland Harbour before entering the Royal Naval College, Dartmouth. He passed out in 1941, and was soon appointed to the cruiser HMS *Trinidad* on Russian convoys. In action in far northern waters, one of *Trinidad*'s own torpedoes went berserk and struck her amidships. She was able to limp into Murmansk but was sunk by enemy aircraft on her return voyage, Graham and many of the crew being taken off by escorting destroyers. He was in the Mediterranean for the North African landings, and returned to Russian convoy duties in 1944.

Graham Mann.

After the war, Graham raced Swallows, Dragons and Darings whenever opportunity arose, so successfully that in 1955 he was appointed sailing master of the Royal Dragon *Bluebottle*. He won a bronze medal in her in the Melbourne Olympics, which led to his selection in 1958 as helmsman of the British challenger for the America's Cup, *Sceptre*. In 1960 he again represented this country in Dragons in the Olympics, and four years later he was team manager for the Tokyo Olympics.

He was meticulous in planning cruises and races, and much in demand as a course-setter in Cowes Week, serving a successful term as Rear Commodore Yachting of the RYS from 1984 to 1988.

Meanwhile, in 1973, he had bought a Rival 34 *Picaroon* for family cruising, graduating in 1987 to a Moody 376, *Sandboy*, both of which he invariably kept in immaculate condition. In these yachts he delighted in applying his navigational skills to explore every nook and cranny of the south coast of England and of north and south Brittany, imparting his love of the sea to his wife Carol and their two daughters. He was elected to the RCC in 1991 but sadly his cruises were curtailed by failing health over the past few years.

JWR

Ursula Martin

Ursula Martin was a Life Member, elected to the Club in 1941. She died at her Cornish home, No. 6 Coastguard Cottages, Helford Passage, on 3rd October 2000. She was 92. She was married first to Tom Worth, a Club member and a nephew of Claud Worth. Tom, an RAF pilot was shot down and killed over the North Sea in 1941, leaving Ursula with two little boys aged four and two.

In 1948, Ursula married Dr Nicholas Martin, a distinguished physician who later became Professor of Chemical Pathology at London University. Dr Martin died in 1981.

In 1941, the year of Tom's death, Ursula was elected to Full Membership of the club, a moving tribute to her late husband. One feels here the influence of the then Hon. Secretary, Donald Cree, a friend and contemporary of Claud Worth. Ursula's election was one of the very few during the war years.

She had lived on the Helford River since 1946, and at the Coastguard Cottages for the last 25 years. We were privileged to be her neighbours for the last 16. We very soon became good friends. The row of cottages overlook the river, and from the vantage point of her favourite chair she could monitor the yachts entering and leaving the river. Much of her early sailing had been in *Bittern* and *Tern IV* and she felt strongly about how a yacht ought to look. She was, to say the least, not keen on the appearance of the modern yacht, but if there was an RCC burgee at the masthead, all was forgiven! She was a devoted and skilful gardener, an industrious and imaginative embroiderer ('tatting', she called it). She will be much missed by her two sons, Michael and Dick, their families, and her many friends. She was warm, gallant and steadfast.

HQD

Meyrick F. (Basil) Payne

Basil had a wonderful and well-lived life with many exciting friends and phases. He lived his life with passion and style. Partially because of his stroke, many who knew Basil in the past twenty years, know little about his early days. Here are a few words about the passages in his life and the lessons he taught his family and friends along the way.

As a Naval officer, he piloted Motor Torpedo Boats across the Channel carrying members of the Dutch and French resistance. He taught the importance of fighting for what you believe in.

He courted Betty in Dartmouth where she was a Wren Officer based at Britannia Royal Naval College. They quietly married in 1942 while enjoying coincident day passes. They have three sons, Meyrick of New York, Antony of Los Angeles and Peter of Melbourne. He taught the importance of seizing the moment with passion and gusto.

Basil joined the United Nations in San Francisco in 1945 trying, as rumor has it, to placate his Mum after a wartime of risks and sacrifices. As a UN mediator, he strove to pacify Gaza and Cyprus, and he served in Greece and Kashmir. Regrettably he did not finish these assignments and those challenges haunt us. Between overseas missions in 1953, he helped allocate offices in the new UN building in Manhattan, skillfully keeping the KGB and CIA from each other's throats. He taught the importance of compromise and peacemaking.

He persuaded Betty that they should leave a well-paid, prestigious future at the UN in New York to acquire Cundell's grocery store in Dartmouth while simultaneously educating three sons at Rugby – an economic feat that would terrify the Chancellor of the Exchequer! Nevertheless, Basil often said 'selling bacon to Mrs. Snooks and quieting the guns in Kashmir require exactly the same skills'. He taught that committed participation is more effective than complaining.

Basil was a long time member of the RCC, RNSA, the Dartmouth Yacht Club and the Royal Dart Yacht Club. Toward the end of his life he even created "Basil's Own Bloody Yacht Club", affectionately known as BOBYC on the caps and blazers of family and friends. He shared ownership of the yacht *Matawa* with Capt. Robert Franks and completed numerous international cruises, many of which have been chronicled in this journal. He, and Robert Franks, taught their collective six sons and respective families the joy of sailing and family participation.

In 1978, Basil suffered a mammoth stroke and nearly died. He had to learn to walk, talk and climb stairs at 65. Few people are brave enough to face their infirmities with such determination and acceptance. He taught persistence and the will to overcome adversity.

In the course of Basil's life, many people helped him; most importantly Betty and those with whom he sailed in both war and peace. Before he died, he wanted to thank each and every one of his fellow travelers along life's rich and rewarding journey.

AP

Loftus Peyton Jones

Loftus Peyton Jones, who has died aged 82, was a tough, fearless Guernseyman, a connection of which he was most proud. Coming from a Service background he joined the Royal Navy through Dartmouth in 1936. He served in the cruiser *Penelope* in the ill-fated Norwegian campaign of 1940, and then as second-in-command of the destroyer *Brocklesby* on convoy escort duty. He joined the destroyer *Achates* as second-in-command in 1942 and took part in two Arctic convoys, earning a DSC and a mention in despatches. After supporting the allied invasion of North Africa in November 1942, *Achates* sailed on a third Arctic convoy in the following month. This convoy, JW 51B, was engaged

Loftus Peyton Jones.

by heavy German warships, during which *Achates* received a direct hit on the bridge from an 8-inch shell. The entire bridge party were killed and Loftus immediately took command and fought the ship, laying smoke to protect the convoy, until *Achates* sank. 81 survivors were picked up by a trawler. Loftus was awarded the DSO.

He then volunteered for the submarine service, but had the misfortune to be sunk and taken prisoner off Sicily on his first mission. He was imprisoned in Italy, and escaped twice, first by throwing himself from a moving train (but was later recaptured) and again when Italy surrendered. He walked 400 miles behind enemy lines before making a hazardous passage with one companion in the only craft he could find, an entirely unsuitable and unseaworthy duck punt, into Allied-held waters. He was appointed MBE for his daring escape.

He commanded the destroyer *Easton* in the Mediterranean before the end of the war, and then held sea-going and staff appointments until retiring from the Navy in 1961. From 1962 to 1966 he set up the Trinidad and Tobago Coastguard *ab initio* and developed it into an efficient and effective force. During his time in the East Indies, Hurricane Hattie struck Belize, and he flew in independently to assist in the emergency. In one incident he organised the tow of a petrol-laden craft from the harbour, for which he was awarded a Queen's Commendation for Brave Conduct. He then joined the Duke of Edinburgh's Award Scheme as Overseas Secretary and later became the Deputy Director (Overseas). He retired again in 1985 having overseen a huge expansion of the Scheme overseas. He was greatly admired and respected for his devotion to this cause, and he was appointed CVO on retirement.

The sea was in Loftus's blood. In Guernsey, the family were brought up from an early age in the small gaff cutter *Naughty Girl*. After the war Loftus acquired a 50-square metre, which became *Rebel Maid*, part-owned with a brother and three cousins. For many intervening years boat ownership was not practicable, but he cruised and ocean raced regularly and frequently either with others or by borrowing. He owned *Valkyrie*, a Kalik 33, and *Calliope*, a Starlight 35, for the last fifteen years. He sailed in them, generally just with his wife, Francie, but sometimes with others too, in home waters, to Scandinavia, round Ireland, and then to the Mediterranean, where *Calliope* has just enjoyed her third full season in that area. He was as fine and fearless a yachtsman as he was a naval officer, and his cruises were often not without incident.

Loftus was a companionable, outgoing and irrepressible person, who made friends wherever he went. He kept in touch with and visited the families that had helped him while he was 'on the run' in Italy, and in 1995, typically, he met again the trawler skipper who picked him up when *Achates* went down in 1942. In addition to the RCC he was a life-long member of the RNSA and the Royal Channel Islands Yacht Club. He was also a member of the Royal Yacht Squadron and in his 81st year he won the Camrose Award of that club for the most notable cruise of the year. He will be sorely missed by Francie and all his large family, and also by his multitude of friends in many callings.

OMR

David Victor Proctor

David Proctor was widely respected as a maritime historian who contributed greatly to better co-operation and understanding between various international bodies studying the maritime past. Overseas countries recognised him as the face of the National Maritime Museum during the 1970s and 1980s. He stayed in public service at the Maritime Museum for 28 years until his retirement in 1989. During this time he served as Education Officer, Museum Secretary and finally as Head of Printed, Manuscript and Technical Records. His lifetime was dedicated to a love of the sea and he had a friend in every port.

It was his appointment as the very first Education Officer at the National Maritime Museum in Greenwich in 1962 that gave him the opportunity to work in the field that he loved. He earnestly believed in making museums more accessible to the general public and not simply 'warehouses' for the national collections. With this in mind one major innovation as Education Officer was to create the 'Half-Deck' – a club for young people designed to encourage and stimulate interest in the nautical world and in the museum itself. The best compliment to its creator was that one or two of those involved in this pioneering scheme were later to join the staff at the museum.

While Head of Printed, Manuscript and Technical Records at Greenwich (1976 to 1989) he oversaw a major expansion of the collections. He retired from his post in 1989 but maintained a keen interest in museum affairs via the Council of Friends. He devoted a lot of time and energy during the 1990s to attending meetings and speaking at international conferences and recently finished a revised study of the navigational equipment called astrolabes.

As well as many contributions to museum publications he wrote two books. *Child O'War* (1972), a documentary of a boy sailor during Nelson's time, was written with Leon Garfield, and *Music of the Sea* (1992) is a work combining two of his great passions and details the importance of music to maritime culture.

In later life he spent much time in the Netherlands aboard his beloved *Bever*, a traditional Dutch sailing barge. Typically he did not want to be an occasional visitor, but grew to know the shipbuilders and sailing community of the region. He even went so far as to study Dutch at night school to be able to communicate better with the local population.

David is survived by his second wife Marion, three sons Andrew, Diccon and Tom, two grandsons and a further six stepchildren.

Cyril Ray

When in 1979 I proposed Cyril Ray for the club Colin McMullen replied saying, 'There is only one thing wrong with this proposal, you should have done it years ago'.

And of course he was so right because, for all of his 92 years, Cyril was an absolutely archetypal club member.

Over a sailing career of some 75 years from when he became one of the youngest, and then by far the oldest, member of the Sussex Yacht Club he ranged far and wide in his later 2½ ton Hillyard *Windflower* a boat of which many of us might admit to some envy as representing our early ambitions. The manner which she regularly appeared in all weathers at Beaulieu meets with a Lymington scow in tow was the epitome of so much that the club stands for. He had a wide circle of friends within the club. He was never backward in his involvement with good causes including the lifeboat, the Sea Scouts and encouraging the young in the ways of the sea. An indefatigable walker despite or perhaps because of his slight frame the mountains of his native Cumbria were another arena over which he ranged widely.

His last long journey with us to Holland at the age of 80 demonstrated his empathy with boats and the sea. My only anxiety was related to thoughts of elderly brittle bones and that it was a lot further across *Foggy Dew's* cabin than *Windflower's* where he had covered so many miles with virtually everything literally to hand.

A splendid profile of him appeared in Yachting Monthly in 1994. The packed congregation in the old Norman Abbey of Shoreham-by-Sea gave witness to the esteem in which his fellows held him. Truly a gentle parfait knight.

MG

Dick Stevens

Dick Stevens, who has died aged 92, was a robust soldier and seaman. He was a member of the Club for 52 years, and one of its great single handers. Coming from a Service family he was commissioned into the Royal Fusiliers from Sandhurst in 1928. He had a very active war from 1939 to 1945, fighting in the Western Desert and in the Eritrean, Normandy and Burma campaigns. He landed in Normandy on D plus 1 in command of an infantry battalion, which was involved in heavy fighting in the beach-head. He was the senior British liaison officer with the Polish parachute brigade in September 1944 and parachuted into Arnhem with the Poles. Before the end of the war he commanded a battalion in Burma, and later commanded the first battalion of his own regiment in action in the Korean war in 1952/53.

Dick retired in 1958 and settled in the Isle of Wight, where he could indulge his chief love – sailing. He had been sailing for a good many years by this time, wherever he could find a boat and a puddle of water – in Japan, Indonesia, Egypt, the Mediterranean and the Baltic. He bought his first cruising boat, the 24ft *Query*, in 1955 and started on his long cruising career, sailing mostly single handed, but occasionally with one companion. He made three cruises to the Baltic, some of the time in company with Rozelle Raynes, also single handed, in *Martha McGilda*. He always fitted out, in the open, in the coldest winter weather and would then be away for one, two or even three separate cruises, generally to north and south Brittany or to Ireland. He was also a robust county commissioner of the Isle of Wight scouts from 1964 to 1972.

He had an unnerving experience in 1961, when he was swept through the Alderney Race on three successive tides in rotten weather, during which one particularly heavy sea caught him off balance and 'decanted me head first over the lee side into the sea. The mainsheet was in my path so I grabbed it when hurtling past and found myself being towed along behind my boat. In an instant I was back aboard and pumping like mad'. The full account of this cruise appeared in the 1961 Journal.

In 1973 he changed boats to *Sausalito*, a 28ft Raymond Wall design built at Wivenhoe. In the two boats he made nineteen cruises to north and south Brittany, including Spain once, three to Ireland and numerous others to the West Country, making many friends along the way. By 1983 he was experiencing difficulty with both hips, but he continued cruising until 1989. Susan Hiscock, by now living at Yarmouth, kept him going for two more years with day sails until at 84 his disability became too severe. Dick was a bachelor, and his last days were spent in the care of a devoted family in Yarmouth who kept him active into his nineties. When asked how he was he would invariably reply 'Rotting', but he never ceased to count his blessings and say how he had enjoyed his cruising in its heyday, with uncrowded harbours and anchorages.

OMR

Dr Noy Trounson

Noy Trounson led full lives in two worlds, medicine and the sea. In Glasgow, he held several academic posts and had a period of military service before becoming Consulting Pathologist for North Warwickshire. He was a founding member of the Royal College of Pathologists and an honorary member of the Warwickshire Union of Mine Workers in recognition of his research into pneumoconiosis.

Noy grew up in Ayr in sight of the sea, and as a young man spent much time on the islands of the Clyde estuary. In 1963, then a widower with two small sons, Noy bought his first yacht, the 35ft sloop *Evening Song*. Two years later he married Doreen, who proved an able and enthusiastic shipmate on cruises from the Baltic to the Aegean. In 1987 Noy retired, sold *Evening Song*, and had built the 42ft Halberg-Rassy ketch *Hesperine* (variously, the evening star or the western horizon).

I first met Noy and Doreen in Corsica in 1988, soon after they had sailed *Hesperine* to the Mediterranean. Noy struck me at once as a person of many talents and interests, overflowing with energy and curiosity, an impression confirmed in the years that followed during which *Hesperine* lay each winter alongside my own *Ardent Spirit* at Ile des Embiez in the South of France. Noy took pleasure in the myriad tasks of yacht husbandry, still more in the annual cruises in *Hesperine* throughout the Med. He was especially fond of Italy. Age and a multiple bypass operation did not seem to slow Noy down. He was 80 when he died suddenly early in 2000.

AB

THE RESIGNATION OF
SIR ARTHUR UNDERHILL

by Sandy Watson

After my mother-in-law, Jean Lowis, died recently I came across a number of old Club newsletters which had belonged to her father, Captain B H Goodhart, who had been elected to the RCC in 1922. Amongst them was one dated 25 January 1937 which was Sir Arthur Underhill's final Annual Letter to members with the arresting title of 'Resignation of the Commodore'. This was largely concerned with a controversy which evidently cast a slight cloud over the final months of his term as Commodore, the office that he had held since 1888, and which is covered briefly on page 137 of *The History of the Royal Cruising Club*. Although, in parts, his letter does not make very comfortable reading, I thought that members might be interested in how he presented the issues to the membership of the day. Although I have done some rearrangement of their order, the excerpts below are taken directly from the letter. The italicized passages obviously reflect key points which the Commodore wished to bring out.

The Commodore begins by quoting a letter from Mr X which had been received by the Hon. Secretary, Donald Cree, on 11 January 1937. It had evidently been sent to many members of the Club. The letter of protest read as follows:

'I feel – and there are others in the RCC who agree with me – that the Club is not being run as it should be and that some effort should be made to improve things. The particular matter on which the protest is based is *only one of several on which I feel that the Club has reasons for dissatisfaction.* Much of the trouble, it seems to me, is *due to the lack of effective Flag Officers. Their absence on account of illness and distant cruising* has left altogether too much power in the hands of the Hon. Secretary, who, grateful as we all must be to him for his work as Secretary, can hardly be expected to combine in his sole person the qualities of Hon. Secretary and three Flag Officers at once.

'I have it on very good authority that Claud Worth wrote on several occasions to the Secretary during the last two years of his own illness, pointing out what would happen if the necessary steps were not taken in time. Whether those letters were personal to Cree or to him as Secretary, I do not know, and no move was made. The result has been that *no Flag Officer has been available for Committee Meetings and Club functions* and this is an undesirable position for any Yacht Club to be in.

'The General Meeting is close upon us, and I should much like to have your views as to what should be done. *I feel myself that it is urgently important that the new Flag Officers should be chosen with careful regard for the actual running of the Club as well as for its prestige.*

'If you agree with the protest, which concerns a matter still more urgent, will you please sign it and return it to me.'

The protest referred to was as follows:

'If it is indeed true that in or soon after July, 1936, the present owner of *Tern 1V* offered to give that vessel to the Club as a memorial to the late Claud Worth and that this offer was not considered by the Committee until October, 1936, and was then rejected, we the undersigned members of the Club wish to bring the following protest to the notice of the Committee:

'We submit that apart from the deep sentimental value of the proffered gift and the opportunities it threw open to the younger members of the Club and to those without boats of their own, its actual money value, equal to several years entire annual income of the Club, would have justified the calling of an Extraordinary General Meeting or the circularising of all members so that the Club as a whole might consider the possibility of keeping up the boat and in any case suitably respond to the extraordinarily generous offer that had been made to it.

'Further, that the Committee by *taking no steps to bring the offer to the knowledge of the members and by their own dilatoriness laid the Club as a whole open to a charge of ungraciousness and even of bad manners.*

'Further, that it is regrettable that the Committee, appointed to carry on the ordinary affairs of the Club, should have come to what is possibly the most important decision in the whole history of the Club at a meeting *at which no Flag Officers were present and without previously ascertaining the opinion of the Club.*

'Finally, we ask that dated copies of the letter making the offer to the Club and the letter refusing it shall be circulated to all members before the General Meeting'.

The protest had been signed by thirty-three members, although several had subsequently withdrawn their signatures.

To understand the background to Mr X's letter, members may wish to be reminded of the senior officers of the Club at this juncture. The Commodore, by then aged eighty-seven, had been in office for nearly forty-nine years. He was evidently not in the best of health. The list of Flag Officers shows that Claude Worth was Vice Commodore from 1919–1937. But he had recently died after a long illness and Vice Admiral Sir Lennon Goldsmith, Rear Commodore since 1931, was now acting Vice Commodore. However, as he was on an extended Mediterranean cruise, he was clearly unable to take much of an active role in the direction of the Club's affairs. Meanwhile the office of Rear Commodore was temporarily vacant. The Hon. Secretary, Donald Cree, had held the office since 1908, apart from a brief spell as Rear Commodore from 1919-21. It is not surprising that with his experience and ability he found himself shouldering more responsibility for the day-to-day running of the Club than could reasonably be expected. Notwithstanding the illustrious personalities involved, all of whom are deservedly legendary in the annals of the Club, it is perhaps understandable that some factions in the Club were not entirely happy with this state of affairs.

After quoting Mr X's letter and its protest, the Commodore's letter goes on to explain the nature of the offer by Mrs McGregor Phillips, a lady member of the Club and the owner of Claud Worth's famous *Tern IV*, by then called *Sea Swallow*, and how it had been handled by himself, the Hon. Secretary and the Committee. The matter had started with a letter from Mrs Phillips to the Hon. Secretary dated 25 July 1936:

'. . . . I have therefore come to the desolate conclusion that I ought to part with her; but she means so much to me, I cannot bear to think of her falling into callous hands. What I should like to do with her is this:— Present her to the Club as a memorial of Claud Worth, to be perhaps at Bucklers Hard or somewhere else as the Sea Headquarters of the Club; or if the Committee thought, she might be on Charter to sailing members of the Club—boys perhaps who could not afford to own such a ship—yet who could afford to share the expenses. Will you *tell me what you think* of this idea? Other Clubs own ships, why not ours?'

This was viewed by both the Commodore and Hon. Secretary as merely being the floating of an idea and the seeking the Hon. Secretary's opinion upon it. Nevertheless, the Commodore instructed the Hon. Secretary to reply to Mrs Phillips explaining that if she if should decide to make a formal proposal to the Club it could not be given proper consideration until 'after the holiday months of August and September were over'.

In October a degree of confusion was introduced when a Commander Nash (Mrs Phillips' agent) wrote to the Hon. Secretary asking if anyone in the Club would be interested in buying the former *Tern IV* for £3,500. Quite reasonably, from this it was presumed that Mrs Phillips had had second thoughts about the idea of donating *Tern IV* to the Club. But further correspondence with her elicited that she would still be willing to consider a gift to the Club.

The proposal was considered by a Committee Meeting on 14 October. The Commodore, being indisposed, could not attend this meeting, but he had communicated his views to the Committee. These were that it would be impractical for the Club to accept *Tern IV*. In the absence of the Commodore and other Flag Officers, the meeting was run by the Hon. Secretary. The eleven members of the Committee unanimously resolved to decline Mrs Phillips' offer. Although not strictly relevant to the greater issue, it may be of interest to read the Commodore's explanation of the reasons for doing so:

'We considered that to use a small vessel of 40 tons as a sort of Club House at Beaulieu or elsewhere for the use of 350 members spread all over the kingdom, was quite impracticable.

'We also considered that to keep her in commission for the use of members was outside our means. It would have meant a skipper and cook-steward, repairs, new sails and ropes occasionally, insurance (which is very heavy), laying up and fitting out expenses and divers other expenses which anyone who (like myself) has owned a 45-tonner knows very well cannot run into less than £400 per annum— and for some years our expenses have slightly exceeded our income. That would have meant doubling the present subscription, and taxing the great bulk of members who have vessels of their own for the benefit of a few of the 'boys' mentioned in Mrs. Phillips' letter who have none, and who, if I may say so without offence, will become far better sailor-men by investing directly they can afford it, in small vessels for single-handed work. It would also most certainly have necessitated the appointment of a paid secretary to manage the vessel and its accounts. Another reason pressing me was that a vessel which, in the ordinary course, would have to be broken up in twenty years, is scarcely a very permanent memorial.

'The idea is outside the objects of the Club. The RCC is not a charitable institution formed to accept extraordinarily handsome gifts from members (gifts which no one of us individually would dream of accepting) with the view of socialising the Club by providing a yacht of some size for the use of members who cannot afford one. That is my deliberate view. If the matter had gone through I certainly would never have used the vessel, and, indeed, would have resigned my membership of the Club, so as to refuse all responsibility.

'At the same time I gratefully acknowledge on behalf of the Club the kind feeling which prompted the offer'.

The Hon. Secretary communicated the Committee's decision to Mrs Phillips on 15 October. The Commodore winds up the *Tern IV* affair:

'I take the entire responsibility on myself. Cree, as Secretary, could only write what I as Commodore told him to write. The Committee took the same view that I did. The only thing with which I can reproach myself is that, perhaps, it would have been better if I myself had answered her as Commodore. But I fail to see any want of courtesy to Mrs. Phillips on the part of any of us; nor do I know on whose authority the protestors allege that such discourtesy has taken place. I now hear, however, that the protestors, or some of them, have been sedulously spreading the charge of discourtesy among members of the Club. Not one of the signatories, who are so shocked at my and Cree's want of courtesy, had the elementary decency, before secretly getting up or signing their bombshell, of communicating with the Commodore of the Club or of verifying the facts.

'At a Committee held on the 15th January [1937] at which (in accordance with his request) Mr. X was present, I asked him why he had carried on this secret conspiracy without communicating with me. To my astonishment and the amusement of the Committee, he answered that he understood that I was 'bedridden.' How and by whom this 'terminological inexactitude' was invented I know not. Possibly it was an euphemism, having regard to my age, for 'senile.' Anyhow, I can assure the Club that I continue to practise and attend Lincoln's Inn every working day. Whether I am senile or not I leave them to infer from this letter.'

Although important, the *Tern IV* affair was but the catalyst for the voicing of serious criticism of the Flag Officers and their management of the Club, which the Commodore naturally took very personally:

'After due consideration and taking the opinion of other qualified persons, it seems quite clear that it is a call for the complete resignation of the Commodore and Vice-Commodore (Admiral Goldsmith, D.S.O.), and possibly the Hon. Secretary and the substitution of more zealous and active officers; with a side allusion to the fact that, notwithstanding the late Vice-Commodore Worth's long and terrible illness, he ought to have been counselled to resign some time ago. I see no alternative to this interpretation, to which (if they read the covering letter) the protestors must be taken to have given their assent.'

The Commodore gives details of the high level of attendance at Committee Meetings by himself and other Committee members, and a plaudit for Donald Cree:

'And now a few words as to the Hon. Secretary. He has given unstintingly many years of his life to the well being of the Club. No one who is not in office knows the time, and indeed money, that he has spent in its service. I do not yet know what course he intends to pursue; but I do know that he is bitterly pained at what has occurred. Some of the letters, copies of which were read by Mr. X at the Committee on the 15th January under stress of cross-examination, were singularly abusive—indeed, might have led to legal proceedings but for the fact that the names of the writers were refused. I warn the Club seriously that, if Cree resigns, it will not only have the greatest difficulty in getting anyone with any knowledge of the time and worry entailed to take on a job which receives such a cruel reward as the protest in question, but that without Cree's assistance the confusion of changing over will be appalling. It seems to me that a paid Secretary will be inevitable.'

As far as the position of the Flag Officers was concerned:

'. . . . As to the suggestion that both I and the late Vice Commodore Claud Worth ought to have retired before this, I have for several years past (certainly seven or eight) offered to resign—nay, have urged the whole Club in my annual letters to elect a new Commodore, but in every case without the slightest response. . . . The suggestion that my dear old friend Worth desired that I should retire is a deliberate falsehood. He, while urging his own retirement, was above all others continually pressing me to remain. I wanted to retire so that while there were hopes of his recovery he might have the satisfaction of becoming Commodore of the Club. Moreover, almost to the end, Claud Worth was not only told what would come up before Committees, but wrote his opinion on it.'

Unknown to X and his fellow protestors, changes in the Flag Officers were already afoot:

'As a matter of fact I had in November, 1936, before I had heard anything whatever of this disturbance, intimated to the Hon. Secretary my irrevocable intention of resigning, as I considered that in my eighty-seventh year, with no yacht, a change was urgent. This came before the Committee in December, and they very carefully considered it and voted on the question as to who should be recommended to the General Meeting as (1) my successor, and (2) as Vice and Rear Commodores. . . . . I request that no attempt be made to induce me to remain. Indeed, after what has happened, I should find no pleasure in remaining. I should resign on the date of this letter but for the fact that it would lead to awkward complications. My resignation, therefore, takes effect after the election of the new Commodore or the 4th March.'

The Commodore summarizes his views on the protest, mostly expressed in a sentence of truly titanic length:

'I am not, however, going to take this attack on myself, my fellow officers and Committee lying down, and I say emphatically, that having regard to the fact that I founded the Club fifty-six years ago with half a dozen members, and that I leave it with an ordinary membership of 300 and a naval membership of 54, with the right to the title Royal and to fly the blue ensign, with three Challenge Cups celebrated throughout the yachting world, and a fourth added in 1936; with imitators not only in Britain, but in the United States of America (where the Cruising Club of America has very kindly made me an Honorary Member), that our Charts are sought for everywhere and our Journal eagerly looked forward to, and that the Navy thinks highly of us and joined in our last Meet, I think the signatories of the protest might have spared me the indignity of demanding my dismissal without communicating with me first—a dismissal in which, I notice, more than one Cadet Member, elected in 1935 or 1936, has joined with a somewhat primitive appreciation of those good manners which used (in my younger days) to be expected from youth to old age, and from new members of a Club to its officers and executive committee; a rebuke which I submit is equally applicable to those older members who have signed the protest, with some of whom I have hitherto had years of friendly relations. I regard their action as most ungracious.'

Notice was given of two resolutions which were to be moved at the forthcoming AGM:

(1)   While recording the warmest thanks of the Club to Mrs McGregor Phillips for her very generous desire to present *Tern IV* to the Club, this Meeting regretfully agrees with the conclusion at which the Committee arrive that the Club should not undertake the responsibility of accepting it.

(2)   This Meeting, having read the Commodore's letter containing the correspondence relating to Mrs. Phillips' offer, and having heard the case for signatories of the protest, is of opinion that the allegations contained in Mr. X's protest and covering letter against the Flag Officers, the Committee and the Hon. Secretary are devoid of foundation, and regrets that such allegations were ever made.

It is presumed that these resolutions were duly passed at the AGM. Also at this meeting Vice Admiral Goldsmith was elected as Commodore, T N Dinwiddy as Vice Commodore, Roger Pinckney as Rear Commodore, and Donald Cree was re-elected as Hon. Secretary. But it cannot have been the finale that Sir Arthur Underhill would have wished for.

BOOK REVIEW

THE JOURNALS OF CAPTAIN JAMES COOK ON HIS VOYAGES OF DISCOVERY

Edited from the Original Manuscripts
Edited by J C Beaglehole

I.   The Voyage of the *Endeavour*, 1768–1771
II. The Voyage of the *Resolution* and *Adventure*, 1772–1775
III. The Voyage of the *Resolution* and *Discovery*, 1776–1780 (in two parts)

Portfolio: Charts and Views Drawn by Cook and his Officers
Boydell Press, Woodbridge & Rochester, NY

ISBN: 0 85115 744 0 Price £595 the set. Special price for RCC members until 31 January 2001, thereafter at list price of £695 the set.

The extraordinary genius of James Cook as explorer, seaman, cartographer and chronicler is celebrated and illuminated by the recently reprinted edition of his *Journals* edited by the great New Zealand scholar J C Beaglehole which was originally published by the Hakluyt Society.

Like successful generals in war, even the ablest explorers need a full measure of luck to survive. James Cook was fortunate in his first superiors in the Royal Navy. How else could he have gone from being the mate of a Whitby collier in 1755 to being chosen by the Royal Society in 1768 to go to the South Pacific to observe the forthcoming transit of Venus across the sun while in command of Her Majesty's bark *Endeavour*?

He served under Captain Palliser in Newfoundland, who taught him trigonometry and became his lifelong patron. Cook's work as a surveyor in the St Lawrence River caused his Admiral, Lord Colvill, to write to the Admiralty in December 1762 that, 'From my experience of Mr Cook's genius and capacity I think him well qualified for greater undertakings.'

The Admiralty recognised, at that early stage, that although Cook had had very little formal education he had quite exceptional qualities. His endurance, self-discipline, unselfishness, humanity and judgement enabled him to survive eleven years almost continuously at sea in a cramped and overcrowded ship.

His first voyage in *Endeavour* from 1768 to 1771 had the most far-reaching consequences. From its early stage he showed his quality as a writer of journals which reported marine intelligence clearly and succinctly. His first major port of call was Rio de Janeiro. He gives meticulous pilotage instructions for the entrance and a comprehensive inventory of the fortifications and of the provisions available. No detail seems to escape him. 'Rum, sugar and molasses are all good and cheap. Tobacco is cheap, but not good. Garden stuff and fruits in plenty, but none that will keep long at sea except Pumpkings.'

Later he drew accurate and elegant charts of New Zealand, and gave the most detailed account of the country. 'It was the opinion of everybody on board that all sorts of European grass fruits and plants would thrive here', he wrote. He circumnavigated both islands and gives us a veritable *Rough Guide* to New Zealand 1770. He did much the same for New South Wales, but his progress up the Australian east coast culminated in running aground on the Great Barrier Reef, holing the vessel on 11 June 1771. First Aid repairs took a month in the Endeavour River. They were beset by shoals. On 14 August Cook writes, 'We have been intangled among shoals more or less since the 26th May in which time we have sailed 360 leagues [about 1000 miles] without ever having a man out of the cheans heaving the lead when the ship was under way.'

It was *Terra Australis Incognita* that was the target of Cook's second voyage, in *Resolution*, from 1772 to 1775. Explorers had long believed there was a great southern continent at the bottom of the Indian or Pacific oceans. The Admiralty's long-winded instructions included, 'You are to endeavour by all proper means to cultivate a friendship or alliance with the inhabitants of the islands, making them presents of such trinquets as they may value, inviting them to traffick and showing them every kind of civility and regard.'

With typical courage and thoroughness Cook left the Cape of Good Hope on 22 November 1772 and headed south, so as to be able to sail eastwards along the ice edge. The weather was daunting, with frequent gales, snow, fog and ice on the ship. They sailed past endless icebergs with only the keen eyes of the watch to prevent them hitting them at night or in fog. On 17 March 1773 he turned northeast and wrote in his Journal, 'After cruising four months in these high latitudes it must be natural for me to wish to enjoy some short repose in a harbour where I can procure some refreshment for my people.' His concern for his 'people' was extraordinary by the standards of the mid-eighteenth century. If the ship acquired some extra food, fresh fish for example, he insisted on its being divided equally among the ship's company. His 'people' had continually to clean the ship and themselves as a measure against disease. He made them eat antiscorbutics – fresh fruit and sauerkraut – often under the threat of punishment. His ships were relatively free of scurvy as a result, and in 1776, the same year that he was elected a Fellow of the Royal Society, he was awarded the Society's Copley Medal for a paper on measures to contain scurvy.

Cook devotes a large part of the Journal to recording his findings in the Pacific Islands and his attempts to establish good relations with the inhabitants, most successfully in his visits to Tahiti where he had some knowledge of the language. In November 1773 he makes a second sweep towards the Antarctic, then via the central Pacific Islands he visits Tierra del Fuego and from there makes a third Antarctic sweep. He then leaves the Cape of Good Hope bound for home, confident that there was no great undiscovered south continent.

When he returns home he is promoted Post Captain and receives his commission from the King, personally. With Elizabeth, his wife, he enjoys the social round in London for a few brief months, and then on 9 January 1777 he makes a mistake with fatal consequences. He was invited to dine with the First Lord, the Earl of Sandwich, and the Comptroller, Admiral Palliser, to discuss who should lead the proposed third expedition to the Pacific. After considering many former colleagues, Cook suddenly stood up and said he would lead it himself. He ignored the health problems he had suffered on the last voyage (probably arising from an intestinal infection) and the strain of commanding yet another expedition in relatively unknown waters.

He duly went on the third voyage with some of his previous officers and crew. He had orders to try to find the western end of the presumed North West Passage. Cook, in *Resolution*, and accompanied by *Discovery* (Captain Charles Clarke) left England on 25 June 1776. This time they encountered many problems: headwinds in the Pacific, troubles with the natives, and perhaps Cook's reluctance to forge ahead as he had used to do. They reached Nootka Sound, Vancouver Island on 26 April 1778, and then laboriously sailed along the shore of Alaska and across the Bering Strait to Kamchatka in Siberia, investigating rivers and inlets without finding anything that might lead through to Baffin.

At the end of the year they went south to Hawaii. Initially they got on very well with the inhabitants and Cook was treated as a king. It is at this point, without any explanation, that Cook's Journal comes to an end, with the entry for 17 January 1779. 'The ship very much crowded with Indians. I have nowhere in this Sea seen such a number of people assembled at one place. All the shore of the place was covered with people.' Why did he stop writing? Did he foresee trouble? We have to rely on the journals of Clarke and others for what followed.

The ships left on 4 February after a magnificent farewell with the island's king, Teneeoboo. On 8 February the foremast was found to be damaged, and Cook decided to return to Keealakakua Bay which they had just left. The natives were displeased to see them return; there was much thieving of fittings from the ships, and things very soon got out of hand. Cook and Bligh, the master of *Resolution*, were bent on restoring order by the use of firearms. On 14 February 1779 Cook went ashore with a marine escort saying that he intended to seize the king and hold him on board. A large and warlike crowd had gathered ashore. In this tense situation Cook set out for the king's house. The crowd became angrier. They set upon the marines who were stabbed and killed. To the horrified watchers on *Resolution* Cook seemed alone. He was struck from behind with a club and then stabbed. He fell into the water and there was an orgy of beating and stabbing. The natives then dismembered Cook's body.

After this tragedy no more was achieved and the voyage's objective was not accomplished. It was not until 1944 that the North West Passage was finally opened up. What the third voyage did achieve was the opening up of northwest Canada as part of the British Empire. In Charles Darwin's words, 'Cook added half a hemisphere to the unknown world'.

With all these staggering achievements, how is it that James Cook never became an English national hero? Do our heroes have to be ones who win wars? In the twentieth century the English had a hero of a sort in Scott of the Antarctic. He was really a romantic failure. Perhaps that is what the English prefer to one whose extraordinary qualities extended an empire and recorded it all with matchless clarity.

The RCC is very grateful for the Publishers' generous gifts of a full set of the Journals to its Library.

David Edwards

INDEX OF AUTHORS

GEOGRAPHICAL INDEX: 2000

Officers of the Club